Comput orks

The **Computer Communications and Networks** series is a range of textbooks, monographs and handbooks. It sets out to provide students, researchers and non-specialists alike with a sure grounding in current knowledge, together with comprehensible access to the latest developments in computer communications and networking.

Emphasis is placed on clear and explanatory styles that support a tutorial approach, so that even the most complex of topics is presented in a lucid and intelligible manner.

Also in this series:

An Information Security Handbook
John M.D. Hunter
1-85233-180-1

Multimedia Internet Broadcasting: Quality, Technology and Interface
Andy Sloane and Dave Lawrence (eds.)
1-85233-283-2

UMTS: Origins, Architecture and the Standard
Pierre Lescuyer (Translation Editor: Frank Bott)
1-85233-676-5

Designing Software for the Mobile Context: A Practitioner's Guide
Roman Longoria
1-85233-785-0

OSS for Telecom Networks
Kundan Misra
1-85233-808-3

The Quintessential PIC® Microcontroller 2nd edition
Sid Katzen
1-85233-942-X

From P2P to Web Services and Grids: Peers in a Client/Server World
Ian J. Taylor
1-85233-869-5

Intelligent Spaces: The Application of Pervasive ICT
Alan Steventon and Steve Wright (eds)
1-84628-002-8

Ubiquitous and Pervasive Commerce
George Roussos (ed.)
1-84628-035-4

Information Assurance: Security in the Information Environment 2nd edition
Andrew Blyth and Gerald L. Kovacich
1-84628-266-7

Alfred Wai-Sing Loo

Peer-to-Peer Computing

Building Supercomputers with Web Technologies

Alfred Wai-Sing Loo, BSc, MSc, PhD, MBCS, MIMA, CEng, CSci, CMath, CITP
Department of Computing and Decision Sciences, Lingnan University,
Tuen Mun, Hong Kong

Series Editor
Professor A.J. Sammes, BSc, MPhil, PhD, FBCS, CEng.
CISM Group, Cranfield University, RMCS, Shrivenham, Swindon SN6 8LA,
UK

British Library Cataloguing in Publication Data
A catalogue record for this book is available from the British Library

Library of Congress Control Number: 2006925862

Computer Communications and Networks ISSN 1617-7975
ISBN-10: 1-84628-381-7 Printed on acid-free paper
ISBN-13: 978-1-84628-381-9

9 8 7 6 5 4 3 2 1

springer.com

To my wife, Rebecca, for her love and support

Contents

1
Overview of Peer-to-Peer System

1.1 Introduction

Peer-to-peer (P2P) computing is the sharing of resources between computers. Such resources include processing power, knowledge, disk storage and information from distributed databases (Kamath, 2001). In the last several years, about half a billion dollars have been invested in companies developing P2P systems.

This kind of interest is due to the success of several high-profile and well-known P2P applications such as the Napster and Oxford anti-cancer projects (Loo, 2003). The concept of sharing resources is not completely new. Indeed, P2P systems are a natural evolution in system architecture. It is worthwhile to have a brief look at this evolution.

1.2 Batch Modes

Mainframe computers were important tools for large enterprises. In the old days, there was only one computer in one organization as the machines were prohibitively expensive. They required special rooms with air-conditioning. The operation of these computers (Fig. 1.1) is described next.

End users used to write down input data on special forms. These forms were passed to the data entry section periodically (*e.g.*, once a day or once a month depending on the nature of the process). Data entry operators typed the data with special machines, which converted the data into punch card, magnetic tape and/or magnetic disk. Such input mediums were passed to computer room. A computer operator then fed the data into computer. The computer processed the data and printed the reports. Such reports were sent back to the users together with their input forms.

Obviously, this 'batch processing' mode of operation suffers from several problems:

1. Input data forms are collected periodically as a batch. It is not uncommon that users need to wait for a few days to get their computer reports. Such kinds of

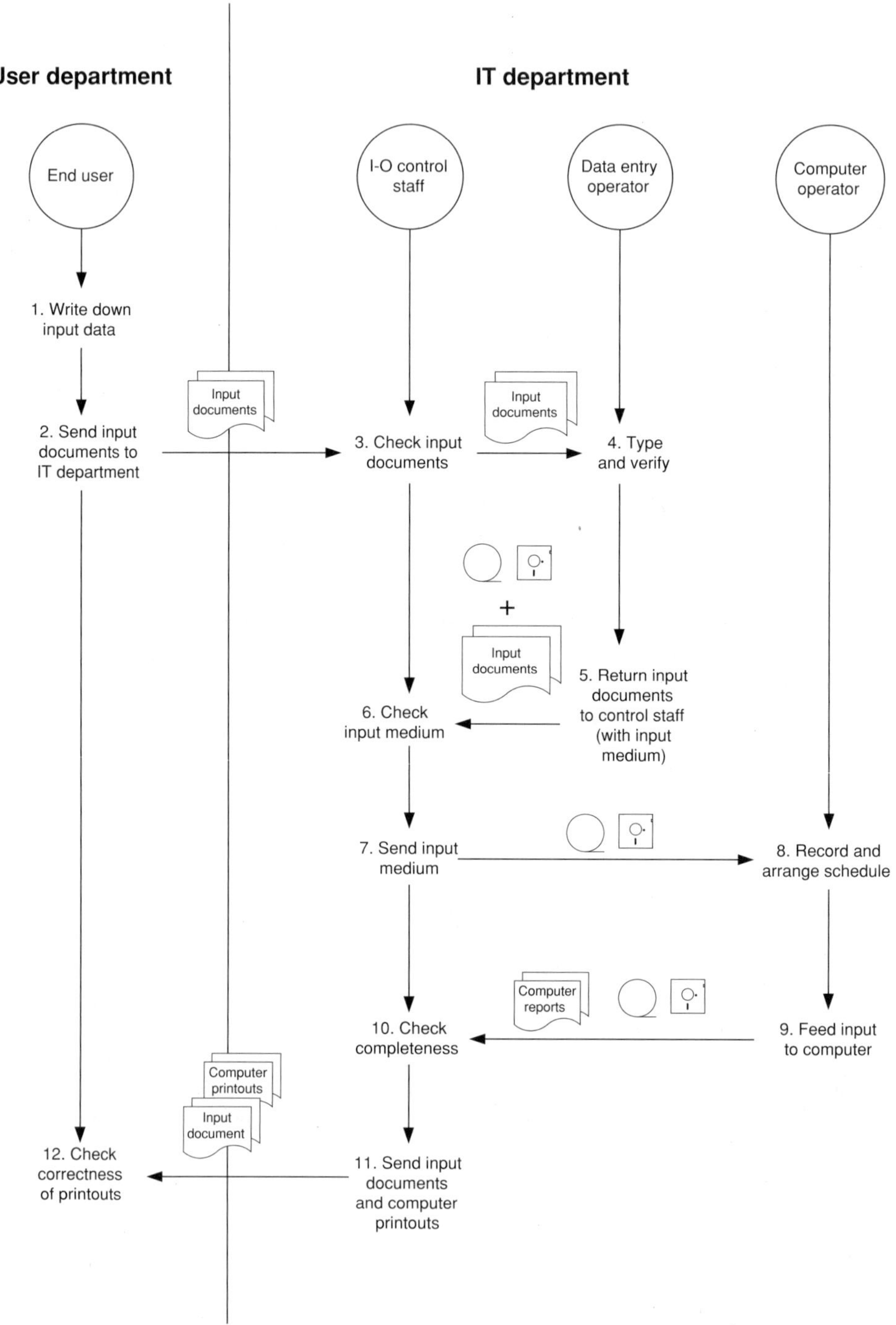

FIGURE 1.1. Operation of batch system.

delays are acceptable for systems such as payroll as they are done periodically. However, it is not satisfactory for systems that need immediate answers, such as an inventory control system.

2. End users collect the data and write them down on input forms. Data entry operators do the typing. As the data entry operators do not have the knowledge of the applications, it is easier to make typing mistakes. It is more difficult for them to detect problems. A 'verifying' process is commonly used to overcome this problem. The idea is simple but the cost is heavy. The input data are typed by one operator. Then another operator types it again. The system compares the first typing with the second typing. Any discrepancy detected will be reported so the data entry operator can check the problem. This process is effective in detecting typing errors but is expensive as we need to type twice for all critical systems. It is also time consuming and causes delays in further processing.

1.3 On-Line Modes

Since hardware costs decreased and technology advanced, the 'on-line processing' mode became available to enterprises. Terminals could be connected to mainframe computers (Fig. 1.2). The first-generation terminal consisted of only two

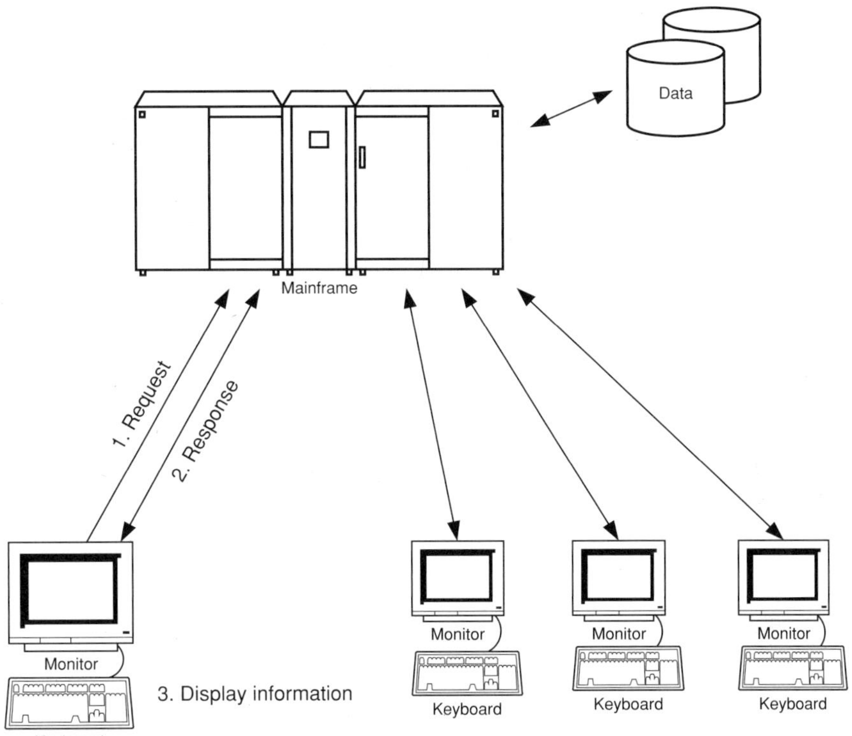

FIGURE 1.2. Mainframe with dumb terminals.

components—a keyboard and a screen. Its function was to allow end users to type in data directly to the computer. After the computer processed the data, the result was displayed on the screen of the terminal. In other words, the terminal's functions are input and output. It does not perform any calculations or formatting at all. Many people refer to this type of terminal as 'dumb terminals'.

On-line processing solves the problems of batch processing. End users can type in their data as soon as possible and thus get the processing faster. However, in the mainframe approach almost everything is done by mainframe computers. Processing in the mainframe quickly becomes a bottleneck in any information system. Enterprises were forced to keep pumping money into mainframe upgrades in order to maintain efficiency under increased processing demands.

In order to alleviate this problem, dumb terminals were replaced by 'intelligent terminals'. Some simple tasks can be performed by intelligent terminals. These tasks include some simple input-data validations and formatting of the display on the screen. Intelligent terminals are much more expensive than dumb terminals, but they reduce some workload from the mainframe computers.

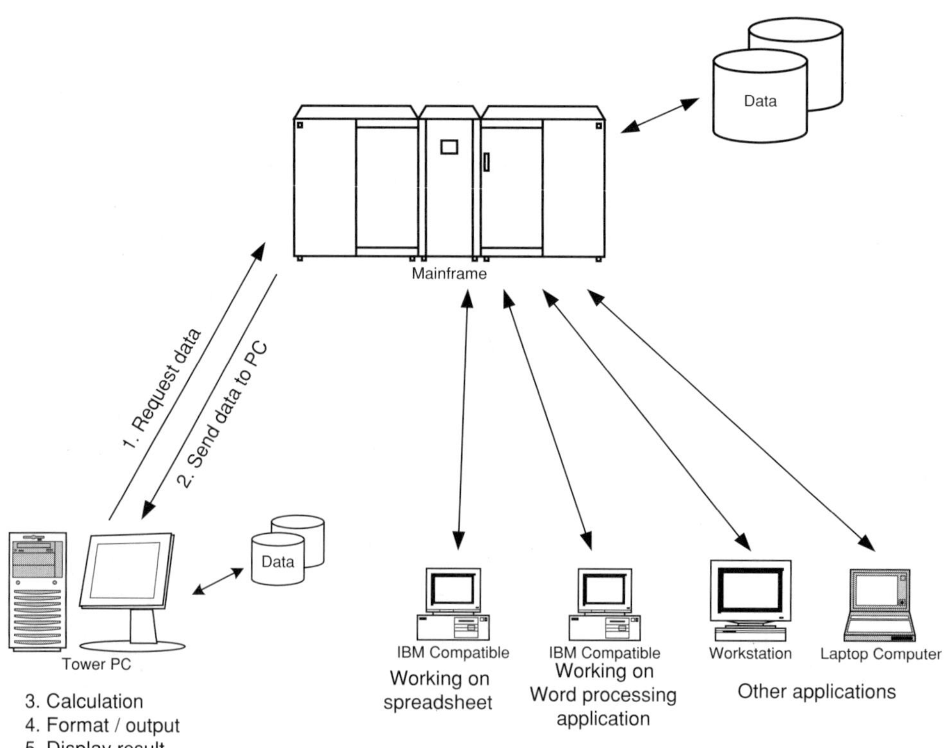

FIGURE 1.3. PCs as intelligent terminals.

In early 1980s, PCs became available in the consumer markets. As demand for PCs was very high, their prices dropped quickly due to mass productions. It was more economic to replace intelligent terminals with PCs (Fig. 1.3). After installing a special 'emulation' program, a PC can 'pretend' to be a terminal and communicate with the mainframe. In addition to lower cost, PCs provide another advantage: Users can use the PC as a stand-alone computer when it is not used as a terminal. It is more cost-effective as the PC can also be used for word processing, spreadsheet and other simple applications.

1.4 Client-Server

The Client-server architecture (Fig. 1.4) for computing systems was first proposed as an alternative to the conventional mainframe systems approach for large

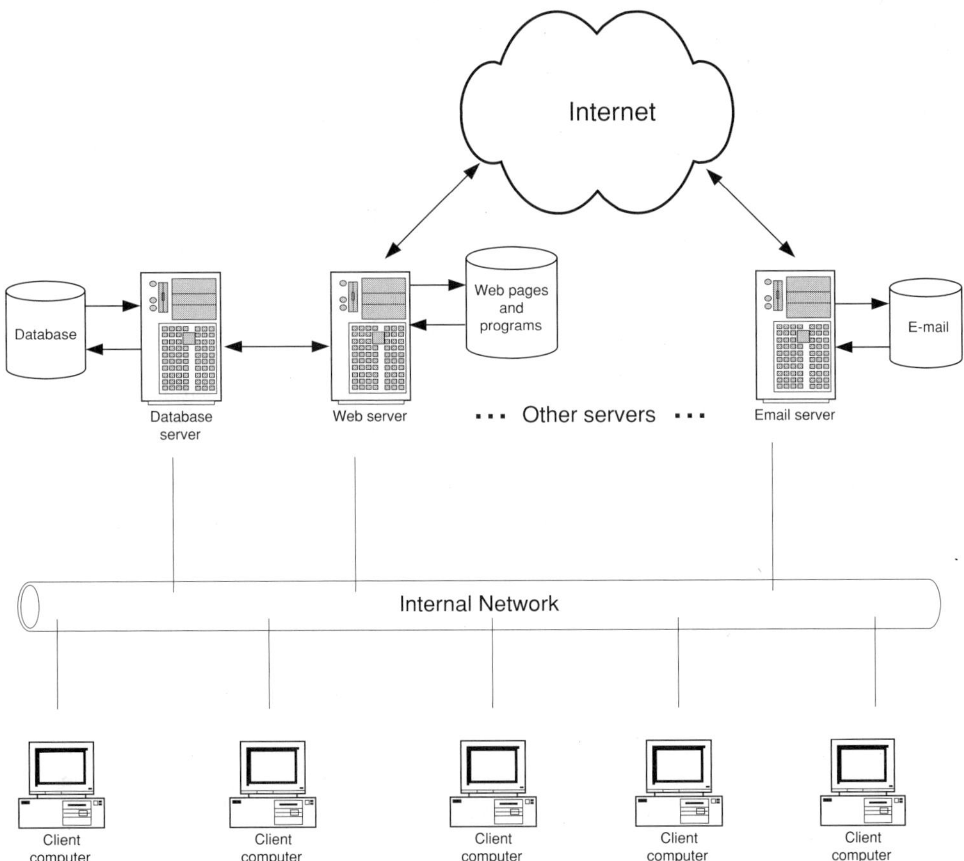

FIGURE 1.4. Client-server model.

enterprises. Client-server models shift the processing burden to the client computer. A client is a computer that requests services from another computer (*i.e.*, the server), while a server is a dedicated computer that provides services to clients in these models. For example, a client may request a database server to retrieve a record. After the server passes the record to the client, the client computer is responsible for further processing (calculating, formatting output, preparation for the graphical user interface, *etc.*). Through workload sharing, client–server systems can improve overall efficiency while reducing budget. Client-server models started gaining wide acceptance in the late 1980s when companies began to seek fresh competitive advantages in an ailing economy.

Both client-server and intelligent terminal–mainframe approaches reduce the workloads of the central computers. However, they differ in several ways:

1. Client-server is more flexible as the client is a general-purpose computer. Users can develop and install proper programs for their particular applications. The client computer can take over as many workloads as possible from the system.
2. Instead having only one or two mainframe, organizations usually have many servers. Each server is dedicated to one particular function. For example, database servers take care of database services, while e-mail servers take care of collection and delivery of e-mail messages. This approach reduces the number of clients which a particular server needs to support.

In other words, the client-server approach is a further improvement in spreading the workloads among different computers. However, there are two major problems in this approach:

1. We need to install application programs on each client computer. Some systems have several hundred or even a thousand clients. Installation alone is a major task. From time to time, we also need to update the programs. It is a daunting task to maintain a system with large number of clients and different applications.
2. Usually one server supports many clients simultaneously so it is extremely busy. On the other hand, client computers are idle most of the time. Corporations need to upgrade their servers while they have unused computing power in the system.

1.5 Peer-to-Peer Systems

In the current global economic recession, companies are again searching for ways to improve their processing power without further investment in new hardware and software. Many client computers are idle most of the time, and they have unused disk storage. The next logical step is to maximize the use of these client computers. The P2P model is the solution to this problem.

In a P2P system, computers can act as both clients and servers. Their roles in any task will be determined according to the requirements of the system at the time.

For example, computer A sends a 'file transfer' request to computer B. During the actual file-transfer process, computer B is the file server and computer A is the client. At a later moment, computer B can send a request for file transfer to computer A. The roles will reverse. This approach minimizes the workload on servers and maximizes overall network performance.

Peer-to-peer computing allows users to make use of collective power in the network. It helps organizations to tackle large computational jobs, which they could not handle before. P2P implementation is also cost-effective for small companies and even individuals. The benefits are lower costs and faster processing times for everyone involved.

1.5.1 Definition of P2P Systems

Is there a universally accepted definition of P2P systems?

Unfortunately, the answer is no. Although there are many definitions (Oram, 2001; Leuf, 2002; Barkai, 2002; Moore and Hebeler, 2002), none of them can be accepted by all practitioners. People also disagree on whether some applications belong to P2P. A lack of agreement on a succinct definition may not be a bad thing as P2P is still evolving. There are new applications and techniques, so it is good to not have a narrow definition. However, there are some common characteristics shared by most P2P systems:

- A 'peer' is a computer that can act as both server and/or client. Its role will be determined by the requirements of the system at a particular time. In some P2P systems, a peer can work as both server and client simultaneously.
- A P2P system should consist of at least two or more peers.
- Peers should be able to exchange resources *directly* between themselves. Such resources include files, storages, information, central processing unit (CPU) power and knowledge.
- Dedicated servers may or may not be present in a P2P system depending on the nature of the applications. However, the roles of the most dedicated servers are limited to enabling peers to discover each other. In other words, they are assuming the role of brokers. P2P systems without dedicated servers are sometimes described as 'pure' P2P systems.
- Peers can join and/or leave the system freely.
- Peers may belong to different owners. It is common for P2P systems to have several millions of owners.

1.5.2 Benefits of P2P Systems

Most P2P systems provide some of the following benefits:

- Workload is spread to all peers. It is possible to have millions of computers in a P2P network, which can deliver huge resources and power.
- It takes a shorter time to complete the task as peers can exchange resources directly without a server, which is always the bottleneck in a network.

- Many computers have unused resources. For example, many office computers are not used at all from 5 PM to 9 AM in the next morning. P2P computer can use these resources and thus maximize the utilization.
- Corporations can save a lot of money through better utilization of existing facilities.
- Centralized control and management are not required. Thus the cost of providing these services can be saved.
- New peers can be added to a P2P easily. The ability to expand a network is also called 'scalability'.
- P2P network will still function when some of its peers are not working properly. Thus it is more fault tolerant than other systems.
- Users can join or leave the system at any time they like. Thus users can maintain the control of their resources.

1.5.3 Drawbacks of P2P Systems

Although P2P systems provide a lot of benefits, they are not a panacea for all problems. A P2P network may not be the right tool for some specific tasks. We list the possible drawbacks as follows:

- The peer will be more vulnerable to hackers' attacks.
- It is difficult to enforce standards in P2P systems.
- For some specific tasks, the workload cannot be shared among the peers.
- A peer can leave the system according to its owner's discretion. A P2P network cannot guarantee that a particular resource will be available all the time. For example, the owner may shut down his computer or delete a file. It is difficult to predict the overall performance of a system.
- It is difficult to generate cash for any participants in the systems.
- It is difficult to prevent illegal uploading and downloading of copyrighted materials.
- A popular P2P system can generate enormous amount of network traffic. For example, the Napster system's overwhelming access slowed down the networks of many universities. As a result, some universities did not allow their students to access Napster inside the campus.

Although P2P has become a buzzword lately, there are still problems in developing large-scale P2P projects. We will look at some high-profile P2P networks as examples and present our solutions in the remaining chapters of this book.

2
File-Sharing Peer-to-Peer System

2.1 Introduction

Although the focus of this book is on CPU power sharing, it is worthwhile to look at the operations of file-sharing P2P systems. It will help us to identify the common features and differences of various types of P2P systems (Oram, 2001; Leuf, 2002; Barkai, 2002; Moore and Hebeler, 2002). We will present several high-profile file-sharing P2P systems in this chapter.

2.2 Famous Napster Model

Shawn Fanning, an 18-year-old student, created Napster in 1999. He was frustrated with the difficulties in finding digital music files on the Web, so he developed his own software.

Napster is a high-profile P2P network, which gives its members the revolutionary ability to connect directly to other members' computers and search their hard drives for digital music files to share and trade.

The operations of Napster are described in Fig. 2.1. Members download a software package from Napster and install it on their computers. The Napster central computer maintains directories of music files of members who are currently connected to the network. These directories are automatically updated when a member logs on or off the network. Whenever a member submits a request to search for a file, the central computer provides information to the requesting member. The requesting member can then establish a connection directly with another member's computer containing that particular file. The download of the target file takes place directly between the members' computers, bypassing the central computer.

The power of Napster and similar applications is that they allow the sharing of widely dispersed information stores without the need for a central file server. Over 36 million people joined the Napster community, and it rapidly accelerated the development and implementation of other P2P models. The limitation is that it can only share music files—participants cannot share other resources.

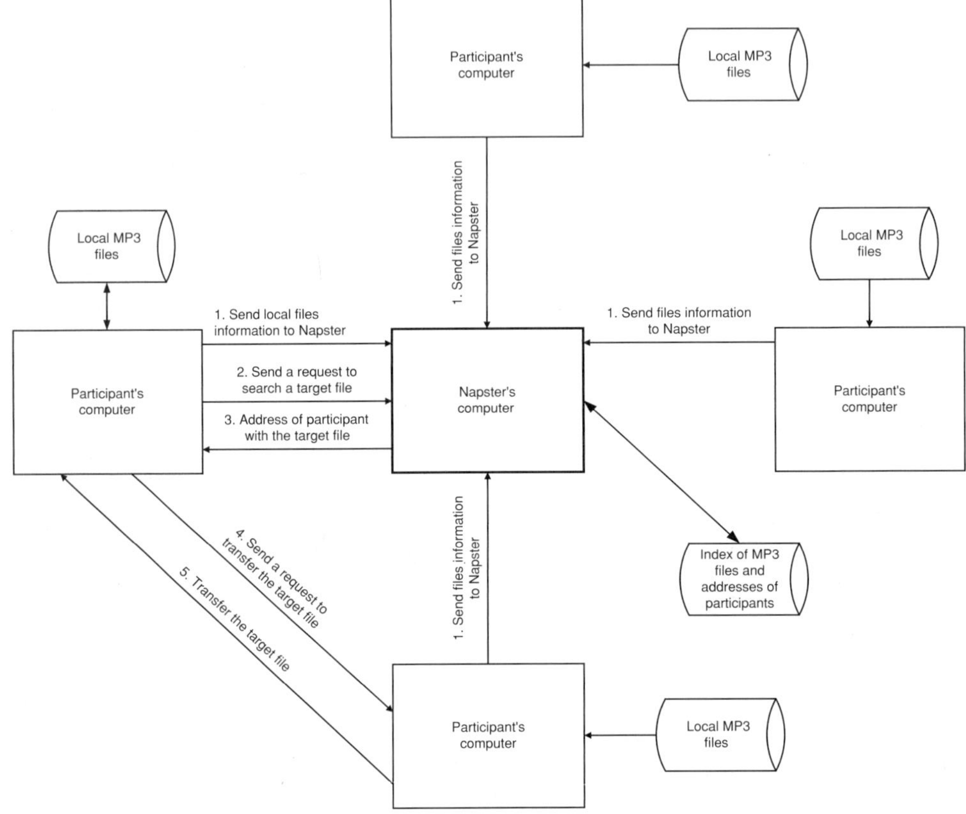

FIGURE 2.1. Napster model.

Napster has also faced considerable legal challenges, unrelated to its technological model, from music-publishing companies who objected to the free copying of copyrighted material. The Recording Industry Association of America (RIAA), a trade group that represents U.S. music publishers, filed its first lawsuit against Napster in December 1999. The court ruled in favour of RIAA. Napster was ordered to block access to copyrighted MP3 files on its system. The appeal court also upheld the ruling. In response to this ruling, Napster deployed various filters to reduce the number of files available for exchange. However, that was not good enough to satisfy Judge Patel. In July 2001, she ordered to close down Napster due to the inefficiency of its filtering.

2.3 Gnutella

Napster was ordered to shut down because it maintained a central directory for its members. Some new file-sharing P2P systems surfaced to replace Napster

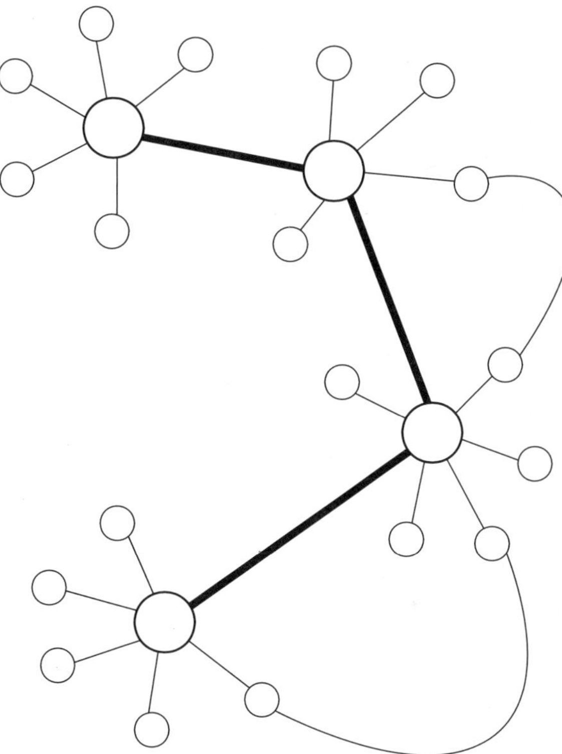

FIGURE 2.2. Structure of Gnutella.

in the wake of its abeyance. These P2P systems can bypass the legal problems as they do not hold a central directory. They do not even need a central server or any company to run the system. Thus, it is impossible to kill the network. These new P2P systems include Gnutella, KaZaA, Direct Connect, *etc.* As Gnutella is one of most prominent networks, its operations will be presented in this section.

The idea of Gnutella is quite simple and similar to the 'search strategies' employed by humans. If you want to get a particular file, you can ask one of your friends nearby. If he/she does not have the file, he/she can ask his/her friends. If everyone is eager to help, this request will be conveyed from one person to another until it reaches someone who has the file. This piece of information will be routed to you according to the original path. The network structure of Gnutella is described in Fig. 2.2.

Computers in the network have different connection speeds. Some computers have high-speed lines such as T3, while others have slow 56K modem connections. A high-speed computer will connect to many computers, while the low-speed computer will connect to only a few computers. Over the course of time, the network will have a high-speed computer in the core.

Gnutella will stop the search according to time-to-live number. The default value of this number is 7. Your request will be conveyed from one computer to another seven times. As each computer in this chain can send the request to multiple computers directly connected to it and this number is counted as 1, the request could reach a large number of computers.

Users need to install a Gnutella client in their computers before they can join the network. Many different packages are available from the Internet. Popular client packages include the followings:

Windows platform
BearShare: http://www.bearshare.com/
Gnucleus: http://gnucleus.sourceforge.net
LimeWire: http://www.limewire.com
Phex: http://phex.sourceforge.net/
Swapper http://www.revolutionarystuff.com/swapper
XoloX: http://www.xolox.nl/
Linux/Unix platform
Gtk-Gnutella: http://gtk-gnutella.sourceforge.net/
LimeWire: http://phex.sourceforge.net/
Mutella: http://mutella.sourceforge.net/
Qtella: http://www.qtella.net/
Macintosh
LimeWire: http://www.limewire.com/
Mactella: http://www.cxc.com
Phex: http://phex.sourceforge.net/
Mactella: http://www.tucows.com/preview/206631
BearShare: http://www.bearshare.com/

Most of the clients are easy to use and provide a lot of functions. Figure 2.3 shows the screen of a popular client—LimeWire. The user does not need to log into the system as there is no central server. A few clicks on the menu of the program will connect the user's computer to the Gnutella network. Alternatively, user can select the option so that the client will connect to the network automatically when the program starts up. The user can also specify that his/her computer automatically run LimeWire when the computer starts. This will allow the user's computer to provide maximum services to the network.

After connection, the client allows users to search for a file by part of its name. For example, typing 'P2P' into user can also focus the search by specifying the type of files. There are five different types in LimeWire:

- image
- video
- documents
- programs
- audio

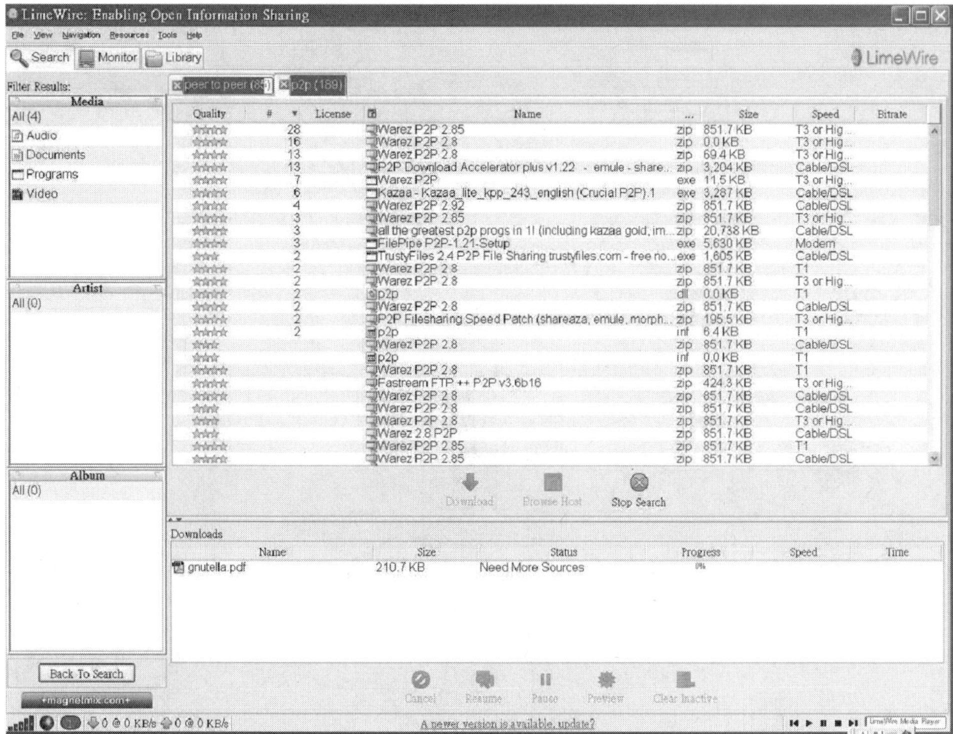

FIGURE 2.3. LimeWire client.

Sharing files is also simple. Users specify the folders they want to share with others. They can then copy or move the files to these folders. LimeWire allows advanced users to control the percentage of bandwidth that can be used for uploading.

2.4 BitTorrent

An analysis by researchers at the Xerox Palo Alto Research Center indicated that 50% of all files for sharing were stored on only 1% of the peers. About 70% of all Gnutella users do not share any files with others. In other word, all they do is 'download'. They are referred to as 'freeloaders' or 'free riders'.

If a network has a large proportion of freeloaders, it will defeat the objective to share workload in a P2P network. When a peer shares a popular file with others in a P2P network, it will attract a large volume of traffic. This successful peer needs to pay more bandwidth costs for more clients as in Fig. 2.4.

BitTorrent (Cohen, 2003) is a new protocol to solve this problem. The idea of this protocol is simple. The peer who plays the role of server breaks down a

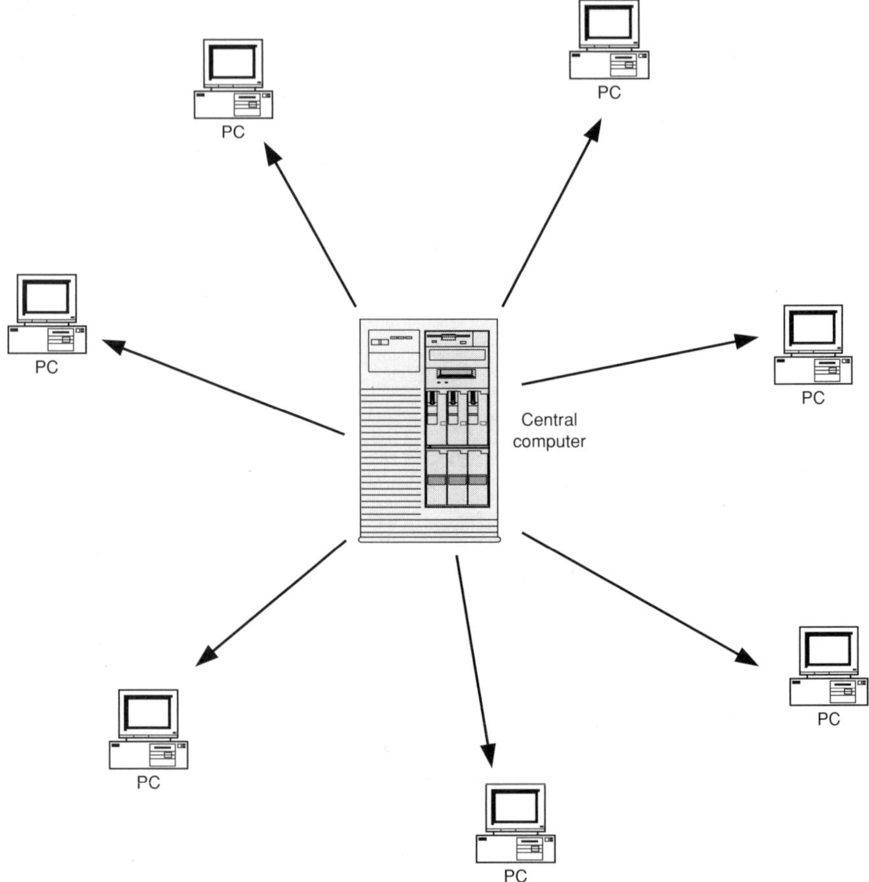

FIGURE 2.4. Traditional downloading.

file into many sub-files. If this file is requested by several clients simultaneously, each client will get a different sub-file. Once a client gets a complete sub-file, it will allow other clients to download this sub-file from this computer while it continues to download the second sub-file from the original server (Fig. 2.5). In other words, the client will assume the role of both client and server simultaneously after it gets the first sub-file. This process will continue until the download is complete.

The BitTorrent protocol is especially good for large files as the downloading process is longer. That means there are more servers in a particular period. More participants will not downgrade the performance of the whole network as the workloads are more or less evenly distributed. Indeed, the performance will be improved because there is no way to turn off the upload function of a BitTorrent program when a computer is downloading.

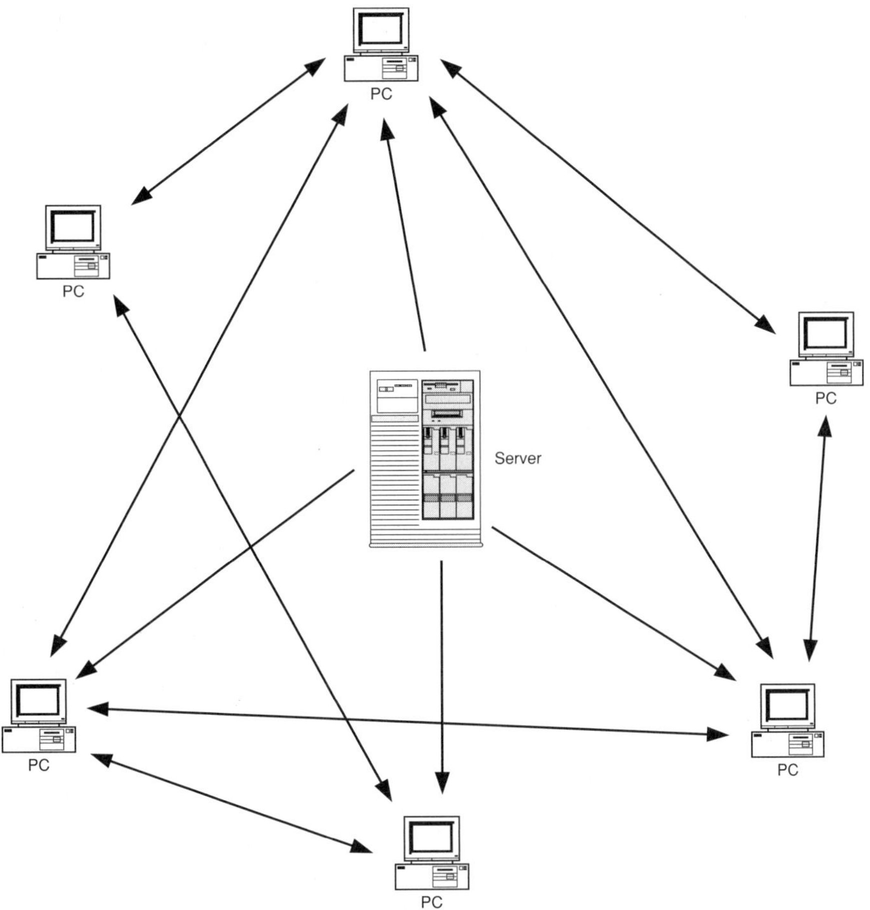

FIGURE 2.5. Cooperation of file sharing.

A schematic diagram is presented in Fig. 2.6. The server computer has four sub-files (*i.e.*, sub-1, 2, 3 and 4) in our example. Each client gets only one sub-file from the server at one time. As described in Fig. 2.6, client 1 gets these four files from different computers. The arrival of each sub-file might not follow the original order. The sequence of arrival in this case is 1-4-2-3 instead of 1-2-3-4. The actual sequence depends on the actual number of participants and sub-files in network. The algorithm of BitTorrent will try to maximize the number of sub-files available for downloading in any particular period.

In order to download a file, a user goes through the following steps:

- Install BitTorrent program.
- Surf the Web.
- Click the file on the server.

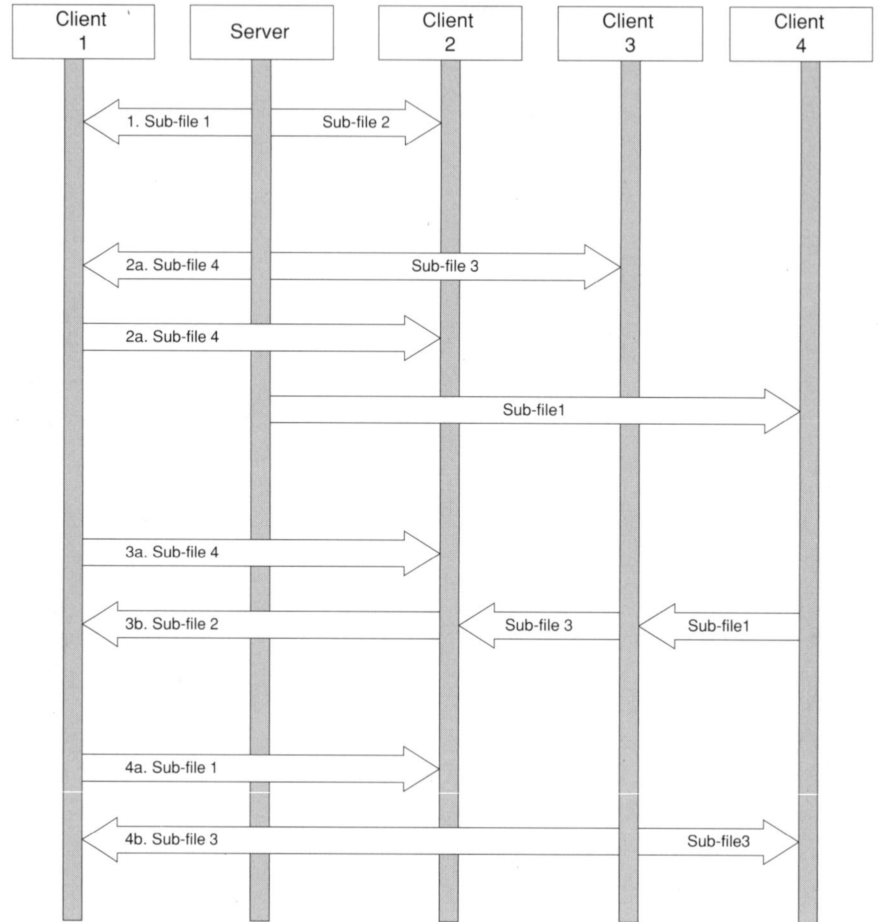

FIGURE 2.6. Example of downloading a file with four sub-files.

- Select the location to save the file.
- Wait for the completion of the process.
- Instruct the program to exit (the uploading process will continue until the user carry out this step).

This method enables the distribution of large files, such as movie files, to a large number of computers within a short time. There are a lot of applications for this technology. For example, some portals provided live video to their customers during the World Cup Final (Soccer). However, they were not able to support the large demand and many requests for connection were rejected. This protocol can solve this type of problems easily.

2.5 Common Features

Although the operations of the aforementioned three P2P systems are different, they provide the following common features:

- They enable users to join and leave the system.
- They allow users to discover each other.
- They allow users to search files which reside on other computers.
- They allow two computers to exchange files directly.

2.6 Legal Challenges

Since a large number of users illegally share copyrighted music, some people might believe that P2P technology is only a tool for piracy. This bad image might scare off some users from using PP network. However, there are still a substantial number of legitimate users who are constantly sharing different kinds of files such as photos, documents, programs, *etc.*

It is interesting to look at the history. In mid-1980s, the movie business believed that the new technology—the VHS recorder—posed a serious threat to their survival. This new technology enabled users to copy movies without the prior permission from studios. They wanted to ban this technology, and the legal battle was fought all the way to the Supreme Court. The court ruled that although some users could use VCR recorder to infringe the copyrights, there were substantial number of legitimate users. Thus VCR should not be banned. Indeed, this ruling is good for both consumers and the movie industry as rental of VCR movies eventually brought huge profits to studios.

History repeats itself. Recently, in addition to suing users for downloading and uploading copyrighted songs to the P2P network, the music industry has also brought the P2P software developers into the courtroom. Movie and music studios asked the courts to hold P2P developers liable for infringement of copyright because people use their products to share files illegally. These kinds of lawsuits create uncertainties and threaten some potential investors in P2P network development.

3
The Need for More Powerful Computers

3.1 Introduction

Dramatic increases in computer speed have been achieved over the past 40 years, but this trend will come to an end with traditional electronic technologies. The limiting factors are the speed at which information can travel and the distance it has to travel within a computer. The former is limited by the speed of light.

For the latter part, the technology used to reduce the size and distance between components is approaching the theoretical limit. Even if we can make the distance shorter than in the present technology, another problem will arise. Simultaneous electronic signal transmission between different pairs of components will start to interfere. In other words, any gains in building faster electronic components will be offset by other technical difficulties.

On the other hand, computer applications are becoming more complex and they demand more computer power. A few examples of current applications that need extremely powerful computers are

- quantum chemistry,
- molecular modelling,
- nanoelectronics,
- computational astrophysics,
- oil explorations,
- genome sequencing and cell modelling,
- drug discoveries,
- modelling of human organs,
- weather prediction and climate change modelling and
- financial market modelling.

One way to get around this problem is to use computers having more than one processor. Such machines are commonly known as parallel computers. In the ideal case, a time-consuming job can be equally divided into many sub-jobs and one processor can then handle each sub-job. These processors can thus cooperate with each other to solve a single problem. If the sub-jobs can be executed independently, then the execution time of the single job will be reduced by a factor of p, where p is the number of processors in the parallel computer. Note that this is the ideal case; other cases will be discussed later in this chapter.

3.2 Problems of Parallel Computers

Although multiprocessor computers had been developed in the past 30 years, more than 90% of the computers sold today are still single processors. Many people view parallel computing as a rare and exotic sub-area of computing; it is interesting but of little relevance to average person (Foster, 1994). The reasons for this phenomenon are simple:

- Parallel computers are still so expensive that many organizations cannot afford to use them.
- It is relatively difficult to find good programmers with parallel computing training and experience. Many universities cannot afford to buy parallel computers for their parallel computing courses.
- Many parallel computers are dedicated to special applications and cannot be used for other general applications. Thus, it is difficult to maximize the utilization of these computers.

Despite these difficulties, parallel processing is still an area of growing interest due to the enormous processing power it offers in solving a lot of computational intensive applications such as aerodynamic simulations, bioinformatics image processing, *etc.* The most important factor among these applications is a 'need of speed' in terms of completion requirements such as calculating a one-week weather forecast in less than one-week. There are two basic models of parallel computer systems, namely processor-to-memory model and processor-to-processor model.

A multiprocessor system consists of p processors plus interconnections for passing data and control information among the computers. Up to p different instruction streams can be active concurrently. The challenge is to put the p processors to work on different parts of a computation simultaneously so that the computation is done at high speed.

Every supercomputer and mainframe company in the world has parallel machines, or plans for parallel machines or an alliance that would lead to the production of parallel machines.

On the other hand, multiprocessor file servers/web servers are common. There is increasing interest in using distributed heterogeneous networks instead of truly parallel machines using various technologies. The latest development is to use P2P systems with millions computers to tackle a single problem. Let us look at two high-profile P2P networks in the next section.

3.3 CPU Power Sharing Examples

There are many CPU power–sharing P2P systems (Oram, 2001; Leuf, 2002; Barkai, 2002; Moore and Hebeler, 2002). Two high-profile examples are selected and presented in the following sections.

3.3.1 SETI@home

Giuspeppe Cocconi and Phil Morrison of Cornell University published an article 'Searching for Interstellar Communications' in the British journal *Nature* in 1959. In that article, they suggested listening to radio signals from space. Collecting and identifying intelligent signals would provide strong evidence of advanced technologies in other planets. Thus, it can be used to prove the existence of life in the stars. Their method leads to a logical and scientific approach for an interesting topic.

Inspired by this suggestion, Frank Drake started his search for life from outer space several months later. He used the equipments in National Radio Astronomy Observatory in West Virginia, United States, to study the signals from two stars—Epsilon Eridani and Tau Ceti. Drake could not find any useful result in his 3-month experiment. However, the discussion of this experiment in a 1961-conference stimulated more interests in scientific community.

Drake's experiment spawned many 'search for extraterrestrial intelligence' (SETI) projects. These projects share a single problem. They do not have the computing power to analyse all collected data. Researchers are forced to select only strong signals for analysis, although weaker signals should also be good candidates for the studies.

David Gedye, a computer scientist in Seatle, came up with the idea to use P2P systems to solve this problem in late 1994. He discussed his idea with his former professor, David Anderson, at the University of California. The SETI@home was officially established in 1999. The project was funded by SETI Institute, the Plantary Society, University of California and Sun Microsystems. Other sponsors include Fujifilm Computer Products, Quantum Corp., Informix, *etc.* About 40 Gb of data is collected daily by the telescope of this project.

The operation (Fig. 3.1) of the SETI@home project is quite simple. The owner of each personal computer downloads a small program from the server. After installation of this program, the personal computer will communicate with SETI@home computer. A work unit will be downloaded to the peer. The analysis job will be conducted by the peer, and results will be sent back to the organiser's computer through the Internet. This P2P system includes several million computers and has generated over 1 million years of computer time.

3.3.2 Anti-Cancer Project

On April 3, 2001 Intel Corporation, the University of Oxford, the National Foundation for Cancer Research and United Devices, Inc. announced a joint P2P

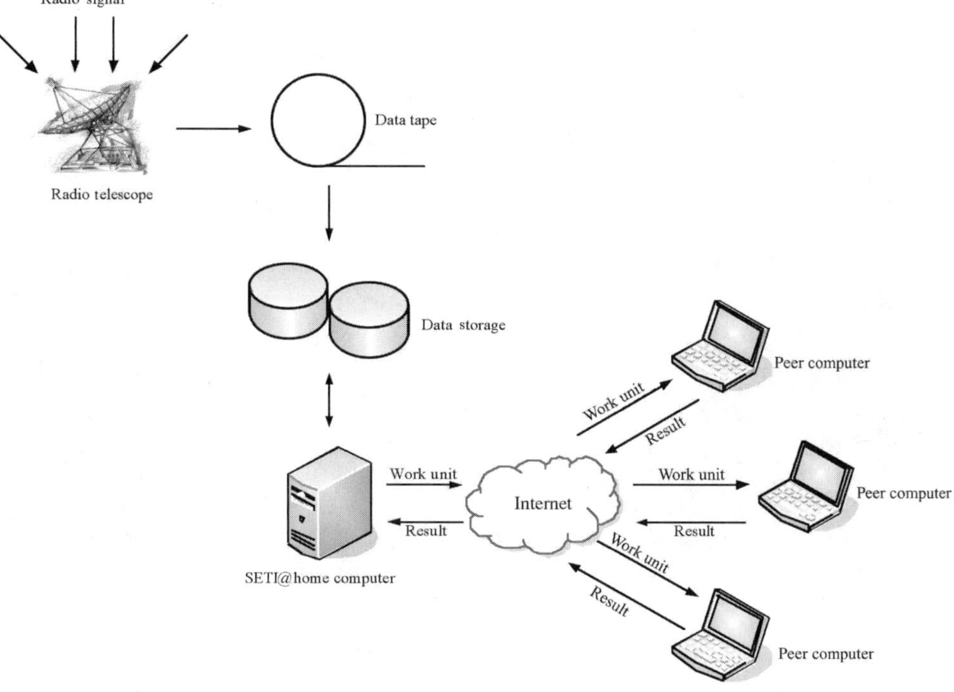

FIGURE 3.1. Operation of the SETI@home project.

computing project aimed at combating cancer by linking millions of PCs in a vast P2P network. While the computing power of each computer in the network is relatively small, linking them in this way creates a resource that is far more powerful than any single supercomputer. This project is quite simple to implement.

Each computer owner downloads a small program to his/her computer via an Internet connection. The program works as a screen saver (Fig. 3.2) and runs only when the computer is idle. The objective of the program is to discover drugs for the treatment of cancer. It will test chemicals by 'bending and flexing' each of hundreds of millions of molecular structures to determine if they interact with proteins involved in cancer.

When a given molecular structure triggers an interaction with target protein, it is referred to as a 'hit'. Hits have different levels of strength, but all of them are potential candidates for an effective treatment. All hits, together with their strengths, are recorded and transmitted back to the coordinator through Internet. In the final phase of the project, the hits will be synthesized and tested in the laboratory for their abilities to cure cancer. The most promising drugs will go through a pharmaceutical process in verifying their anti-cancer abilities.

This project is succeeding in the sense that it has attracted about 3 millions of PC owners to participate and a total donation of 410,000 years of CPU time as of

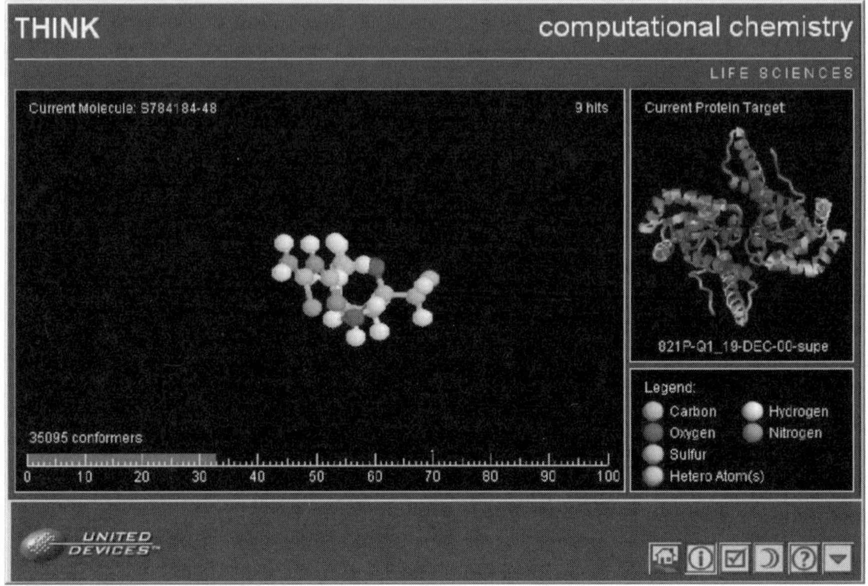

FIGURE 3.2. Screensaver of the anti-cancer project.

April 2005. About 3 billion small molecules have so far been screened against 16 protein targets.

3.4 Need for Parallel Algorithms

Using multiple computers alone cannot solve our problems. As is in the case of single computer, efficient parallel algorithms are required to realize the benefits of using multiple computers in a P2P network. As mentioned earlier, computers need to cooperate to complete a single job and there will be additional overheads in the cooperation process. Indeed, it is rather similar to human society as cooperation is quite common in real life.

We can look at a simple numerical example. A person is given 100 million numbers and is required to calculate the sum of them. If he/she can perform one 'add' operation in 1 s, then he will be able to add 28,800 numbers in a day. He would thus require about 3570 days to complete the job.

If we want to complete this task of calculation in a shorter period, a simple approach is to employ more people and divide the numbers into many parts. One worker is then assigned to each part and then all of them can work independently and simultaneously. If one person can calculate the sum in 3570 days, then theoretically 100 persons will be able to complete it in approximately 35.7 days. However, this argument will break down quickly if we increase the number of people to a very large number. If we increase the number of people to 1 million, then common sense tells us that the sum cannot be obtained within 100 s although each one of them can complete 100 'add' operations in 100 s.

Looking more deeply at this example reveals that people involved in the adding process need to communicate with each other and this kind of communication might be time consuming. Some processes cannot start until other processes are finished. The output of one process will be used for the input to another process. Some person might be idle as they are waiting for other people to finish their job before they can begin. Management is required so that each process will be delegated to the right person, and a schedule is required.

In the aforementioned example, each person is assigned 100 numbers and only gets the sub-total of these 100 numbers after all finish their own process. There are one million sub-totals at the end of this phase. We still need to add up these sub-totals to get the sum, and it is not a simple task. The people who add the sub-totals must wait for them to arrive. Careful planning is required for such a job with its huge amount of data and processes, otherwise the job will never be completed.

Indeed, a similar case happened in 1880, when the United States conducted a census of all its citizens. Although the necessary information had been collected and simple calculation was involved, they were not able to tabulate the statistics in that year due to the large volume of data. The problem was not solved until Herman Hollerith, an employee of the Census Bureau, devised a tabulating and sorting machine to handle the problem.

From this 'adding' example, we can see that the procedure to complete a job with one person will be quite different to the procedure with many people. An efficient procedure involving many people will be more complex than the procedure for one person. We need to take care of the problems of duty allocation, synchronization, resource sharing, scheduling, *etc.*

Similarly, a serial algorithm cannot usually be used efficiently in a parallel computer. Parallel algorithms are needed, which take care of the problems of synchronization, resource sharing and scheduling if they are to be efficient. For any given problem, the optimum parallel algorithm may be radically different from the optimum serial algorithm. The design goal of any parallel algorithm is to divide the task into independent sub-tasks that require little synchronization and communication. Efficient parallel algorithms result from the efficient use of process resources and the maximization of the computation–communication ratio.

3.5 Metrics in Parallel Systems

Efficient parallel algorithms are required to realise the benefits of the parallel computers. This section will present the major metrics used to measure the efficiency of parallel systems.

3.5.1 Speedup

The strongest argument against the future of parallel computing is Amdahl's Law (Quinn, 1994), which indicates that a small number of sequential operations in a parallel algorithm can significantly limit the speedup of the whole process. The term 'speedup' is defined as the ratio of the time required to complete the process with the fastest serial algorithm using one processor to the time required to complete the same process with the parallel algorithm using p processors.

If f is the fraction of operations in a process which must be executed in a sequential way, then the maximum speedup which can be achieved by a computer with p processors (Amdahl, 1967) will be:

$$\text{speedup} <= \frac{1}{f + (1 - f)/p} \tag{3.1}$$

This effect is illustrated in Figs. 3.3 and 3.4. Increasing the size of the sequential part of the problem quickly causes the speedup to saturate. Even when only 5% of the problem is executed sequentially, speedup is limited to less than one-third of what could be achieved in principle. Thus research is being focused on building efficient algorithms with few (or almost no) sequential operations, thus minimizing the idle time of each processor.

3.5.2 Efficiency

In general, only ideal systems can achieve a speedup of p for a p-processor system. This implies that the fraction of operation, f, is 0. In practice, the ideal case cannot be achieved as processors cannot devote all of their time to computing the

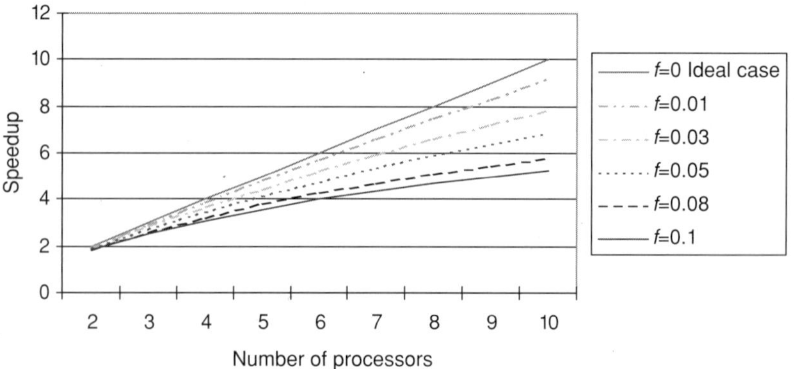

FIGURE 3.3. Speedup vs. number of processors/computers with different f values ($2 \leq p \leq 10$).

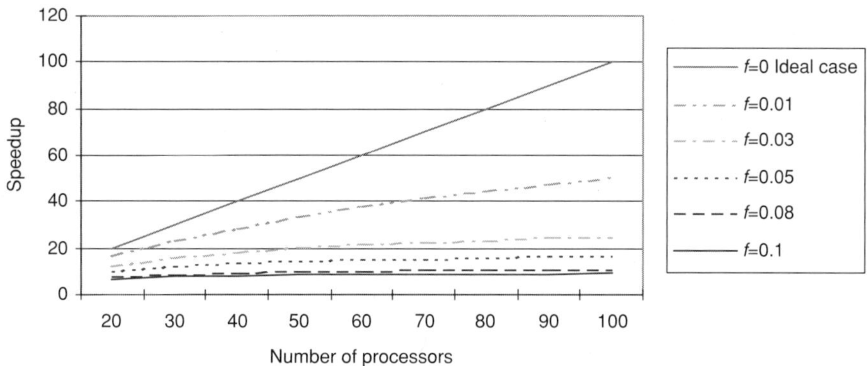

FIGURE 3.4. Speedup vs. number of processors/computers with different f values ($10 \leq p \leq 100$).

problem. There are overheads embedded such as inter-processor communication, synchronization, *etc.*

Efficiency (E) is then proposed as a measure of the fraction of time for which processors are usefully employed. In the ideal case, speedup is p when the efficiency is 1. In practice, speedup usually is less than p and efficiency is a value between 0 and 1. If E is the efficiency and p is the number of processors, they are related by the following formula:

$$E = \text{speedup}/p \tag{3.2}$$

where p is the number of processors per computers in the system.

By combining Eqs. (3.1) and (3.2), we have:

$$\begin{aligned} E &\leq \frac{\frac{1}{f + (1 - f)/p}}{p} \\ &\leq \frac{1}{fp + (1 - f)} \\ &\leq \frac{1}{f(p - 1) + 1} \end{aligned} \tag{3.3}$$

Efficiency is again a function of f. It decreases quickly when f increases. The effect is demonstrated in Figs. 3.5 and 3.6.

3.5.3 Scalability

As discussed in Section 3.5.1, the speedup usually does not increase linearly when the number of processors increases. A constant speedup tends to be achieved as overheads due to communication, synchronization, *etc.*, increase. On the other hand, an increase in the problem size yields a higher speedup and efficiency for

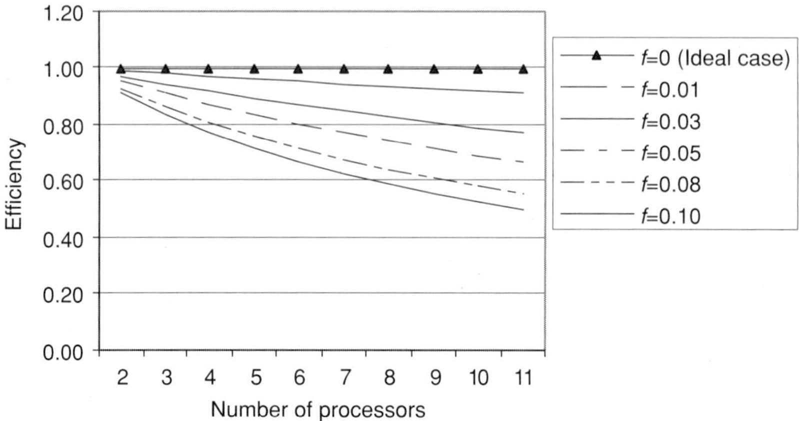

FIGURE 3.5. Efficiency vs. number of processors/computers with different f values ($2 \leq p \leq 10$).

the same number of processors. These two phenomena are common for a lot of parallel systems.

An ideal scalable parallel system maintains efficiency as the number of processor increases under the condition that the problem size is also increased. Such parallel systems are called scalable parallel systems.

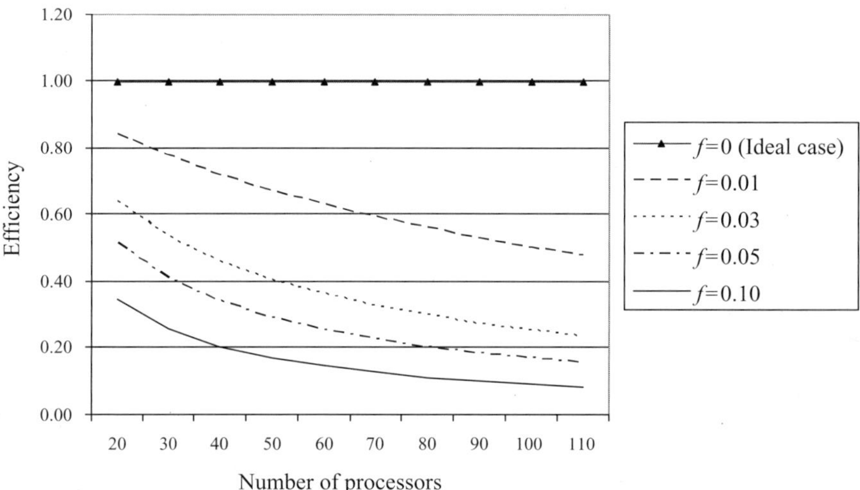

FIGURE 3.6. Efficiency vs. number of processors/computers with different f values ($20 \leq p \leq 100$).

3.6 Summary

A parallel system consists of a parallel algorithm and the parallel architectures on which it is implemented. Its performance depends on a design that balances hardware and software. The cost-effectiveness of a network depends on a large number of factors discussed in this chapter.

4
Problems and Solutions

4.1 Problems

The successful operation of the anti-cancer project is discussed in Charter 3. However, it is extremely difficult for other organizations or individuals to develop similar P2P projects according to the method used in this project. The weaknesses of this method are discussed in the following sections.

4.1.1 Security

Participants (individual PC owners) need to completely trust the research organization before they download the programs. Allowing P2P programs to run on your own computer greatly increases vulnerability to security breaches. Such breaches could include the following:

- Deleting files or directories on your computer
- Reading from or writing to the files on your computer
- Creating new files or directories on your computer
- Execute programs or commands such as deleting files, making long distance calls with your modem and telephone line, *etc.*
- Connecting to other computers and perform illegal operations such as hacking other computers

It is very difficult to secure P2P applications against these misuses, especially where participating computers use operating systems like Microsoft Windows. Any organization less famous than Intel or the University of Oxford would have problems assuring participants of the safety of their network.

4.1.2 Motivation

Participants do not get any benefits from participating in this type of project. They donate computer time only because they believe in the project's objective. Although it may well benefit humanity as a whole, it will still fail to attract the more sceptical computer owners.

Many public or commercial organizations have thousands of PCs lying idle after the 9 AM to 5 PM working hours. They are ideal 'donors' but they do not join the projects. Why not?

First of all, the research result will be the sole and exclusive property of Oxford University. Other academic institutions might not like this idea. Although the other two project partners in the cancer project, Intel and United Devices, Inc., do not in fact receive any direct benefit from this project, many people assume that they must benefit from it—even if only in public relation or marketing terms. The thought bothers many organizations and deters them from participating. For other projects with explicit commercial objectives, it may be almost impossible to attract donors.

4.1.3 Performance Efficiency

In the aforementioned project, each participant needs to download a program and then install the program on his/her computer. If the participants want to donate processing time to a new project, they will need to repeat this process. Even if the number of participants was limited to a mere 1000, the process of distributing the software to all the participating machines would take a long time to complete. It is also extremely difficult to maintain the system and perform tasks like upgrading the programs on the participants' computers. What is needed is an automatic method of storing and updating the programs on remote computers.

4.1.4 Compatibility

The software used in the cancer project can only be executed on PCs. There are a large number of workstations which use Unix or other operating systems, many of which are enterprise-based and therefore unused after office hours. These machines are usually more powerful than PCs. It is a pity that workstations cannot join this project due to compatibility problems. Another large-scale P2P project,SETI@home from the University of California (see http://setiathome.berkeley.edu for more information), which searches for extraterrestrial intelligence, uses different version of programs for different platforms to solve this problem. Participants can download their versions according to different operating systems such as MacOS, Unix, *etc.* This approach makes more computer power available to the researchers but increases the cost of maintenance as many versions need to be kept and updated.

4.2 Desirable Characteristics of P2P Systems

In a P2P architecture, participating computers communicate directly among themselves and can act as both clients and servers. Their roles will be determined according to what is most efficient for the network at the time. In order to make the power of large P2P system accessible to small organizations or even individuals, the system must have the following characteristics:

1. We need the ability to initiate a program on a remote server from a client computer. A software package to achieve this must be installed on both servers and clients. It must be inexpensive (or even free) if we want to attract individuals to join the projects. Although there are a number of P2P products on the market, all are very expensive.
2. The program must be easy to use.
3. It must be safe to use. The user should not have to examine every program from other users, which will be executed on his computer.
4. It must require a minimum amount of user intervention. Effort from the user for first-time installation is acceptable, but the maintenance work should be reduced to a minimum—the ideal would be no maintenance.
5. It should not rely on a software product from a single vendor. If there is any existing product that can achieve the task, we should not reinvent the wheel. We should be able to simply extend the features of these products. A model based on existing web server technologies can be used for P2P products; we will present this model in next section.
6. Client computers should be able to reach a large number of power-server computers within a short period. We define servers in the sense that these computers serve CPU power to other users.

4.3 Enabling Technologies

All of the earlier requirements can be met. Some problems can be solved with the latest enabling software while others need to be handled by building infrastructures. We will discuss the technologies first and present the infrastructure solutions in a later chapter.

4.3.1 Java Language

In many P2P systems, we will have heterogeneous systems with different operating systems and hardware platforms. Portability of programs is of the utmost importance in such structures. Java is the only language which delivers the 'write once, run anywhere' promise. More P2P programs will be written in Java in the future.

4.3.2 Security Managers

Java is designed with security in mind and a 'security manager' is one of its special features. A user can specify security policy in the security manager. By identifying programs to run under the security manager, we can control the programs' behaviour according to our pre-defined security policy.

4.3.3 Web Servers and Servlets

When we surf the Internet, we select a desired web page via an embedded 'link' and our browser (such as Internet Explorer or Netscape) sends a message to the

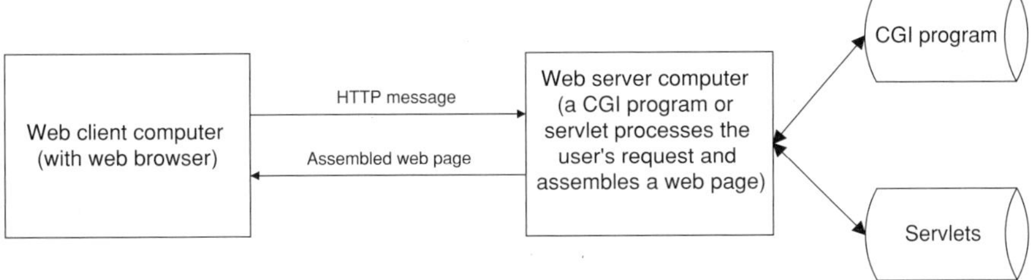

FIGURE 4.1. Process user's request with CGI or servlets.

remote web server. The message is encoded in a format referred to as hypertext transport protocol (HTTP). The web server then locates the appropriate web page and sends it back to the browser. This simple model is sufficient as long as the user only wants to view static web pages.

On the other hand, some applications require more processing and a 'dynamic' web page is required. In a typical example, the web server needs to access several records and do some calculations before it can assemble a dynamic web page. In this case, the HTTP message will invoke a program on the web server as in Fig. 4.1. Such programs on the server side are referred as Common Gateway Interface (CGI) programs or servlets. CGI programs are programs written in any language except java, while servlets are simple small java programs. Servlets are better than CGI programs as they are Java programs and have no compatibility or security problems.

4.4 Overview of Our Solution

This ability to invoke a program on a web server can be used in P2P applications. A 'power server' model using server and servlet is shown in Fig. 4.2. In this model, we introduce a new concept: a single 'client' computer can use the computing power of many 'servers' simultaneously. It is different from conventional networks which consist of many 'clients' working with one 'server'. In traditional client–server systems, servers usually serve data to the client. However, in this model we define power servers in the sense that these computers serve CPU power to other users. Every computer in the system will become a power server by installing 'web server' package and a few Java programs.

One computer acts as a client. A Java application program is executed on the client. It divides a single, computation-intensive task into many small sub-tasks and queues them in the system. The application program invokes a servlet on the server and transfers a small part of the task to the servlet. The servlet can then complete the task on the server. The computed results are sent to the client. A performance test of this model is available in Loo et al., 2000.

The behaviour of web servers is well defined. Many good server-software packages are available, and many of them are freeware/shareware (*e.g.*, vqserver). These

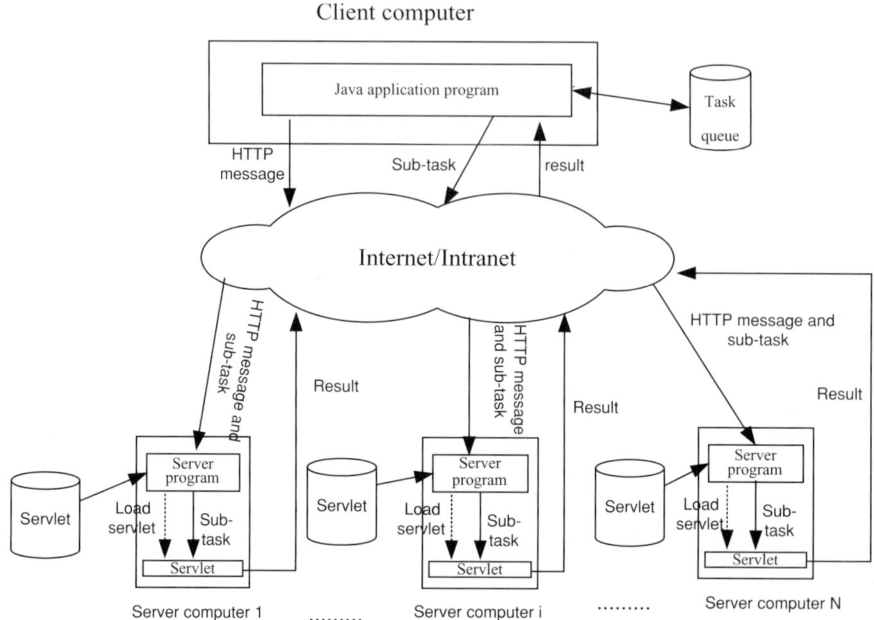

FIGURE 4.2. Power server model.

packages are quite small and easy to install. Any computer user should be able to install a web server package and allow their computer to act as a power server.

We need to update the server machines one by one in the power server model. If we have a large number of servers, this maintenance is very time consuming. This drawback can be overcome by automation. Because most web servers have upload functions, the maintenance job can be alleviated by using this function. This can be achieved by uploading the new version of the servlets and is automated by use of a special program on the client computer. The maintenance job can be further reduced if all participants are within one organization and their computers are connected in a local area network (LAN). Only one copy of the web server and servlet is installed on the network drive. Every computer invokes the web server and servlet using the single version on the network drive, and thus the maintenance job is streamlined.

4.5 Comparison

In addition to overcoming all the problems of the anti-cancer project, the following are the power server model's advantages:

- Participants can initiate new projects any time without upgrading or adding software to the power servers.

TABLE 4.1. Comparison of P2P models.

Characteristics	Napster	Cancer research project	Power server model
Resources shared	MP3 music files	CPU computing power	CPU computing power
Those who will benefit	All participants	Organizer only	All participants
Projects supported	Single project (only for MP3 file sharing)	Single project (only for drug development)	Multiple projects
Abilities for participants to start a new project	No	No	Yes
Role of participant's computer	Client and server	Server only	Client and server
Type of platforms support	Microsoft Windows, Linux	Microsoft Windows only	All platforms
Security	Participants need to entirely trust the organizer's software	Participants need to entirely trust the organizer's software	Security is enforced by the 'security manager' of the participant's computer

- Each computer owner is sure that his/her computer is safe as it is safeguarded by his/her own version of the 'security manager'.

The limitation of this model is that the programs must be written in Java as it is the only language which can run across all platforms.

The differences between all three models are summarized in Table 4.1.

4.6 Impact

Many enterprises are waiting for vendors to come up with software products that allow them to share CPU power with each other. Existing web server technologies can be easily extended using the model described in this chapter. In addition to save the expenditure on expensive dedicated P2P software packages, P2P systems using web server technologies will be easier to maintain as the features of web servers are already well understood. The web server will become a power server by adding a few java programs. We have presented an inexpensive way to dramatically increase computing power. Peer-to-peer networks for power exchange will be popular in the future. Many organizations and individuals will discover that they can do things in different, more powerful ways as they obtain increased access to computing power.

5 Web Server and Related Technologies

5.1 Introduction

This chapter introduces the basic concepts of web servers and servlets as we do not assume readers to have prior knowledge in these areas. Five power server models will be presented in Chapter 9 to 13. As three of them are run under a web server, readers need to have some knowledge of web servers and servlets. After reading this chapter, readers will be able to install a web server.

However, this is not a manual for server or servlet writing. Many features of servlets will not be covered and only those that are related to our models will be discussed. Readers interested in finding out more advanced features should refer to other books on servers and/or servlets. Equally, if you are familiar with servers and servlets, you can skip to Chapter 9.

5.2 Web Servers

When we surf the Internet, we select a desired web page via an embedded 'link' and our browser (such as, Internet Explorer or Netscape) sends a message to the remote web server. The message is encoded in a format referred to as HTTP. The web server then locates the appropriate web page and sends it back to the browser as in Fig. 5.1. This simple model is sufficient as long as the user only wants to view static web pages.

On the other hand, some applications require more processing and a 'dynamic' web page is required. In a typical example, the web server needs to access several records and do some calculations before it can assemble a dynamic web page. In this case, the HTTP message will invoke a program on the web server as in Fig. 5.2. Such programs on the server side are referred as CGI programs or servlets. CGI programs are programs written in any language except java, while servlets are simple small java programs. Servlets are better than CGI programs as they are Java programs and have no compatibility or security problems. These differences will be discussed in Chapter 6.

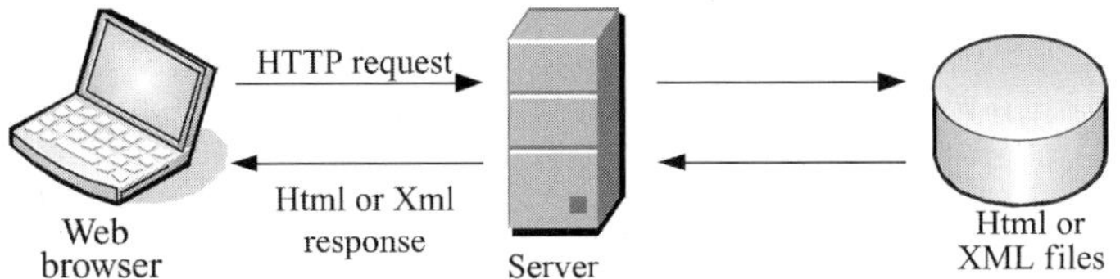

FIGURE 5.1. Web server with static web files.

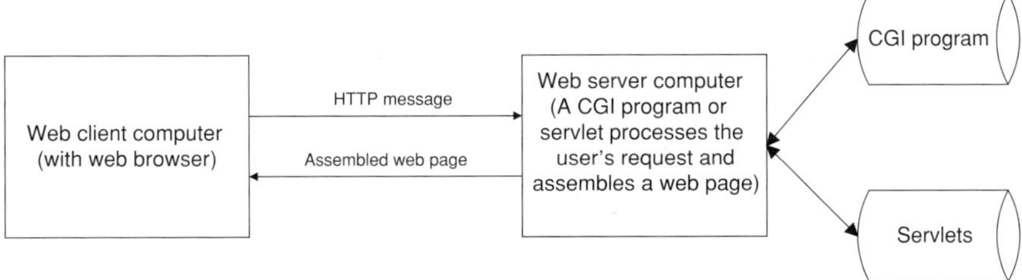

FIGURE 5.2. Process user's request with CGI or servlets.

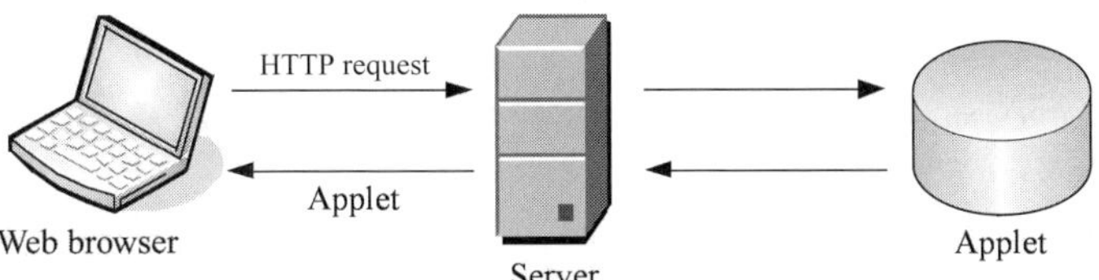

FIGURE 5.3. Applet.

In the CGI-servlet approach, everything is done in the server computer. In the traditional design, there is only one server in the system. If there are a large number of clients, the server will become a bottleneck quickly. Applets can be used to solve this problem.

Applets are Java programs which are stored in the server's hard disk as in Fig. 5.3. However, they will not be executed in the server. Whenever a user sends the HTTP message to the server, an applet will be delivered to the web browser of the client computer. The applet will be executed automatically under the web browser.

5.3 Apache Tomcat

The ability to invoke a program on a web server can be used in P2P applications. As servlet programs are used in this book, you need a web server to test these programs. We will demonstrate the installation of Apache Tomcat in the following sections.

5.3.1 Installation of J2SE Development Kit (JDK)

Download the latest java development kit from http://java.sun.com. At the time of writing this chapter, the latest version is JDK5.0. (Note that one should not select JRE as it is only a sub-set of JDK.) The installation of this package is quite easy. Double click the downloaded package and follow the steps.

After the installation of JDK, you need to check the environmental variables. If you are using Windows XP or a later version, you can set the environmental variables by the following steps:

1. Click Start from the Window
2. Click Settings
3. Click Control panel
4. Click System option
5. Select the Advanced tab
6. Click new in the 'System variables' window
7. Type 'JAVA_HOME' in the field of 'Variable name'
8. Type the path of the installation in the field of 'Variable value', *e.g.*, c:\program files\java\jdk1.5.0_05\bin

   Note that when you try to invoke a program with commands, the system will search in the current directory. If it is not successful, the system will search the directories specified in the 'path' variable.
9. Click OK (Note that a new row should be inserted into the 'system variables' window)
10. Click the row with 'path' inside the 'System variables' window
11. Click Edit inside the System variables window
12. Insert %JAVA_HOME%\bin; as the first entry in the field of directory (Note that entries are separated by a';'. Do not forget the'' in the insertion.)
13. Click OK in the ' "Edit System Variable' window
14. Click OK in the 'Environment Variables' window

You can test the installation with the following command in DOS:

java –version

The computer will display the version as illustrated in Fig. 5.4.

You can also display the version of javac by typing the following command in DOS:

javac –version

```
C:\>java -version
java version "1.5.0_05"
Java(TM) 2 Runtime Environment, Standard Edition (build 1.5.0_05-b05)
Java HotSpot(TM) Client VM (build 1.5.0_05-b05, mixed mode, sharing)
```

FIGURE 5.4. Java version

The computer will display the version as follows:

```
C:\>java -version
java version "1.5.0_05"
Java(TM) 2 Runtime Environment, Standard Edition (build 1.5.0_05-b05)
Java HotSpot(TM) Client VM (build 1.5.0_05-b05, mixed mode, sharing)
```

If anything goes wrong, you can type 'set' in DOS to check the variables. The computer will display contents of all variables as follows:

$USERNAME=alfred
ALLUSERSPROFILE=C:\Documents and Settings\All Users
APPDATA=C:\Documents and Settings\english\Application Data
CLASSPATH=C:\Program Files\Java\j2re1.4.1_02\lib\ext\QTJava.zip;.;\jsdk2.1\serve r.jar;\jsdk2.1\servlet.jar
CommonProgramFiles=C:\Program Files\Common Files
COMPUTERNAME=BUG10-ALFRED
ComSpec=C:\WINDOWS\system32\cmd.exe
FP_NO_HOST_CHECK=NO
HOMEDRIVE=C:
HOMEPATH=\Documents and Settings\english
JAVA_HOME=c:\program files\java\jdk1.5.0_05
LOGONSERVER=\\BUG10-ALFRED
MAPROOTOFF=1
NUMBER_OF_PROCESSORS=2
OS=Windows_NT
path=c:\program files\java\jdk1.5.0_05\bin

5.3.2 Installation and Testing of Tomcat

1. Download the latest version of Apache Tomcat from http://jakarta.apache.org. If you are using a system with windows, the easiest way is to use the 'executable' version. (At the time when this chapter was written, the latest version was Tomcat 5.5.12.)
2. Type the installation directory of Tomcat, *e.g.*, c:\Tomcat 5.5\. (Note that we will use c:\Tomcat 5.5 as the installation directory for the rest of this chapter.)
3. Select Examples and Webapps boxes as in Fig. 5.6.
4. The system will automatically pick up the right path of java as in Fig. 5.7. However, you can select the path if it picks up the wrong directory.
5. The default port for HTTP connection is 8080 for Tomcat as in Fig. 5.8. You can change the port to other numbers. Port 8080 and 80 are the most common ports for web servers. As the default number is 80 for most web rowsers (*e.g.*, Internet explorer and Netscape), you do not need to include the port number in the universal resource locator (URL) if the server uses port 80. However, port 8080 is used for our discussion for the rest of this book.

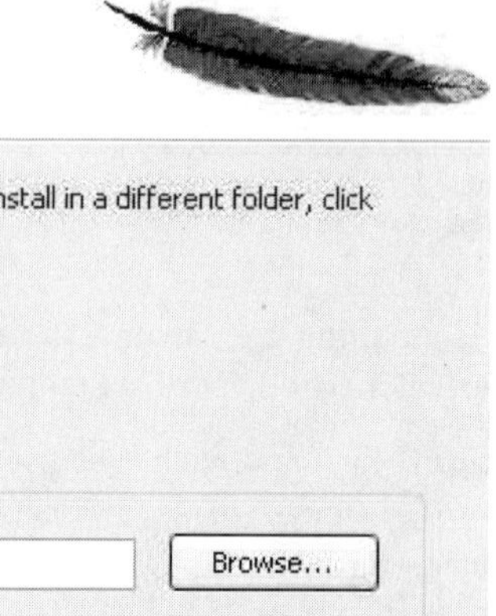

FIGURE 5.5. Installation directory of Tomcat.

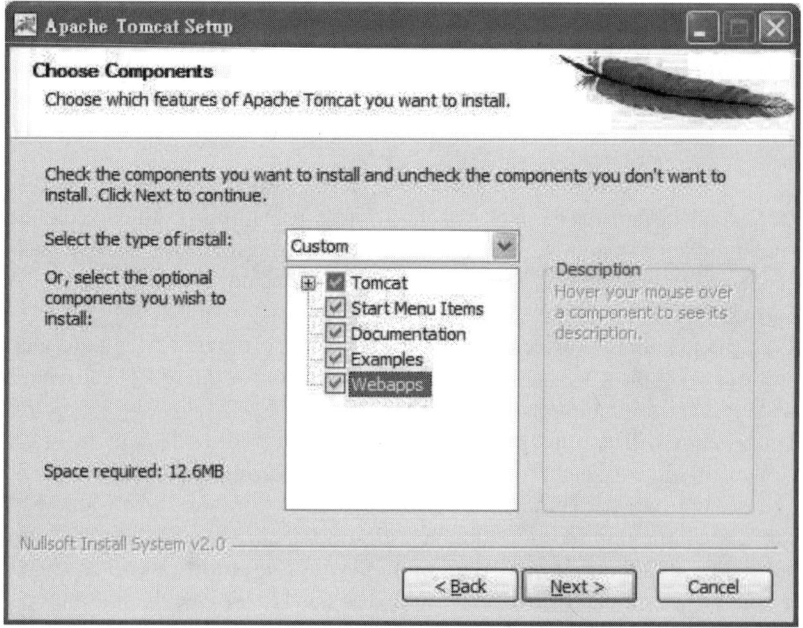

FIGURE 5.6. Components of Tomcat.

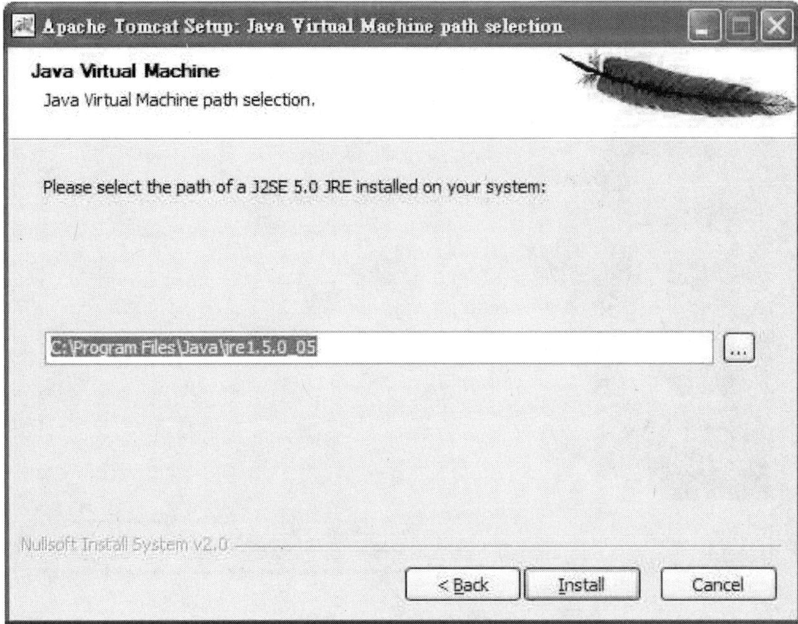

FIGURE 5.7. Path of Java virtual machine.

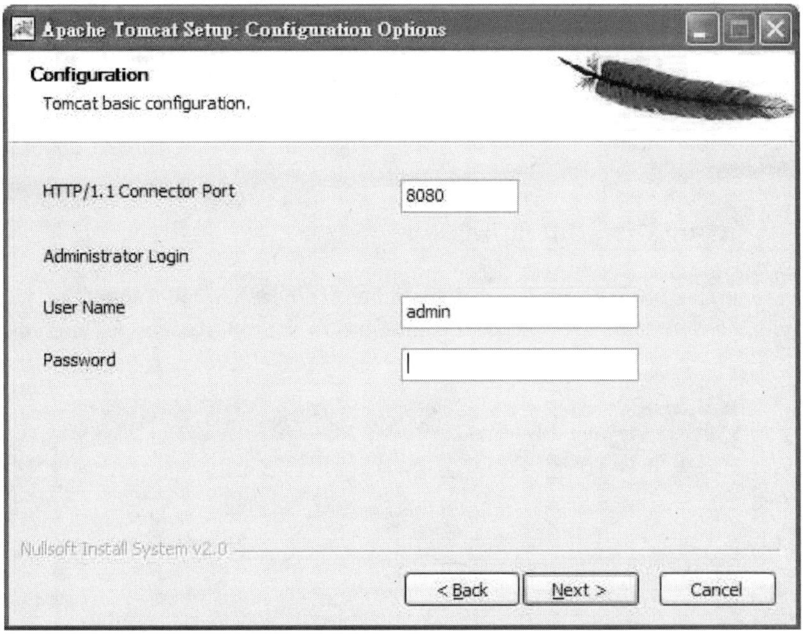

FIGURE 5.8. Port and administration password.

FIGURE 5.9. Starting Tomcat.

6. Select your own password for the administrative task in the future. Click Next.
7. Click the box of 'Run Apache Tomcat' (in Fig. 5.9) as it will allow you to test the completeness of the installation.
8. If your installation is successful, you will see the window in Fig. 5.10. You need to wait for a while depending on the speed of your computer.
9. Start a web browser and type http://localhost:8080. The computer will display the windows in Fig. 5.11 if everything is fine.

5.4 Starting the Tomcat Server

The executable programs of Tomcat are in the \Tomcat 5.5\bin folder (Fig. 5.12). (Note that \Tomcat 5.5\ is the installation folder of Tomcat in your com-

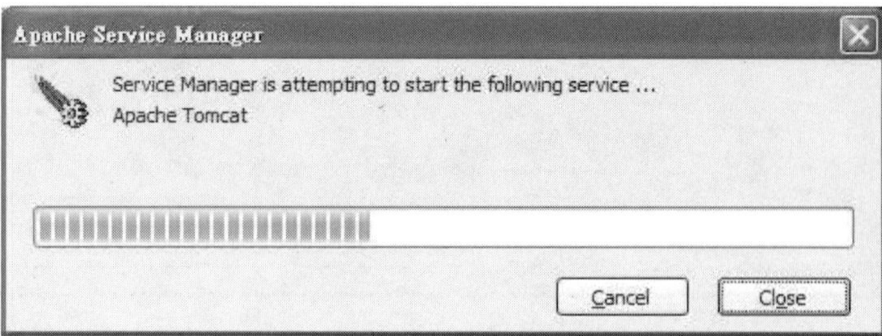

FIGURE 5.10. Starting service.

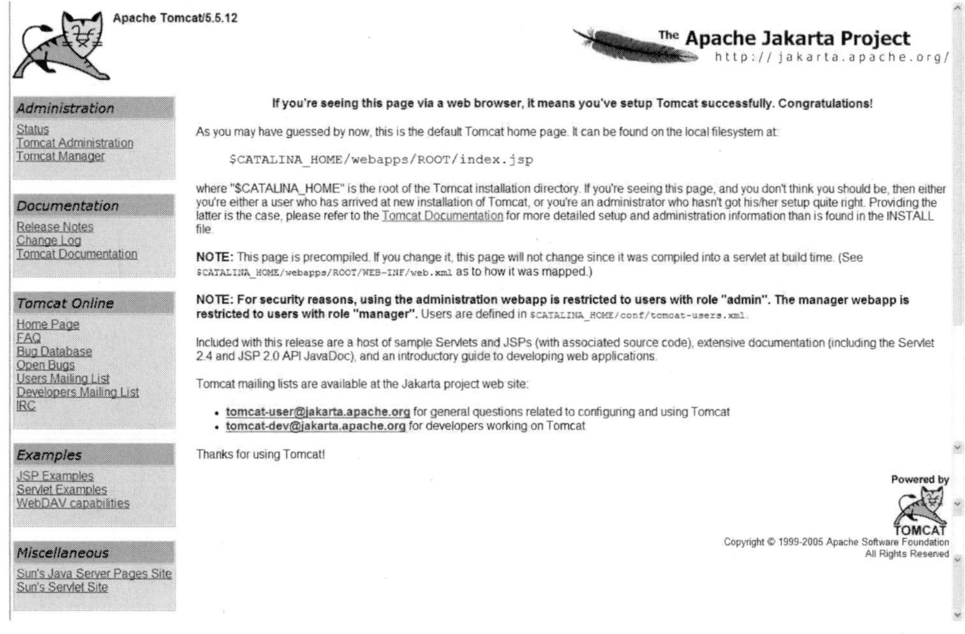

FIGURE 5.11. Default home page of Tomcat.

puter.) You can double click either tomcat5 or tomcat5w program to start the server.

The tomcat5w provides more user-friendly control features, thus it is more suitable for implementation phase (*i.e.*, after you fully test and debug your application programs). Double clicking the tomcat5w icon will bring up the window shown in Fig. 5.13. You can choose the following 'Startup type':

- Automatic
- Manual
- Disabled

You can also start or stop the service by clicking the 'Start' or 'Stop' box in Fig. 5.13.

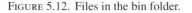

FIGURE 5.12. Files in the bin folder.

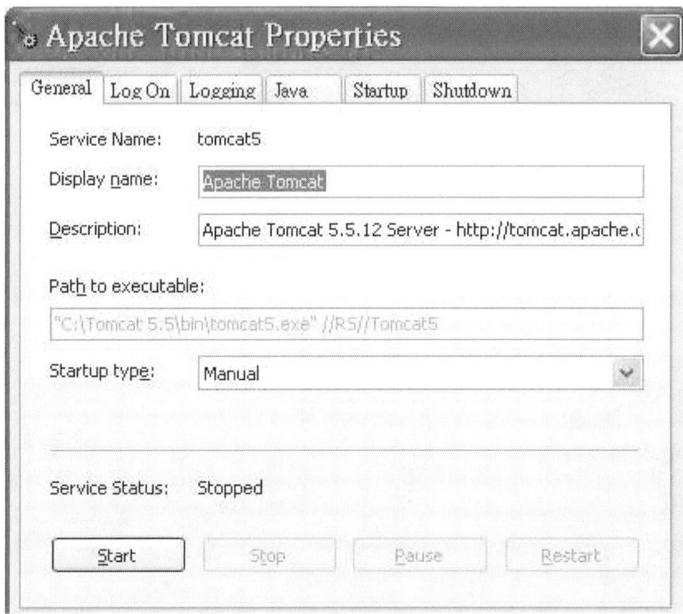

FIGURE 5.13. Window of Tomcat5w.

On the other hand, the tomcat5 provides more instant information on the activities of the server. Thus, it is more useful in the testing and development phase. Figure 5.14 is the window of tomcat5 program. Program tomcat5 will be used for demonstration in the rest of this book.

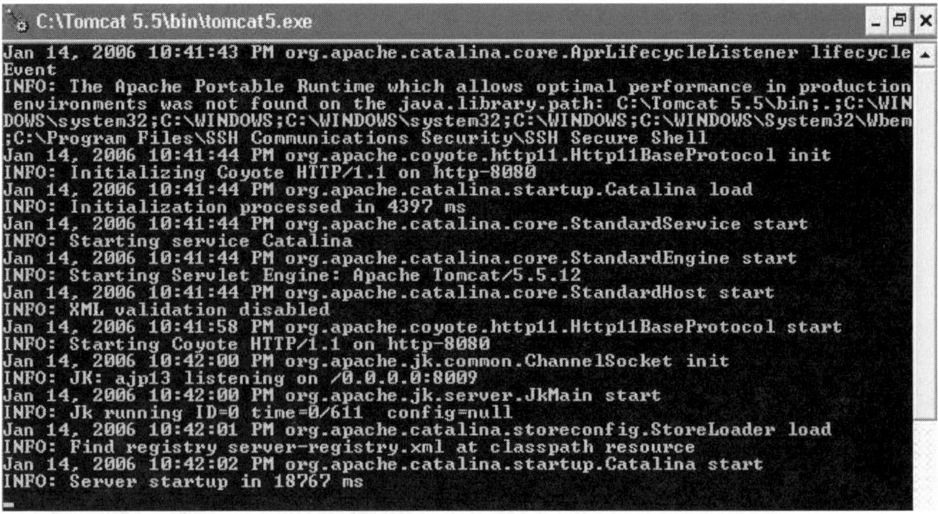

FIGURE 5.14. Window of Tomcat5.

5.5 Better Development Environment

After the installation of Apache Tomcat, you can modify the settings so it is easier and more efficient to develop your systems.

5.5.1 Servlet Compilation

Servlet features are not the core of Java servlet development kit (JSDK). Unless you are using an IDE (Integrated Development Environment such as Jbuilder) or similar tools, you need another library when you compile a servlet program. This library is included in the Apache Tomcat. You can modify the environmental variables with the following steps:

1. Click Start from the Window.
2. Click Settings
3. Click Control panel
4. Click System option
5. Select the Advanced tab
6. Click 'New' in the 'System variables' window
7. Type 'CATALINA_HOME' in the field of 'Variable name'
8. Type the path of the installation in the field of 'Variable value' *e.g.*, c:\Tomcat 5.5
9. Click OK (Note that a new row should be inserted into the 'System variables' window.)
10. Click the row with 'classpath' inside the 'System variables' window

    Note that if 'classpath' does not exist in your computer, click New inside the 'System variables' window and type 'classpath' in the 'Variable name' in the 'New System Variable' window. Jump to step 12.
11. Click Edit inside the System variables window
12. Insert *%CATALINA_HOME%\common\lib\servlet-api.jar;.;* as the first entry in the field of directory (Note that the entries are separated by a';'. Do not forget the';' in the insertion.)
13. Click OK in the 'New System Variable' window
14. Click OK in the 'Environment Variables' window

You can test the installation by compiling the simple.java program of this book. Type the following command in DOS:

javac simple.java

A new simple.class will be generated if the compilation is successful.

If you want to compile a servlet program on a computer without the Apache Tomcat, you can download another development kit (JSDK) for servlets from http://java.sun.com.

5.5.2 'Reloadable' Feature of Tomcat

You need to modify and compile your servlet program many times in the normal development and testing process. It will be extremely troublesome to stop and start the web server each time you compile a program. You can turn on the 'reloadable' feature of Tomcat by modifying the context.xml file in the *conf* path under the Tomcat installation directory. Contents of *c:\Tomcat 5.5\conf\context.xml* file are as follows:

```
<!– The contents of this file will be loaded for each web application –>
<Context>

  <!– Default set of monitored resources –>
  <WatchedResource>WEB-INF/web.xml</WatchedResource>

  <!– Uncomment this to disable session persistence across Tomcat restarts –>
  <!–
  <Manager pathname=" "/>
  – >

</Context>
```

Change <context> in second line to <context reloadable="true"> with a text editor. The servlet class will be reloaded automatically when a new version is available.

5.5.3 Invoker Servlet

All application web pages and programs should be installed under the webapps path. The simplest way is to deploy web pages and JSP programs in the webapps\root path, while servlet programs should be deployed in the webapps\root\classes path in the testing phase.

If you have many applications in your system, it will be difficult to manage them as programs of different applications mixed together. A better way is to create a folder for each application under the webapps path.

The web server needs to know how to find the servlet programs when it receives a URL from the browser. The mapping between the URL and the actual location is done by searching the web.xml files. (There will be more than one web.xml under the Tomcat directories.)

In other words, you need to modify the corresponding web.xml file whenever you deploy a new servlet program into the web server. A simpler way is to enable the invoker servlet in the Tomcat. After enabling this function, you can drop the servlet in the webapps\root\classes directory and invoke it by typing the following URL:

http://localhost:8080/servlet/yourServletName

It is useful and more convenient in the learning and testing process. I recommendyou to enable the invoker servlet if you are not familiar with Tomcat. You can enable this function by modifying the web.xml under the *conf* path.

Steps to enable the invoker servlet are as follows:

1. Locate the following two blocks in the web.xml file in the *conf* directory.

```
<!--
    <servlet>
        <servlet-name>invoker</servlet-name>
        <servlet-class>
          org.apache.catalina.servlets.InvokerServlet
        </servlet-class>
        <init-param>
            <param-name>debug</param-name>
            <param-value>0</param-value>
        </init-param>
        <load-on-startup>2</load-on-startup>
    </servlet>
-->

<!–
    <servlet-mapping>
        <servlet-name>invoker</servlet-name>
        <url-pattern>/servlet/*</url-pattern>
    </servlet-mapping>
-->
```

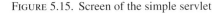

2. Remove the first line and last line of the above two blocks (*i.e.*, <!--and -->).
3. Save the web.xml file. You can turn off this function by adding back the first and last line to the blocks.
4. Create *classes* path under the C:\Tomcat 5.5\webapps\ROOT\WEB-INF.
5. Copy the simple.class of this book to the following path: C:\Tomcat 5.5\webapps\ROOT\WEB-INF\classes
6. Start a web browser.
7. Type http://localhost:8080/servlet/simple as the URL. The browser will display the screen as illustrated in Fig. 5.15.

FIGURE 5.15. Screen of the simple servlet

5.5.4 Deployment of Servlets

It will be better to put the source files and compiled files (*i.e.*, the class files) in different directories when you have a lot of programs in your application. If you are using an IDE tool (such as Jbuilder), then the IDE will take care of compilation and put the class file in the right directory. However, if you do not have an IDE on your computer, you can use the following command:

javac –d directory_of_the_class_name.java

For example, the following command will compile a simple.java program and store the simple.class file in the c:\Tomcat 5.5\webapps\ROOT\WEB-INF\classes.

e.g.,javac –d c:\Tomcat 5.5\webapps\ROOT\WEB-INF\classes simple.java

You can also use a wild card character '*' to compile all programs in the current directory.

*e.g.,javac –d c:\Tomcat 5.5\webapps\ROOT\WEB-INF\classes *.java*

It is not an interesting task to type these commands many times a day. It is also an error-prone exercise unless you have very good typing skills. You can use a batch file (or script file in unix or linux environment) to make your life easier. A tom.bat file can be found in the website of this book. The contents of this file are quite simple:

javac -d "c:\Tomcat 5.5\webapps\root\web-inf\classes" %1.java

Format of the command to invoke the batch file is *tom servlet_name*

The following command will compile the simple.java program with the batch file:

tom simple

Note that there is no need to type .java.

5.6 Directories

Tomcat has a lot of sub-directories, so it is quite complicated for beginners. You need some basic understanding of the directories and the mapping mechanism of Tomcat.

5.6.1 First Level Sub-directories

There are eight directories under the installation directories:

- bin
- common
- conf
- logs
- server
- shared
- temp
- webapps
- work

We will discuss only four of them as it will be enough for the basic operations of this book:

- bin: All executable files are stored in this directory (see Fig. 5.12 for details).
- conf: This directory stores files which control the behaviour of Tomcat server. You can modify the files with a text editor. See Sections 5.5.2 and 5.5.3 for details.
- logs: This directory stores different log files, so users can check the activities of the web server. You can view or print these files with a text editor.
- webapps: All application programs (*e.g.*, JSL and servlets) and web pages should be installed under the sub-directories of this directory.

5.6.2 Webapps Directory

There are six sub-directories under webapps if you follow the installation procedures of this chapter:

- balancer
- JSP—examples
- ROOT
- servlets-examples
- tomcat-docs
- webdav

We will discuss only four of them as follows:

- JSP—examples. This directory stores the JSP examples. Beginners can learn JSP by modifying and testing JSP programs here.
- ROOT. The simplest way is to place your application programs and web pages under this directory. This is an important directory, so we will discuss more about it in the next section.

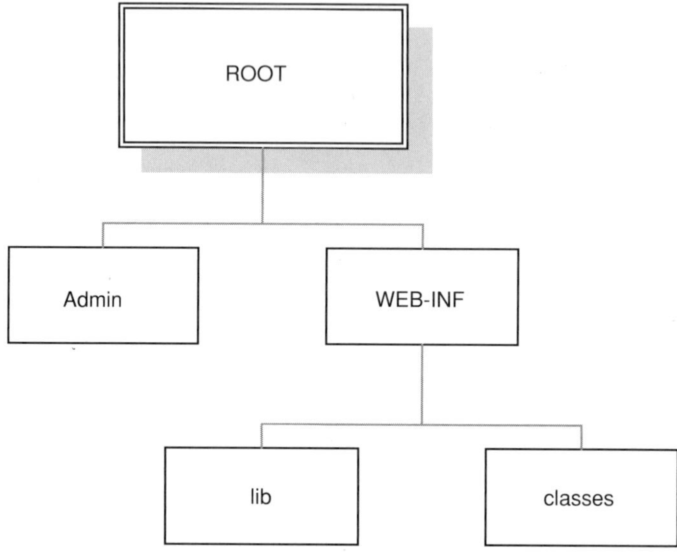

FIGURE 5.16. Structure the ROOT directory.

- servlets-examples. This directory stores the servlet examples. You should study these examples if you are not familiar with servlets. You can also test these servlets to decide whether the Tomcat installation is stalled properly.
- tom-docs. This directory stores the documentations of Tomcat.

5.6.3 ROOT Directory

This directory has the structure as shown in Fig. 5.16.

JSP and web pages should be placed directly under the ROOT. Classes of servlets should be placed under the classes directory which is created by users (if necessary). The lib directory stores the library file of Tomcat. If you have only one application or you are in the learning/testing process, storing everything under this directory will be fine. Otherwise you should create application directories as will be described in next section. A web.xml file which controls the program mapping is stored in the WEB-INF directory. The format of web.xml will be discussed in a later section.

The contents of different directories are summarized in Table 5.1.

TABLE 5.1. Important contents in directories.

Directory	Contents
ROOT	JSP and web pages (*e.g.*, index.html)
WEB-INF	web.xml
lib	Library file(s) (*e.g.*, cataline-root.jar)
classes	Class files of servlet programs

5.6.4 Application Directories

Instead of storing all programs in the ROOT of the Tomcat directories, it is better to store them on separate directories as shown in Fig. 5.17.

The structure of application directory is quite similar to that of ROOT. Users might wish to create additional sub-directories depending on the application. The following example (Fig. 5.18) is one of the possible sub-directories. A summary of contents in a typical application setting is presented in Table 5.2.

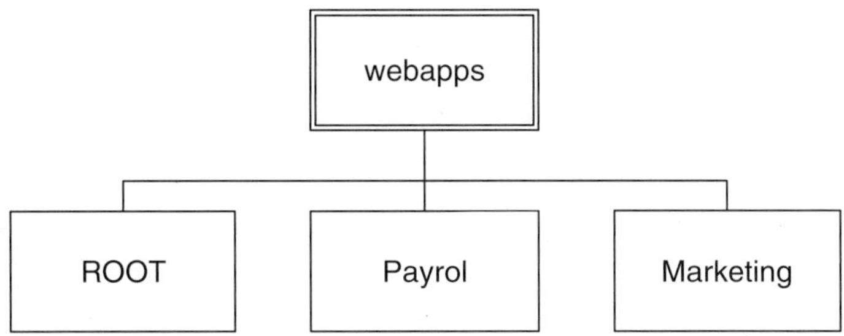

FIGURE 5.17. Example of application directories.

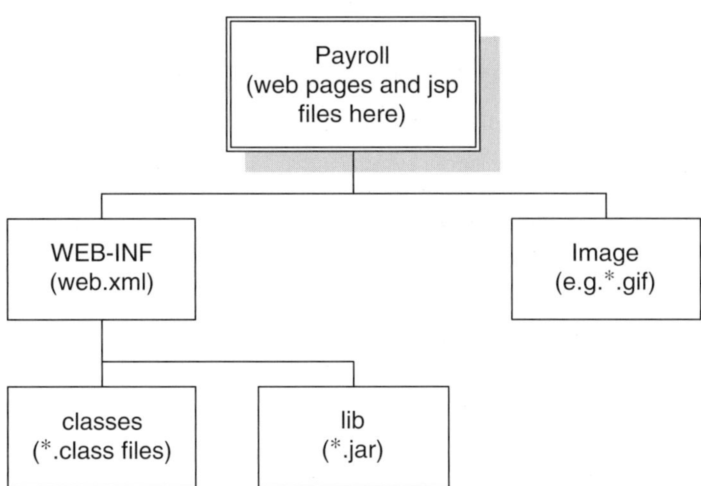

FIGURE 5.18. Example of sub-directories.

TABLE 5.2. Contents under the application directories

Directory	Contents
Application name	JSP and web pages (*e.g.*, index.html)
Image	Picture files (*e.g.*, *.gif)
WEB-INF	web.xml
lib	Library files (*e.g.*, jar files)
classes	Class files

5.7 Mapping Between URL and Servlet

After enabling the invoker servlet as in Section 5.5.3, users can install the servlet class file in the classes directory of the ROOT. Users can invoke the servlet with the following URL:

http://webSiteName:8080/servlet/servletName

For example, you can invoke the servlet simple.class in ROOT\WEB-INF\classes with the following URL:

http://localhost:8080/servlet/simple

If you create an application directory as discussed in Section 5.6.4, you need to add the name of the directory in your URL. For example, you can invoke the servlet simple.class in the payroll\WEB-INF\classes with the following URL:

http://localhost:8080/payroll/servlet/simple

5.7.1 Using web.xml for Mapping

Instead of using the default mapping of invoker servlet, you can use the web.xml to control the mapping. You modify the mapping by defining the following three variables:

- Servlet-name—the logical name of the servlet assigned by you.
- Servlet-class—the physical name of the servlet (the real name of the class).
- URL-pattern—the URL to invoke the servlet.

The format to define these three variables are as follows:

```
<servlet>
    <servlet-name>logical name of servlet</servlet-name>
    <servlet-class>physical name of servlet</servlet-class>
</servlet>
<servlet-mapping>
    <servlet-name> logical name of servlet </servlet-name>
    <url-pattern>url from web browser</url-pattern>
</servlet-mapping>
```

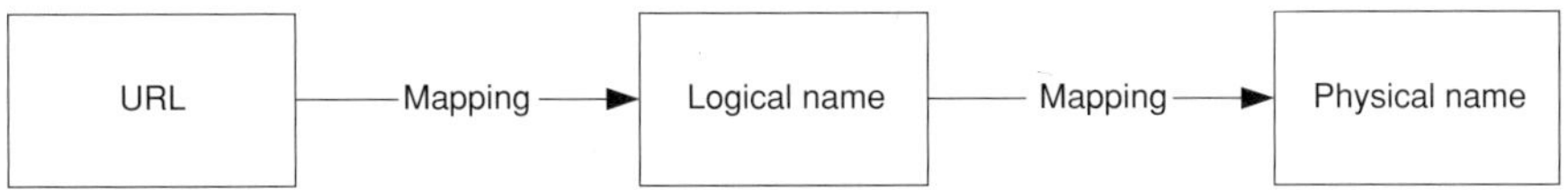

FIGURE 5.19. Mapping process.

The URL will be mapped to a logical name first. Then the logical name will map to the physical name of the servlet as in Fig. 5.19 .

5.7.2 Example 1

In this example, you modify the web.xml file in the ROOT\WEB-INF directory by the following steps:

1. Copy simple.class to ROOT\WEB-INF\classes directory.
2. Insert the following blocks to ROOT\WEB-INF\web.xml file.

```
<servlet>
        <servlet-name>simpleProgram</servlet-name>
        <servlet-class>simple</servlet-class>
</servlet>
<servlet-mapping>
        <servlet-name>simpleProgram</servlet-name>
        <url-pattern>/go</url-pattern>
</servlet-mapping>
```

   The variables are defined as follows:
   - Servlet-name—*simpleProgram.*
   - Servlet-class—*simple* (note that no need to type .class).
   - URL-pattern—*/go* (note that do not forget to type the first character '/').
3. Start your web server.
4. Start your web browser.
5. Type the following URL.

   . *http://localhost:8080/go*

The simple.class will be invoked in the server, and the screen shown in Fig. 5.15 will be displayed in the web browser. The source codes of simple.java are presented as described in Fig. 5.20.

5.7.3 Example 2

In this example, you modify the web.xml file in the payroll\WEB-INF directory by the following steps:

1. Create a directory payroll under the webapps directory
2. Create a directory WEB_INF under the payroll directory

```
import java.io.*;
import javax.servlet.*;
import javax.servlet.http.*;
public class simple extends HttpServlet
{
    public void init() throws ServletException
    {
        System.out.println("***** simple program started ******");
    }

    public void doGet(HttpServletRequest request, HttpServletResponse response)
                    throws ServletException, IOException
    {
        PrintWriter output=response.getWriter();

        output.println("<html>");
        output.println("<head>");
        output.println("<title> simple servlet</title>");
        output.println("</head>");
        output.println("<body>");
        output.println("<h1>Simple " + "</h1>");
        output.println("</body>");
        output.println("</html>");
        output.close();
    } // end of method
    public void destroy()
    {
        System.out.println("destroy method of simple servlet called");
    }
}
```

FIGURE 5.20. Simple java

3. Create a directory classes under the WEB-INF directory
4. Copy simple.class to payroll\WEB-INF\classes directory
5. Create a web.xml file in the payroll\WEB-INF directory with a text editor as:

```
<web-app>

  <servlet>
    <servlet-name>payroll</servlet-name>
    <servlet-class>simplePayroll</servlet-class>
  </servlet>

  <servlet-mapping>
    <servlet-name>payroll</servlet-name>
    <url-pattern>/pay</url-pattern>
  </servlet-mapping>

</web-app>
```

The variables are defined as follows:
- Servlet-name—*Payroll.*
- Servlet-class—*simplePayroll* (note that no need to type .class).
- URL-pattern—*/pay* (note that do not forget to type the first character '/').

6. Start your web server.
7. Start your web browser.
8. Type the following URL:

   . *http://localhost:8080/payroll/pay*

   Note: Do not forget the type the directory name 'payroll'.

The simplePayroll.class in the payroll directory will be invoked in the server. You can still invoke the same servlet by typing the following URL if the invoker servlet is effective.

http://localhost:8080/payroll/servlet/simplePayroll

The source codes of simplePayroll.java are shown in Fig. 5.21, and the output of this program is shown in Fig. 5.22.

5.7.4 Further Testing

I recommend you to modify the web.xml files (*i.e.*, modify the servlet-name and URL-pattern) of the earlier two examples and conduct more testing until you understand the mapping.

5.7.5 Advantages of Mapping

The actual deployment of servlet (*i.e.*, the actual name and location) can be hidden from the users with web.xml mapping method. It will provide better security. You can minimize changes to URLs if you change the name and location of the servlet after the implementation.

5.8 Selection of Web Servers

There are a large number of web servers. You should consider the following factors:

- Cost of the web server—As users might have a large number of servers, cost in purchasing the web server might be huge. Although there are a large number of free web servers, some of them are free only for non-commercial uses.
- Portability—Some servers can only run on a particular platform such as Microsoft Windows. This factor is more important if you have a large number of computers with different platforms.

```
import java.io.*;
import javax.servlet.*;
import javax.servlet.http.*;
public class simple extends HttpServlet
{
    public void init() throws ServletException
    {
        System.out.println("***** Simple Payroll started ******");
    }

    public void doGet(HttpServletRequest request, HttpServletResponse response)
                    throws ServletException, IOException
    {
        PrintWriter output=response.getWriter();

        output.println("<html>");
        output.println("<head>");
        output.println("<title> Simple Payroll</title>");
        output.println("</head>");
        output.println("<body>");
        output.println("<h1>Simple " + "</h1>");
        output.println("</body>");
        output.println("</html>");
        output.close();
    }// end of method
    public void destroy()
    {
        System.out.println("destroy method of simple servlet called");
    }
}
```

FIGURE 5.21. Simple payroll java

- Compatibility—Some servers do not support servlets. Some servers need to install another piece of software to extend their abilities to run servlets. If you need to support other languages, such as C, php, *etc.*, in the future, you need to study the specifications of the servers carefully.
- User interfaces—Some servers are more difficult to use than others. For example, Tomcat Apache is probably one of most popular web servers as it provides rich

Simple Payroll

FIGURE 5.22. Output of simple payroll.

set of features. The administrator needs to edit the xml files which control the behaviours of the server. Although it is faster for users to change the settings in this way, this process is error prone for inexperienced users. On the other hand, some web servers use the Window and mouse interface method to modify their settings. This kind of server is more suitable for beginners.

6
Introduction to Servlets

6.1 Introduction

This chapter introduces the basic concepts of servlets. After reading this chapter, readers will be able to modify the servlets in these models.

6.2 Servlets

A servlet is a java program that runs under a web server. It can be invoked by an HTTP message, which is received by the web server. The HTTP message can be sent either from a web browser (*e.g.*, Internet Explorer, Netscape, *etc.*) or a program from the client computer. The servlet will conduct some activities in the server and then return the result to the client (usually in the form of html).

Although the idea of 'servlets' was not created with P2P systems in mind, this method provides an easy way to control the calculation in a remote computer. It can be used in our P2P model, and it provides many advantages, which will be discussed in later chapters in more detail.

Although CGI programs can perform the same functions as servlets, we used the servlet technology for our models for the following reasons:

- *Heterogeneous parallel computing*. CGI programming can be done in almost any language, including C and C++. None of these languages are truly portable on different platforms (*e.g.*, Windows and Unix). Only the Java language is 'write once, run everywhere'. As the servlet is a pure Java solution, the actual server in our system can be any combination of hardware and operating system. The only requirement of the server computer is that it supports the execution of servlets. Indeed, we have tested our system in a heterogeneous environment consisting different Pentium computers and Sun Sparc workstations. In terms of operating systems, these included Windows 95, 98, NT, 2000, XP, Unix and Linux. We did not need to change a single line of our programs.
- *Persistency*. A servlet stays in the memory of the computer as an object after it completes its operation. It can thus respond and execute faster than a CGI

program. As it is persistent, it can maintain its state and hold external resources such as database connection, communication sockets, *etc.* Obtaining such external resources might take several seconds. The states of the program might be important for some applications. It is almost impossible for a CGI program to achieve the same as it will disappear from memory after its execution.

- *Software engineering principles.* Java is an object-oriented language and supports most software engineering principles such as objects, inheritance, strong type safety, *etc.*, while some CGI programming languages do not have the same level of support.
- *Web server's ability.* The servlet can work together with a web server in that it can obtain information from the server and use the server's functionality to perform some tasks (Hunter, 1998). Examples of such tasks include file path translation, authorization, *etc.*
- *Concurrency and communication support.* A Java servlet has built in concurrency support (Lea, 1997) by creating separate threads. Its concurrency support is better than that of C and other popular high-level CGI programs. This feature is very useful for many applications and is particularly important for parallel programming. It is much easier to write programs for communications using sockets, datagrams and multicast techniques in Java than in other languages.
- *Portability.* Since the language Java used in this implementation is highly portable, it can be run on any platform. Programs developed on one platform can be run without any modification on other platforms.
- *Safety.* In our P2P system, each server will allow servlets written by an unknown party to run on its machine. Security is an important issue as users will not be able to scrutinize them one by one. Servlets are safer than CGI programs in the following senses:
  - A servlet is written in java, and it is executed under the control of a web server. It is impossible to have pointer and invalid memory access. Thus, it cannot bring down the server if it is designed poorly or maliciously.
  - The operations of a servlet are restricted by the security manager. A properly configured security manager can restrict servlets from carrying out the following activities in the server's computer:
    - Reading or writing files.
    - Deleting files.
    - Transmitting information to other computers rather than the client which initiated the HTTP message to invoke the servlet.
  - A servlet can verify the identity of the client easily with SSL or similar technologies.

6.3 Servlet Lifecycle

Before we write a servlet, it is important to know its lifecycle. The sequence of its operations is presented in Fig. 6.1. Basically, servlets will follow these steps:

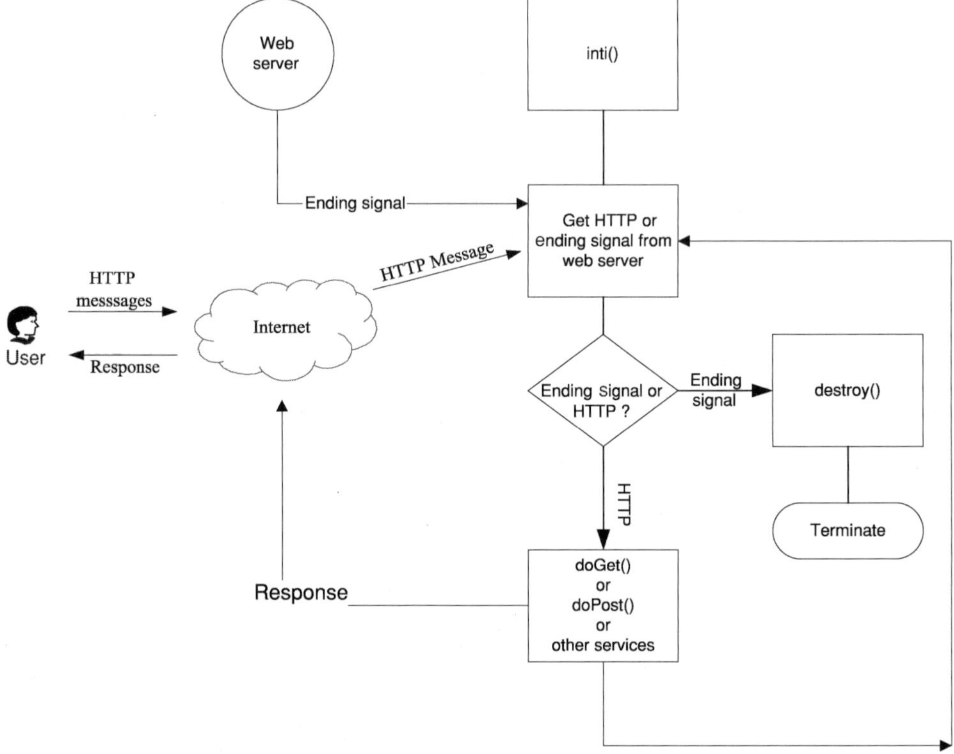

FIGURE 6.1. Lifecycle of servlet.

1. Create and initialize the servlet. The initialization is done by the following method:
   - Init()
2. Wait for the request from client. It will usually perform one of the following methods:
   - doGet()
   - doPost()
   - doHead()
   - doDelete()
   - Service()
3. Destroy the servlet. Before the termination of the servlet, you can release resources or conduct other activities (such as saving information to a file or passing information to other servlets) in the following method:
   - Destroy()

6.4 Servlet Collaboration

Servlets can cooperate with each other through a 'servlet chaining' process as shown in Fig. 6.2. You can pass the control from one servlet to the other. In other

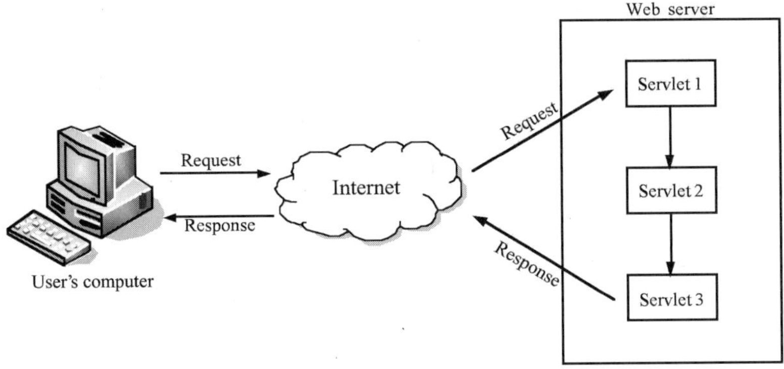

FIGURE 6.2. Servlet chaining.

words, a request from a client is handled by a series of servlets. The last servlet is responsible for sending the final answer to the client.

6.5 Basic Structure of Servlet

The basic structure of a servlet's example is as follows:

```
import java.io.*;
import javax.servlet.*;
import javax.servlet.http.*;
public class yourFileName extends HttpServlet
{
   public void init(ServletConfig config) throws ServletException
   {
         ... ... ... ...
         Your initization routine here!
   }
   public void doGet(HttpServletRequest request, HttpServletResponse response)
                        throws ServletException, IOException
   {
         Get the input
         Do something here
         Assemble and send an html file to the client
   }
   public void destroy()
   {
         Anything you want to do before termination!
   }
}
```

Servlets differ from other java programs in the following ways:

- You must include the following lines before the 'public class' statement:

  import javax.servlet.*;
  import javax.servlet.http.*;

- You must extend HttpServlet in the first line of your program. For example, public class student extends HttpServletwhere 'student' is the name of your servlet class.
- The init() and destroy() method are optional. They can be omitted if they are not necessary.
- Usually you will have at least one of the following methods in your servlet:
  - doGet()
  - doPost()
  - doHead()
  - doDelete()
  - Service()

  Most likely you perform the following functions in this method:
  - Obtain the input data.
  - Process the data (such as reading records from a file, doing some calculation, *etc.*).
  - Assemble an html file and return it to the client computer.

6.6 Sending and Receiving Information

Since only doGet() method is used in our models, we will explain how to send and receive information from the client with this method.

In order to carry out a simple test, usually we need two files:

- An html file which will send an HTTP message to the server.
- A servlet which takes the request (HTTP message) and returns an answer.

The following example asks the user to type the student ID and name in the client computer. These two fields are sent to the server. The servlet will format these two fields to an html file and send it back to the client computer. The html file (student.html) is presented in Fig. 6.3, while the servlet file (student.java) is presented in Fig. 6.4.

This program creates an output object with the following line:

PrintWriter output=response.getWriter();

Syntax of the line:

PrintWriter ***NameOfOutputObject*** *=response.getWriter();*

The following line gets the value of the variable 'name' from the browser:

```
<HTML>
 <HEAD>
        <TITLE>Get the student name</TITLE>
 </HEAD>
 <BODY>
 <FORM ACTION="/servlet/student" METHOD="get">
          <H1>
            Please type your name<BR/>
            <INPUT TYPE="Text" NAME="name" VALUE=""></INPUT>

            <INPUT TYPE="Submit"></INPUT>
          </H1>
      </FORM>
 </BODY>
</HTML>
```

FIGURE 6.3. Student.html

```
String studentName= request.getParameter("name");
```

Syntax of the line:

*request.getParameter("**NameOfVaribleFromBrowser**");*

The following line specifies the type of output. This piece of information is sent to the browser.

```
response.setContentType ("text/html");
```

Syntax of the setContentType statement:

NameOfOutputObject.setContentType ("TypeOfFile");

A new web page is assembled by the following statements:

```
output.println("<html>");
output.println("<head>");
output.println("<title> This is your first servlet</title>");
output.println("</head>");
output.println("<body>");
output.println("<h1>Your name is: <br/>");
output.println(studentName + "</h1>");
output.println("</body>");
output.println("</html>");
```

Syntax of the lines:

NameOfOutputObject.println“... ... ”); // send output to browser

```
import java.io.*;
import javax.servlet.*;
import javax.servlet.http.*;
public class simple extends HttpServlet
{
    public void init() throws ServletException
    {
    System.out.println("***** student program started ******");
    }

  public void doGet(HttpServletRequest request, HttpServletResponse response)
                throws ServletException, IOException
    {
        PrintWriter output=response.getWriter();
        String studentName= request.getParameter("name");
        response.setContentType ("text/html");
        output.println("<html>");
        output.println("<head>");
        output.println("<title> This is your first servlet</title>");
        output.println("</head>");
        output.println("<body>");
        output.println("<h1>Your name is: <br/>");
        output.println(studentName + "</h1>");
        output.println("</body>");
        output.println("</html>");
        output.close();
    } // end of method

    public void destroy()
    {
        System.out.println("destroy method called");
    }
}
```

FIGURE 6.4. Student.java

6.7 Testing your First Servlet

You can test the servlet with one computer as it can be both server and client simultaneously. We assume you have some understanding of html files. However, if you have problem in understanding html files, you can skip to Section 6.7 for a simpler version of servlet that does not use any html at all. We do not use any html in our models. Html file is presented here for academic purposes since many applications need html files (but not ours).

FIGURE 6.5. Screen on the client computer.

1. Copy the student.html file to the default html path of your web server. (Usually it is the /public path under the server directory, consult the documentation of your server if you have problems.)
2. Copy the student.class file to the default servlet path of your web server.
3. Start the web browser in your computer. If you are using only one computer, type the following line in the URL field:
   http://localhost:8080/student.html
4. You will get a screen as shown in Fig. 6.5. Type in the data and submit the form.
5. You will get the answer as in Fig. 6.6.

The browser receives the following lines from the server:

```
<html>
<head>
<title> This is your first servlet</title>
</head>
<body>
<h1>Your name is: <br/>
David</h1>
</body>
</html>
```

The sequence of the operations is presented in Fig. 6.7.

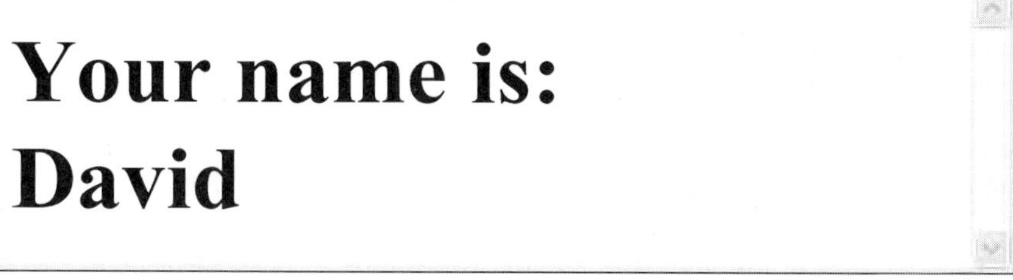

FIGURE 6.6. Answer from the server.

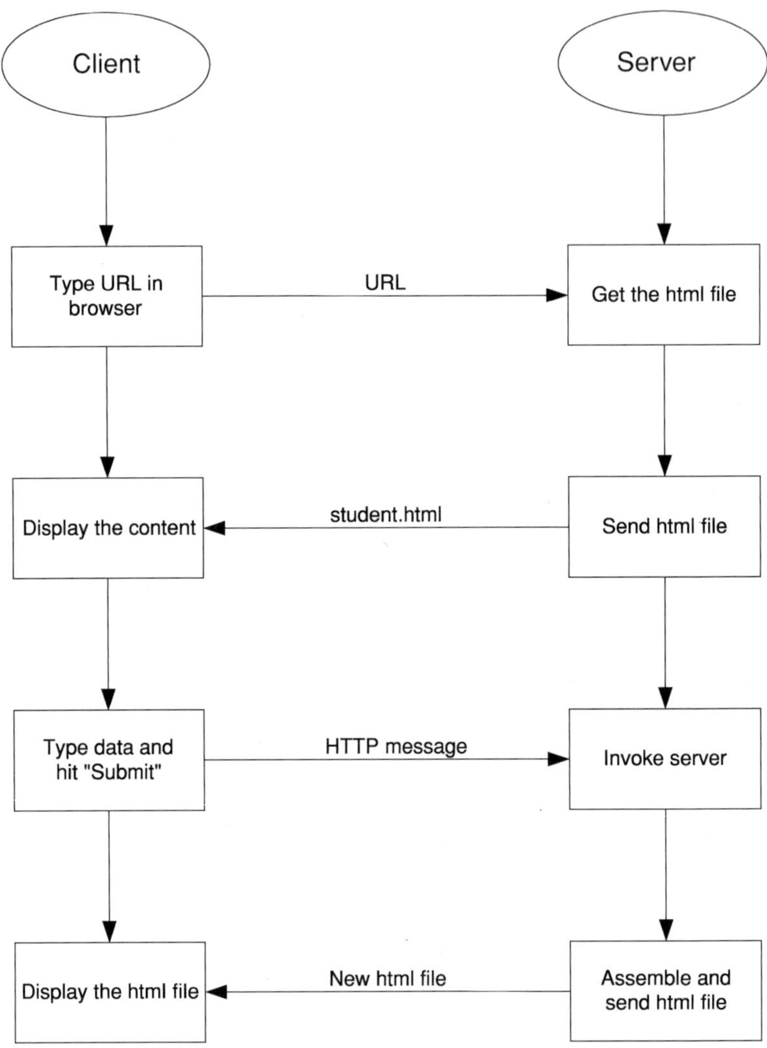

FIGURE 6.7. Sequences of the operations.

6.8 Testing Second Servlet (Without html File)

A simpler version of servlet, studentNoHtml.java, is presented in Fig. 6.8. The difference is that it will return a string of characters to the client, not html statements. A browser can still display such strings although the format is less elegant.

You can test this program with the following steps:

- Copy the program studentNoHtml.class to the default servlet path of your web server.

```
import java.io.*;
import java.net.*;
import java.util.*;
import javax.servlet.*;
import javax.servlet.http.*;
public class simple extends HttpServlet
{
    public void init() throws ServletException
    {
    System.out.println("***** student program started ******");
    }

  public void doGet(HttpServletRequest request, HttpServletResponse response)
                throws ServletException, IOException
    {
        PrintWriter output=response.getWriter();

        String studentName= request.getParameter("name");
        String studentName= request.getParameter("name");
        output.println("Your name is: " + studentName);
        output.close();
    }
    public void destroy()
    {
        System.out.println("destroy method of simple servlet called");
    }
}
```

FIGURE 6.8. StudentNoHtml.java

- Start the web server.
- Start your web browser (*e.g.*, Internet Explorer or Netscape).
- Type the following url in the browser http://localhost:8080/servlet/studentNoHtml?name=David.

The client screen is shown in Fig. 6.9.

```
Your name is: David
```

FIGURE 6.9. Client screen after the test.

6.9 Further Tests

If the tests in Sections 6.6 and 6.7 are fine, you should perform more tests with two computers. Simply modify 'localhost' to the IP address of the server computer.

6.10 Compiling the Servlet

It will be a good exercise to modify and then test the aforementioned programs to gain better understanding of the servlets. As servlet features are not the core part of JSDK, you need to download the java development kit (JSDK) from www.sun.com. Before you can compile any servlets, you need to install the development kit to your hard disk. You also need to append the directory of the development kit to the classpath. For example, if you have installed the version 2.1 JSDK to the directory of \jsdk2.1 in your hard disk, you can use the following command to add the library to the classpath:

set classpath=%classpath%;.;\jsdk2.1\server.jar;\jsdk2.1\servlet.jar;

7
Java Network Programming

7.1 Introduction

Since there are many computers in a P2P system, these computers need to communicate with each other. Knowledge of Java network programming (Courtois, 1997) is required. We will discuss the following methods in this chapter:

- URL connections
- Socket communication
- Datagram

7.2 URL Connection

When a user surfs the Web, he/she sends a URL to the remote server with a web browser. The server then returns an object according to the specification of the URL. This process is very simple and hides all technical details from the user. That is why Internet surfing is so popular.

Java is designed with Internet programming in mind. It is very easy to write a java program that can send a URL to the server. An example is presented in Fig. 7.1. It establishes a URL connection and retrieves an object (*i.e.*, a file in our example) from the web server.

First try block—The connection is established in the first try block:

```
httpMessage = new URL(args[0]);
URLConnection connection = httpMessage.openConnection();
in = new BufferedReader(new InputStreamReader(
                               connection.getInputStream()));
```

The first line picks up the URL from the first argument of the command line.

The second line creates an object *connection* from the class *URLConnection*.

The third and fourth lines create an object *in* from the class *BufferedReader*.

```
//  This program demonstrates how to:
//     1. send a url to a web server
//     2. get a text/html file according to the url
//     3. read and display the first line of the file
//
import java.net.*;
import java.io.*;
public class sendHttp
{
    public static void main (String[] args)
    {
        URL httpMessage;
        String answer;
        BufferedReader in= null;
        if (args.length >= 1)
        {
                System.out.println("your URL is:" + args[0]);
        }
        else
        {
                System.out.println("Please type the URL");
                System.out.println("Format: sendHttp URL");
                System.exit(-1);
        }

        try
        {
        httpMessage = new URL(args[0]);
        URLConnection connection = httpMessage.openConnection();
        in = new BufferedReader(new InputStreamReader(
                                connection.getInputStream()));
        }
        catch (IOException e)
        {
            System.out.println("Please check the url.");
            System.out.println(e);
            System.exit(-1);
        }
        try
        {
            answer = in.readLine();
            System.out.println("The first line of the file is: ");
            System.out.println(answer);
            in.close();
        }
        catch (IOException e)
        {
            System.out.println("problem in reading the file");
            System.out.println(e);
        }
    }
}
```

FIGURE 7.1. sendHttp.java

```
C:\add>java sendHttp http://cptra.ln.edu.hk/~alfred
your URL is:http://cptra.ln.edu.hk/~alfred
The first line of the file is:
<!DOCTYPE doctype PUBLIC "-//w3c//dtd html 4.0 transitional//en">
```

FIGURE 7.2. Screen of URL client.

Syntax of *URLConnection:*

URLConnection ***nameOfConnectionObject***= *httpMessage.openConnection();*

Syntax of *BufferedReader:*

nameOfBufferReaderObject *in = new BufferedReader(new InputStreamReader(* ***nameOfConnectionObject***.*getInputStream()));*

Second try block.—This block reads the first line of a file downloaded from the web server with the following statement:

answer = in.readLine();

You can change the statements in this block as follows if you want to read and display all lines of the file:

while ((answer = in.readLine())!=null)
System.out.println(answer);
in.close();

The complete coding of the modified program (sendHttpAll.java) can be found in the website of this book.

7.2.1 Testing

Syntax of testing command: java sendHttp URL. For example, java sendHttp http://cptra.ln.edu.hk/∼alfred

java sendHttp http://localhost:8080/phone.html

The program will display the information on the screen as shown in Fig. 7.2.

7.3 Socket Communication

Communication via the URL connection method (Courtois, 1997) is very simple. It is easy to write programs to implement this method. The protocol is well defined, and application programmers do not need to take care of the technical details. Process in the server is completely handled by the web server. However, if we need more flexibility in communication, we need to use more complex methods. Socket communication is one of them. It is similar to a phone conversation. The communication process with phones consists of the following steps:

- Dial the number.
- Wait for the other side to pick up the phone.
- Talk to each other once the connection is established.
- Hang up the phone.

It has the following characteristics:

- The connection must be established before the communication.
- Connection is maintained even if the line is idle. For example, your friend asks a question in the phone conservation. You need to think for several seconds before you can answer so there is an idle period.
- The connection is closed only after the communication process is completed.

7.3.1 Client Side Program—Socket

The following client program sends a request to establish connection with the server. It despatches a simple message 'How are you?' to the server and waits for the answer. It then displays the answer on the screen. The program is presented in Fig. 7.3.

First try block. —
The connection is established with the following lines. The first line sends a request for connection to the server. The second and third lines initialise the PrintStream object (for output) and BufferReader object (for input).

```
powerSocket = new Socket(IP, 3333);
out = new PrintStream(powerSocket.getOutputStream());
in = new BufferedReader(new InputStreamReader(
                        powerSocket.getInputStream()));
```

The syntax for defining the socket is:

Socket ***nameOfSocket***; :
nameOfSocket = *new Socket(IP, 3333);*

The syntax for defining the output object is:

PrintStream ***nameOfOutputObject*** *=null ;*
nameOfOutputObject = *new PrintStream(****nameOfSocket****.getOutputStream());*

The syntax for defining the input object:

BufferedReader ***nameOfInputObject*** *=null;*
nameOfInputObject = *new BufferedReader(new InputStreamReader(*
nameOfSocket*.getInputStream()));*

```
import java.net.*;
import java.io.*;
public class socketClient {
    public static void main(String[] args) throws IOException {
        String IP;
        PrintStream out=null ;
        BufferedReader in =null;
        Socket powerSocket;
        // ************ get parameter from command argument *******
        if (args.length >= 1)
            {
                IP =args[0];
                System.out.println("IP address:" + IP);
            }
        else
            {
                IP = "localhost";
            }
        // ************* connect to server ****************
        try
        {
            System.out.println("connecting site: "+IP);
            powerSocket = new Socket(IP, 3333);
            out = new PrintStream(powerSocket.getOutputStream());
            in = new BufferedReader(new InputStreamReader(
                                powerSocket.getInputStream()));
        }
        catch (UnknownHostException e)
        {
            System.err.println("unknown host: "+IP);
            System.exit(1);
        }
        catch (IOException e)
        {
            System.err.println("connection to: "+IP);
            System.exit(1);
        }
        System.out.println("connection ok");

        // *********** start to communicate ****************
        out.println("How are you?"); // transmit to power server
        String answer;
        if ((answer = in.readLine())!= null)
            System.out.println("server's answer: "+answer);
    } // end of main method
}
```

FIGURE 7.3. socketClient.java

Sending and receiving messages.—The following line sends a message to the server:

```
out.println("How are you?"); // transmit to power server
```

The following lines receive messages from the server:

```
String answer;
if ((answer = in.readLine())!= null)
        System.out.println("server's answer: "+answer);
```

7.3.2 Server Side Program

This program is presented in Fig. 7.4.

First try block.—This program creates a socket with the following line:

```
serverSocket = new ServerSocket(3333);
```

Second try block.—The following statement accepts the connection request from client.

```
powerSocket=serverSocket.accept();
```

Third try block.—The following lines initialise the input and output objects:

```
out = new PrintWriter(powerSocket.getOutputStream(), true);
in = new BufferedReader(new InputStreamReader(
                    powerSocket.getInputStream()));
```

Fourth try block.—The server receives a message from the client with the following lines:

```
fromClient = in.readLine();
System.out.println ("Client's Message:" +fromClient);
```

The server sends a message to the client with the following lines:

```
toClient = "Thank you! I am fine.";
out.println(toClient);
```

7.3.3 Sequences of Operations

The sequences of operations in client and server are summarized in Table 7.1.

7.3.4 Testing 1

Programs can be tested with the following steps as in Fig. 7.6:

1. Type the following command in your server machine:

```
java socketServer
```

TABLE 7.1. Sequences of operations.

	Client	Direction	Server
1	Nil		Create socket *serverSocket = new ServerSocket(3333);*
2	Create socket by sending a request to server *powerSocket = new Socket(IP, 3333);*	→ ⟶	Listen to connection request power*Socket=serverSocket.accept()*
3	Create input and output objects		Create input and output objects
4	Send a message to server *out.println("How are you?");*	⟶→	Receive a message from *fromClient = in.readLine();*
5	Receive an answer from server *answer = in.readLine()*	← ⟵	Send a message to client *out.println(toClient);*
6	Close the socket		Close the socket

2. Type the following command in your client machine as in Fig. 7.5:

   java socketClient IPaddress

   where IPaddress is the IP address of your client computer.
   e.g., java socketClient 192.168.1.2
   The client program will use 'localhost' as the IP address if the user does not type it in the command line.

7.3.5 Multi-Threads Server

The server program is fine if the system has only one client. However, you need to modify the program if the system supports many clients simultaneously. One way to handle multiple requests from clients is to generate one thread for one client's request. A new version of server program is presented in Figs. 7.7 and 7.8, and it consists of two modules:

- *mSocketServer*
  - Create a socket.
  - Listen to client's request.
  - Generate a socket.
  - Generate a thread to handle the request.
- *mSocketServerThread* (thread created by *mSocketServer*)
  - Create input and output objects.
  - Receive a message from client.
  - Send a message to client.
  - Close the socket.

```
import java.io.*;
import java.net.*;
import java.util.*;
public class socketServer

{
    public static void main (String[] args)
                throws IOException
    {
        ServerSocket serverSocket = null;
        boolean listening = true;
        Socket powerSocket= null;
        System.out.println("************************************");
        try
        {
            serverSocket = new ServerSocket(3333);
        }
        catch (IOException e)
        {
            System.err.println("please check port 3333");
            System.exit(-1);
        }
        while (listening)
        {
            try
            {
            System.out.println("waiting for Client ******");
            powerSocket=serverSocket.accept();
            }
            catch (IOException e)
            {
            System.err.println("accept failed");
            }
        // ***************************************
        String fromClient= " ";
        String toClient= "initial value";
        PrintWriter out =null;
        BufferedReader in=null;
        try
        {
        out = new PrintWriter(powerSocket.getOutputStream(), true);
        in = new BufferedReader(new InputStreamReader(
                        powerSocket.getInputStream()));
        } // END TRY
```

FIGURE 7.4. socketServer.java

```
catch (IOException e)
      {
            System.out.print ("io exception in input/output");
      }
// ************** get data from client *******
try
{
fromClient = in.readLine();
System.out.println ("Client's Message:" +fromClient);
// ************** send information to client ************
toClient = "Thank you! I am fine.";
out.println(toClient);

} // END TRY
catch (IOException e)
{
            System.out.print ("io exception in input/output ");
}

      // ****************** closing down *****************
try
{
      out.close();
      in.close();
      powerSocket.close();
}
catch (IOException e)
{
      System.out.print ("io exception in CLOSING");
}
} // end of while
}// end of main method
}
```

FIGURE 7.4. (*Continued*)

```
C:\add>java socketClient 192.168.1.2
IP address:192.168.1.2
connecting site 192.168.1.2
connection ok
server's answer: Thank you! I am fine.
```

FIGURE 7.5. Screen of client.

```
C:\add>java socketServer
***********************************
waiting for Client ******
Client's Message:How are you?
waiting for Client ******
```

FIGURE 7.6. Screen of server.

```
import java.io.*;
import java.net.*;
import java.util.*;
public class mSocketServer

{

    public static void main (String[] args)
                throws IOException
    {
        ServerSocket serverSocket = null;
        boolean listening = true;
        Socket powerSocket= null;
        System.out.println("*****************************");
        try
        {
            serverSocket = new ServerSocket(3333);
        }
        catch (IOException e)
        {
            System.err.println("please check port 3333.");
            System.exit(-1);
        }
        while (listening)
        {
            try
            {
            System.out.println("waiting for Client ******");
            powerSocket=serverSocket.accept();
            new mSocketServerThread(powerSocket).start();
            }
            catch (IOException e)
            {
            System.err.println("socket accept failed");
            }
        } // end of while
    } // end of method
}
```

FIGURE 7.7. mSocketServer.java

```
import java.io.*;
import java.net.*;
import java.util.*;
import java.net.*;
public class mSocketServerThread extends Thread
{
    Socket powerSocket=null;
    public mSocketServerThread (Socket powerSocket)
                  throws IOException
    {
        this.powerSocket=powerSocket;
        String fromClient= " ";
        String toClient= "initial value";
        PrintWriter out =null;
        BufferedReader in=null;
        try
        {
        out = new PrintWriter(powerSocket.getOutputStream(), true);
        in = new BufferedReader(new InputStreamReader(
                       powerSocket.getInputStream()));
        } // END TRY
        catch (IOException e)
            {
                System.out.print ("io exception in/out ");
            }
        //--------------------------------- get data --------------
        try
        {
        fromClient = in.readLine();
        System.out.println ("Client's Message:" +fromClient);
        // ***************** send information to client *****************
        toClient = "Thank you! I am fine.";
        out.println(toClient);
        } // END TRY
        catch (IOException e)
        {
                System.out.print ("io exception in input/output ");
        }

    // ****************** closing down ******************
        try
        {
            out.close();
            in.close();
            powerSocket.close();
        }
        catch (IOException e)
        {
            System.out.print ("io exception in CLOSING");
        }
    } // end of method
}
```

FIGURE 7.8. mSocketServerThread.java

TABLE 7.2. Sequence of the thread operation.

Steps	Client	Direction	Server
1	Nil		Create socket *serverSocket = new ServerSocket(3333);*
2	Create socket by sending a request to server *powerSocket = new Socket(IP, 3333);*	⟶ ⟶	Listen to connection request *powerSocket=serverSocket.accept()*
3	Nil		Create a thread *new mSocketServerThread (powerSocket).start();*
4	Create input and output objects		Create input and output objects
5	Send a message to server *out.println("How are you?");*	⟶ ⟶	Receive a message from *from Client = in.readLine();*
6	Receive an answer from server *answer = in.readLine()*	⟵ ⟵	Send a message to client *out.println(toClient);*
7	Close the socket		Close the socket

The following lines accept the request from the client and create a socket 'powerSocket'. A thread is generated with the socket object in the second line.

powerSocket=serverSocket.accept();
new mSocketServerThread(powerSocket).start();

The syntax of the statements:

NameOfSocket*=serverSocket.accept();*
*new mSocketServerThread(****NameOfSocket****).start();*

The sequences of the operations are summarized in Table 7.2.

The module *mSocketServer* performs steps 1 to 3 on the server's side. The module *mSocketServerThread* performs steps 4 to 7.

7.3.6 Testing 2

Programs can be tested with the following steps as in Figs. 7.9, 7.10, and 7.11:

1. Type the following command in your server machine:

   java mSocketServer

```
C:\add>java mSocketServer
************************************
waiting for Client ******
```

FIGURE 7.9. Server in waiting state.

```
C:\add>java socketClient
connecting site localhost
connection ok
server's answer: Thank you! I am fine.
```

FIGURE 7.10. Screen of client.

```
C:\add>java mSocketServer
*********************************
waiting for Client ******
Client's Message:How are you?
waiting for Client ******
```

FIGURE 7.11. Screen of server after the communication.

2. Type the following command in your client machine:

   java socketClient IPaddress

   where IPaddress is the IP address of your client computer. For example, *java socketClient 192.168.1.2*

The client program will use 'localhost' as the IP address if user does not type it in the command line.

7.4 Datagram

Datagram communication (Campione and Walrath, 2001; Deitel, 2005) is similar to mailing a letter to your friend. You insert your messages into an envelope and drop it in the post office. The advantage is that there is no need to establish a connection before you send the letter. However, the letter might not reach your friend. If the letter is important, you need to set up the mechanism to ensure that your friend receives the letter. For example, you might ask him/her to acknowledge your letter.

You insert your messages into packets via the datagram method. If one packet is not enough for your message, you can use several packets. The datagram has the following advantages and disadvantages compared with the socket communications in the previous section.

Advantages

- No need to establish connection.
- No need to wait for the other computer as there is no connection.
- Requirement of resources is minimized as we do not need to maintain the connection during the communication process.

Disadvantages

- The packet might be lost in the process.
- Packets might not be received in the original sending order.
- Programmers need to build their own error checking routine if the messages are important.

There are three forms of datagram communication:

Unicast.—A message is received by only one computer. In other words, the communication takes place only between two computers. It is quite different from multicast and broadcast methods.

Multicast.—More than one computer can receive a single message. Each computer in the network can decide whether it wants to join the multicast group.

Broadcast.—A message is sent to all computers on the network in this mode.

7.4.1 Unicast

An example with unicast is presented in this section. The client program (Fig. 7.12) sends a datagram to the server. The server sends an acknowledgement back to the client.

Datagram client program—This program accepts the user's input (the port number and IP address of the server) with the following statements. If these two pieces of information are not specified, the default values will be used (*i.e.*, 3334 for port number and localhost for address).

```
if (args.length >= 1)
  {
          serverSite = args[0];
  }
    else
      {
          System.out.println("please type the server address:");
          System.out.println("DatagramClient serverAddress portNumber");
          System.exit(-1);
      }
if (args.length ==2) portNum=Integer.parseInt(args[1]);
```

This program sends a message 'How are you?' to the server with the following statements:

```
DatagramSocket socket = new DatagramSocket();
InetAddress address = InetAddress.getByName(serverSite);
byte[] ServerMsg = new byte[28];
String msg="How are you?";
ServerMsg = msg.getBytes();
DatagramPacket toServerPacket;
```

```
//     Operations of this program:
//     1. send a datagram to server
//     2. receive a datagram from client
//
import java.io.*;
import java.net.*;
import java.util.*;

public class DatagramClient
{
      public static void main(String[] args) throws IOException
      {
        int portNum =3334;
        String serverSite=null;
   if (args.length >= 1)
      {
            serverSite = args[0];
      }
      else
         {
            System.out.println("please type the server address:");
            System.out.println("DatagramClient serverAddress portNumber");
            System.exit(-1);
         }
      if (args.length ==2) portNum=Integer.parseInt(args[1]);
      System.out.println("port : " + portNum);
      DatagramSocket socket = new DatagramSocket();
      InetAddress address = InetAddress.getByName(serverSite);
      byte[] ServerMsg = new byte[28];
      String msg="How are you?";
      ServerMsg = msg.getBytes();
      DatagramPacket toServerPacket;
      toServerPacket = new DatagramPacket(ServerMsg, ServerMsg.length,
                              address,portNum);
      socket.send(toServerPacket);
      // ****** receive datagram **********
      DatagramPacket packet;
      packet = new DatagramPacket(ServerMsg, ServerMsg.length);
      socket.receive(packet);
      String fromServer = new String(packet.getData());
      System.out.println("Server's Address: " + packet.getAddress());
      System.out.println("Server's message: " + fromServer);

   socket.close();
      }
}
```

FIGURE 7.12. DatagramClient

```
toServerPacket = new DatagramPacket(ServerMsg, ServerMsg.length,
                        address,portNum);
socket.send(toServerPacket);
```

Syntax of the statements:

```
DatagramSocket nameOfSocket = new DatagramSocket();
DatagramPacket nameOfPackett;
nameOfPackett= new DatagramPacket(NameOfMesssage,
                                  NameOfMesssage.length,
                                  AddressOfOtherComputer,
                                  portNumberOfOtherComputer);
nameOfSocket.send(nameOfPackett);
```

The statements which receive a message from other computer are simpler. It does not need to know the details of the sender (such as address and port number). Only three lines are required:

```
DatagramPacket packet;
packet = new DatagramPacket(ServerMsg, ServerMsg.length);
socket.receive(packet);
```

Syntax of the above three lines:

```
DatagramPacket NameOfPacket;
NameOfPacket = new DatagramPacket(NameOfMessage,
                                  NameOfMessage.length);
NameOfSocket.receive(NameOfPacket);
```

Datagram server program.—The server waits for a request (a simple ‘How are you?’ message in this example) from the client. It sends a reply (‘I am fine!’ message) to the client. The server can entertain up to 100 messages before it terminates the program. The source codes of the program are presented in Fig. 7.13.

This program waits for message with the following statement:

```
socket.receive(fromClient);
```

The server can obtain the client’s information with the following statements:

```
int clientPort =fromClient.getPort();
System.out.println("Client's site: " +fromClient.getAddress());
System.out.println("Client's port: " + clientPort);
int clientLength=fromClient.getLength();
```

In order to send a reply to the client, the server needs to know the port number and address of the client. However, there is no need to send these two pieces of information to the server in the client program.

```
//    This thread sends the answer to client 100 times.
//
import java.io.*;
import java.net.*;
import java.util.*;

public class DatagramServer
{
      public static void main(String[] args)
      {
        int portNum =3334;
   if (args.length >= 1)
      {
           portNum =Integer.parseInt( args[0]);
      }
         byte[] dataMsg = new byte[29];
         String msg;
         System.out.println("port of client: " + portNum);
         try
         {
              DatagramSocket socket = new DatagramSocket(portNum);
              //    the server is receiving in our example
         System.out.println("socket created");
              for (int i = 1; i < 101; i++)
                {
                   DatagramPacket fromClient =new DatagramPacket(dataMsg,
                                                                   dataMsg.length);
                   // waiting for message from client
                   socket.receive(fromClient);
                   int clientPort =fromClient.getPort();
                   System.out.println("Client's site: " +fromClient.getAddress());
                   System.out.println("Client's port: " + clientPort);
                   int clientLength=fromClient.getLength();
                   String clientMsg = new String(fromClient.getData(),0,clientLength);
                   System.out.println("Client's message: " +clientMsg);
                   System.out.println("Length of Msg: " + clientLength);
                   msg = "I am fine! " ;
                   dataMsg = msg.getBytes();

                   DatagramPacket toClient = new DatagramPacket(dataMsg,
                                                          dataMsg.length,
                                                          fromClient.getAddress(),
                                                          clientPort);
                   socket.send(toClient);
                   System.out.println("just sent " + i + " packets\n");
                } // end of for loop
                socket.close();
         }

         catch (IOException e)
         {
         e.printStackTrace();
         }

      }
}
```

FIGURE 7.13. DatagramServer.java

```
C:\add>java DatagramServer 3335
port of client: 3335
socket created
Client's site: /127.0.0.1
Client's port: 1382
Client's message: How are you?
Length of Msg: 12
just sent 1 packets

Client's site: /192.168.1.3
Client's port: 1096
Client's message: How are you?
Length of Msg: 12
just sent 2 packets
```

FIGURE 7.14. Screen of Datagram Server.

Syntax of the methods:

NameOfSocket*.receive(****NameOfIncomingMessage****)****—receive a message***
NameOfIncomingMessage*.getPort()* - *obtain port number*
NameOfIncomingMessage*.getAddress()* - *obtain address*
NameOfIncomingMessage*.getLength()* - *obtain length of the message*

Testing.—These programs can be tested with following steps:

- Type the following command in the server window (Fig. 7.14):

  java DatagramServer **3335**

  where **3335** is the port number (default=3334)
- Type the following command in the client window (Fig.7.15)

  java DatagramClient **localhost 3335**

If the test is successful, you can start the client program on a second computer. The syntax of the command is:

java DatagramClient **AddressOfServer PortNumberOfServer**
e.g., java DatagramClient 192.168.1.2 3335

The server program will remain in the memory until it serves 100 messages.

```
C:\add>java DatagramClient localhost 3335
port : 3335
Server's Address: /127.0.0.1
Server's message: I am fine!
```

FIGURE 7.15. Screen of datagram client.

7.4.2 Multicast

In some applications, we need to send a message to many computers. It will be time consuming if we use the unicast method. The same message needs to be sent many times. A better approach is to use the multicast method as a message can be sent to multiple computers simultaneously. It is much faster. Furthermore, the message is sent only once.

Although both multicast and broadcast methods can send messages to multiple computers, multicast provides greater flexibility. The broadcast method sends a message to all computers in the network. On the other hand, clients can decide whether they need a particular message by joining and leaving multicast group. This allows us to involve a selected group of computers in a network in our communication process.

7.4.2.1 Multicast Client Program

This program joins a multicast group and picks up five messages from the server. It does not need to know the IP address of the server. However, it needs to specify the port number of the server. The default port is 3334 in both server and client programs in our example. Users can override the port number by supplying it in the command that invokes the program (see Fig. 7.16).

The following lines allow the user to override the default value of the port number which is used by the server.

```
if (args.length >= 1)
{
    portNum =Integer.parseInt( args[0]);
}
```

The following lines enable the client to join the multicast group:

```
MulticastSocket socket = new MulticastSocket(portNum);
InetAddress address = InetAddress.getByName("230.0.0.1");
socket.joinGroup(address);
```

Syntax of the aforesaid lines:

MulticastSocket ***NameOfSocket****= new MulticastSocket(portNumberOfServer);*
InetAddress ***NameOfAddress****= InetAddress.getByName("****MuticastChannel****");*
NameOfSocket*.joinGroup(****NameOfAddress****);*

where MulticastChannel is a value from 224.0.0.1 to 239.255.255.255

The program obtains a message from the server with the following line:

```
socket.receive(packet);
```

```
import java.io.*;
import java.net.*;
import java.util.*;

public class MulticastDemoClient
{
    public static void main(String[] args) throws IOException
    {
      int portNum =3334;
    if (args.length >= 1)
    {
        portNum =Integer.parseInt( args[0]);
    }
      System.out.println("port : " + portNum);
      MulticastSocket socket = new MulticastSocket(portNum);
      InetAddress address = InetAddress.getByName("230.0.0.1");
      socket.joinGroup(address);
      byte[] ServerMsg = new byte[28];
      DatagramPacket packet;
      packet = new DatagramPacket(ServerMsg, ServerMsg.length);
      for (int i = 0; i < 5; i++)
          {
            socket.receive(packet);
            String fromServer = new String(packet.getData());
            System.out.println("Server's Address: " + packet.getAddress());
            System.out.println("Time of Server : " + fromServer);
          }
    socket.leaveGroup(address);
    socket.close();
      }

}
```

FIGURE 7.16. MulticastDemoClient

7.4.2.2 Server Side Program

This server program sends 100 messages (the current date and time) to the network. It does not wait for the client to take any actions. It does not have any knowledge of the number of clients in the network.

If you multicast a large number of messages in a prolonged period, it will overload the network. Other computers will not be able to communicate. In our example, the program sleeps for 3 s after it sends a message so it will not overload the network. The whole process will take about 300 s (*i.e.*, 5 min) if it is not interrupted by user. The default port is 3334 but user can override it (if necessary).

```
//   This program sends 100 multicast messages
//
public class MulticastDemoServer
{
     public static void main(String[] args)
     {
       int portNum =3334;
     if (args.length >= 1)
     {
          portNum =Integer.parseInt( args[0]);
     }

       new MulticastDemoServerThread(portNum).start();
     }
}
```

FIGURE 7.17. MulticastDemoServer.java

This program consists of two modules:

- *MulticastDemoServer* (Fig. 7.17)
- *MulticastDemoServerThread* (Fig. 7.18)

The *MulticastDemoServer* module performs only two functions:

- Accept user's input (*i.e.*, port number) with the following lines:

```
if (args.length >= 1)
{
     portNum =Integer.parseInt( args[0]);
}
```

- Create a thread to handle the multicasting with the following lines:

```
new MulticastDemoServerThread(portNum).start();
```

The new thread is presented in Fig. 7.18. The constructor accepts the port number from the *MulticastDemoServer* module.

This program multicasts the message with the following lines:

```
InetAddress group = InetAddress.getByName("230.0.0.1");
DatagramPacket packet = new DatagramPacket(now, now.length,
                                            group, portNum);
socket.send(packet);
```

```
//    This thread sends the time of server 100 times.
//
import java.io.*;
import java.net.*;
import java.util.*;

public class MulticastDemoServerThread extends Thread
{
      int portNum;
      public MulticastDemoServerThread (int portNum)
      {
            this.portNum=portNum;
      }
      public void run()
      {
       long ONE_SECOND = 1000;
       byte[] now = new byte[29];
       String msg;
       System.out.println("port of client: " + portNum);
       try
       {
            MulticastSocket socket = new MulticastSocket();
            // no need to specify the port number
            //       as the server is not receiving anything in our example
            for (int i = 0; i < 100; i++)
               {
                     msg = new Date().toString() ;
                     now = msg.getBytes();

                 InetAddress group = InetAddress.getByName("230.0.0.1");
                 DatagramPacket packet = new DatagramPacket(now, now.length,
                                                          group, portNum);
                 socket.send(packet);
                 System.out.println("just sent " + i + " packets");
                    // sleep for a while
                 try
                    {
                        sleep((long)(3 * ONE_SECOND));
                  }
                        catch (InterruptedException e)
                    {
                        System.out.println("cannot sleep?");
                    }
            } // end of for loop
            socket.close();
      }

      catch (IOException e)
      {
            e.printStackTrace();
      }

   }
}
```

FIGURE 7.18. MulticastDemoServerThread.java

```
C:\add>java MulticastDemoServer
port of client: 3334
just sent 0 packets
just sent 1 packets
just sent 2 packets
just sent 3 packets
just sent 4 packets
just sent 5 packets
just sent 6 packets
just sent 7 packets
just sent 8 packets
just sent 9 packets
just sent 10 packets
```

FIGURE 7.19. Screen of multicast server.

Syntax of the aforementioned lines:

InetAddress ***NameOfGroup****= InetAddress.getByName(****MulticstChannel****);*
DatagramPacket ***NameOfPacket****= new DatagramPacket(****NameOfMessage****,*
NameOfMessage*.length,*
MulticstChannel,
PortNumber*);*

NameOfSocket*.send(****NameOfPacket****);*

The following line causes the thread to enter 'sleep"' state for 3 s.

*sleep((long)(3 * ONE_SECOND));*

7.4.2.3 Testing

The testing procedures are very simple:

- Type 'java MulticastDemoServer' in the server computer (Fig. 7.19).
  Syntax of the command: java MulticastDemoServer portNumber
  where port number is optional.

```
C:\add>java MulticastDemoClient
port : 3334
Server's Address: /192.168.1.2
Time of Server   : Tue Feb 07 14:03:16 CST 2006
Server's Address: /192.168.1.2
Time of Server   : Tue Feb 07 14:03:19 CST 2006
Server's Address: /192.168.1.2
Time of Server   : Tue Feb 07 14:03:22 CST 2006
Server's Address: /192.168.1.2
Time of Server   : Tue Feb 07 14:03:25 CST 2006
Server's Address: /192.168.1.2
Time of Server   : Tue Feb 07 14:03:28 CST 2006
```

FIGURE 7.20. Screen of first multicast client.

```
C:\add>java MulticastDemoClient
port : 3334
Server's Address: /192.168.1.2
Time of Server  : Tue Feb 07 14:03:25 CST 2006
Server's Address: /192.168.1.2
Time of Server  : Tue Feb 07 14:03:28 CST 2006
Server's Address: /192.168.1.2
Time of Server  : Tue Feb 07 14:03:31 CST 2006
Server's Address: /192.168.1.2
Time of Server  : Tue Feb 07 14:03:34 CST 2006
Server's Address: /192.168.1.2
Time of Server  : Tue Feb 07 14:03:37 CST 2006
```

FIGURE 7.21. Screen of second multicast client.

- Type 'java MulticastDemoClient' in the two client computers. Each client joins the multicast group at a different time so the contents in their screens (Figs. 7.20 and 7.21) are different in our example.
  Syntax of the command: java MulticastDemoServer portNumber
  where port number is optional

7.5 Differences

The differences between socket, unicast, multicast and broadcast are summarized in Table 7.3.

TABLE 7.3. Differences of communication methods.

Communication methods	Server-client ratio	Reliability	Communication directions
Socket	One to one (for each connection)	Reliable	Two ways
Unicast	One to one	Unreliable	One way
Multicast	One to many	Unreliable	One way
Broadcast	One to all	Unreliable	One way

8
Testing and Enhancements of Servlets

8.1 Introduction

Servlets are java programs, and they are executed under the control of a web server. They provide the following advantages:

1. The life cycle of a servlet is well defined and so it is easier to follow the program's logic.
2. Communications and initialization of servlets are actually handled by the web server. The server hides the technical details from developers so programmers can concentrate in writing the logic of their applications.
3. A servlet can support the requests of multiple clients at the same time.

However, it is more complicated to test the servlets than other java programs. We will introduce some features that can enhance the testing and performances of servlets in this chapter.

8.2 Debugging Techniques

Writing communication programs is usually more complicated than developing other programs because they involve at least two computers. In some cases, there are many computers communicating simultaneously in the system. If you are using an integrated development environment (IDE) such as Borland JBuilder, it will make your life easier. However, these tools still have their limitations. It is extremely difficult to simulate communications of multiple computers (*i.e.*, multiple servers and browsers) with one IDE. It might be inconvenient or expensive to install the IDE on every computer in the network.

One common debugging technique in the old days was to insert 'print' statements to the programs when there were hardly any debugging tools. This technique is still useful for the testing of communication programs involving large numbers of computers. It provides the following information to the programmers:

- Confirmation that a particular block is executed.
- The value of a variable at a particular time.

After the completion of the debugging process, these statements should be removed. Users will be bothered if you supply them with too many irrelevant pieces of information. However, if you insert a large number of 'print' statements in the program, it will be a time-consuming and error-prone exercise to remove them later. Furthermore, you might still need them in a later stage as some bugs are still not discovered in the testing phase.

This problem can be overcome by incorporating a test indicator (a variable) in the program. The 'print' is active only if the indicator is 'on'. You can change the value of the test indicator by specifying the parameter in the command invoking the program.

Nevertheless, you cannot change the test indicator of a servlet with a command as it is invoked by the web server. We will discuss methods that can modify the parameters in a servlet.

8.2.1 Parameters in web.xml File

The value of the test indicator can be controlled by modifying the web.xml file in the web server. The following example controls the value of a parameter 'debugInd'. Its value is '0' in the example.

```
<servlet>
   <servlet-name>init</servlet-name>
   <servlet-class>init</servlet-class>
   <init-param>
         <param-name>debugInd</param-name>
         <param-value>0</param-value>
   </init-param>
</servlet>

<servlet-mapping>
   <servlet-name>init</servlet-name>
   <url-pattern>/init</url-pattern>
</servlet-mapping>
```

Syntax of the lines is as follows:

```
<servlet>
   <servlet-name>logical name of servlet</servlet-name>
   <servlet-class>physical name of servlet</servlet-class>
   <init-param>
         <param-name>Name of parameter</param-name>
         <param-value>Value of parameter</param-value>
   </init-param>
</servlet>
```

```
import java.io.*;
import javax.servlet.*;
import javax.servlet.http.*;
public class init extends HttpServlet
{
    String ind;
    public void init() throws ServletException
    {
        System.out.println("***** init program started ******");

        ServletConfig cfg = getServletConfig();
        ind= cfg.getInitParameter("debugInd");
        System.out.println("Test Indicator:"+ind);
    }

    public void doGet(HttpServletRequest request, HttpServletResponse response)
                throws ServletException, IOException
    {
        PrintWriter output=response.getWriter();
        response.setContentType ("text/html");
        output.println("<html>");
        output.println("<head>");
        output.println("<title> simple servlet</title>");
        output.println("</head>");
        output.println("<body>");
        output.println("<h1>Simple " + "</h1>");
        if (ind.equals("1"))
            output.println("<h2>testing</h2>");
        output.println("</body>");
        output.println("</html>");
        output.close();
    } // end of method

    public void destroy()
    {
        System.out.println("destroy method of init called");
    }
}
```

FIGURE 8.1. init.java

```
<servlet-mapping>
   <servlet-name>logical name of servlet </servlet-name>
   <url-pattern>url from web browser</url-pattern>
</servlet-mapping>
```

The program shown in Fig. 8.1 gets the value of the test indicator from the block. It displays 'simple' on the browser's screen. It displays an additional message 'testing' on the client's screen if the value of the test indicator is '1'.

FIGURE 8.2. Screen of the browser (test indication off).

The following statements retrieve the value of the indicator from the web.xml file:

ServletConfig cfg = getServletConfig();
ind = cfg.getInitParameter("debugInd");

Syntax of the aforementioned line is

ServletConfig **NameOfConfig** = *getServletConfig();*
NameOfVariable = **NameOfConfig**.*getInitParameter("***NameOfParameter***");*

Testing (test indicator off)

1. Insert the block (in Section 8.2.1) into the web.xml file and save it.
2. Start the web server.
3. Start your browser.
4. Type http://localhost:8080/init.

Figure 8.2 shows the screen of the browser. The value of the test indicator is also displayed on the console of Tomcat.

Testing 2 (indicator on)—We turn on the test indicator in this test.

1. Start the web server.
2. Change the value of the indicator to '1'as in the following block. Note that you do not need to close the Tomcat server when you update the web.xml file. The server will automatically re-load the context file as in Fig. 8.3. 'Destroy' methods of servlets will be called.

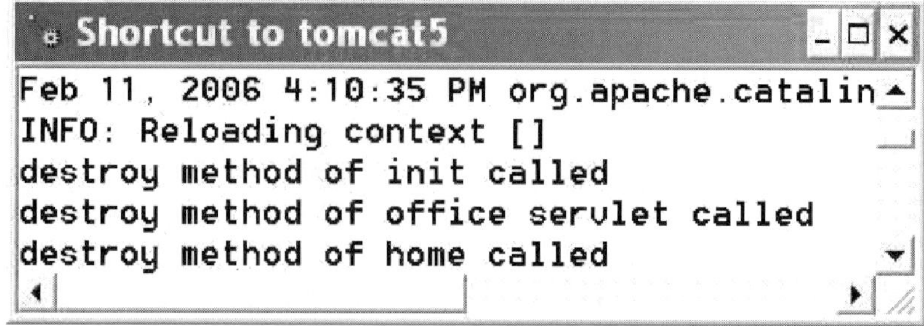

FIGURE 8.3. Reloading context.

FIGURE 8.4. Screen of program *init* (test indicator on).

Simple

testing

```
<servlet>
   <servlet-name>init</servlet-name>
   <servlet-class>init</servlet-class>
   <init-param>
        <param-name>debugInd</param-name>
        <param-value>1</param-value>
   </init-param>
</servlet>

<servlet-mapping>
   <servlet-name>init</servlet-name>
   <url-pattern>/init</url-pattern>
</servlet-mapping>
```

3. Start your browser.
4. Type http://localhost:8080/init.

Figure 8.4 shows the screen of the browser. The value of the test indicator is also displayed on the console of Tomcat.

8.3 Global Parameters

In addition to controlling the test indicator, parameters can be used to change the operations of servlets in run time. For example, instead of coding the file name inside the servlet, it can be stored in the parameter. Parameters in the web.xml file provide more flexibility in your program. It can minimize maintenance work if this technique is used properly.

In the previous section, you learn how to specify a parameter for one servlet. If several servlets share the same parameter, you still need to insert one block for one servlet. This is a tedious task. Besides, maintenance will be more difficult if there are a large number of such parameters. A better way is to use the 'context parameter' to define global variables. A 'context parameter' can be accessed by all servlets of an application system.

8.3.1 Example of a Context Parameter

This example defines a parameter 'global'. Its value is 'ip.txt'.

```
<context-param>
   <param-name>global</param-name>
   <param-value>ip.txt</param-value>
</context-param>
```

Syntax of the block is as follows:

```
<context-param>
   <param-name>Name of the global parameter</param-name>
   <param-value>Value of the global parameter</param-value>
</context-param>
```

8.3.2 office.java

The program shown in Fig. 8.5 extracts two file names from the web.xml file. The first file name is a global file, which is also used by other servlets. The second file is used by this program only.

The following statements retrieve the global file name:

```
ServletContext global = getServletContext();
GlobalFile=global.getInitParameter("global");
System.out.println("Global value:"+GlobalFile);
```

The following statements retrieve the private file name:

```
ServletConfig cfg = getServletConfig();
LocalFile= cfg.getInitParameter("FileName");
System.out.println("Local value: "+LocalFile);
```

The corresponding lines for the private file name in the web.xml are as follows:

```
<servlet>
   <servlet-name>office</servlet-name>
   <servlet-class>office</servlet-class>
   <init-param>
         <param-name>FileName</param-name>
         <param-value>File_1.txt</param-value>
   </init-param>
</servlet>

<servlet-mapping>
   <servlet-name>office</servlet-name>
   <url-pattern>/office</url-pattern>
</servlet-mapping>
```

```
import java.io.*;
import javax.servlet.*;
import javax.servlet.http.*;
public class office extends HttpServlet
{
    String GlobalFile;
    String LocalFile;
    public void init() throws ServletException
    {
        System.out.println("*** office program started ***");
        ServletConfig cfg = getServletConfig();
        LocalFile= cfg.getInitParameter("FileName");
        System.out.println("Local value: "+LocalFile);

        ServletContext global = getServletContext();
        GlobalFile=global.getInitParameter("global");
        System.out.println("Global value:"+GlobalFile);
    }

    public void doGet(HttpServletRequest request,
                          HttpServletResponse response)
                 throws ServletException, IOException
    {
        PrintWriter output=response.getWriter();
        response.setContentType ("text/html");
        output.println("<html>");
        output.println("<head>");
        output.println("<title> office</title>");
        output.println("</head>");
        output.println("<body>");
        output.println("<h1>");
        output.println("Globle File: "+GlobalFile);
        output.println("<br/>");
        output.println( "Local File: "+LocalFile);
        output.println("</h1>");
        output.println("</body>");
        output.println("</html>");
        output.close();
    } // end of method

    public void destroy()
    {
        System.out.println("destroy method of office called");
    }
}
```

FIGURE 8.5. office.java

The following statements send the value of both parameters to the browser:

```
output.println("Globle File: "+GlobalFile);
output.println("<br/>");
output.println( "Local File: "+LocalFile);
```

8.3.3 Testing of office.java

1. Start your web server.
2. Insert the following blocks to the web.xml file.

```
<context-param>
   <param-name>global</param-name>
   <param-value>ip.txt</param-value>
</context-param>
<servlet>
   <servlet-name>office</servlet-name>
   <servlet-class>office</servlet-class>
   <init-param>
         <param-name>FileName</param-name>
         <param-value>File_1.txt</param-value>
   </init-param>
</servlet>

<servlet-mapping>
   <servlet-name>office</servlet-name>
   <url-pattern>/office</url-pattern>
</servlet-mapping>
```

3. Sart the web browser.
4. Type the following URL
   http://localhost:8080/office

Figure 8.6 shows the screen of the browser, while Fig. 8.7 shows the screen of server.

FIGURE 8.6. Screen of browser.

FIGURE 8.7. Screen of browser.

8.3.4 *home.java*

The program shown in Fig. 8.8 is almost identical to office.java except the name of the class. However, it picks up a different private file name from the web.xml file.

8.3.5 *Testing of home.java*

1. Start your web server.
2. Insert the following blocks into the web.xml file.

```
<servlet>
   <servlet-name>home</servlet-name>
   <servlet-class>home</servlet-class>
   <init-param>
      <param-name>FileName</param-name>
      <param-value>File_2.txt</param-value>
   </init-param>
</servlet>

<servlet-mapping>
   <servlet-name>home</servlet-name>
   <url-pattern>/home</url-pattern>
</servlet-mapping>
```

3. Sart the web browser.
4. Type the following URL
   http://localhost:8080/home
   Figure 8.9 shows the screen of the browser, while Fig. 8.10 shows the screen of server.
5. Compare the output of both office.java and home.java.

```
import java.io.*;
import javax.servlet.*;
import javax.servlet.http.*;
public class home extends HttpServlet
{
    String GlobalFile;
    String LocalFile;
    public void init() throws ServletException
    {
        System.out.println("*** home program started ***");
        ServletConfig cfg = getServletConfig();
        LocalFile= cfg.getInitParameter("FileName");
        System.out.println("Local value: "+LocalFile);

        ServletContext global = getServletContext();
        GlobalFile=global.getInitParameter("global");
        System.out.println("Global value:"+GlobalFile);
    }

    public void doGet(HttpServletRequest request,
                      HttpServletResponse response)
            throws ServletException, IOException
    {
        PrintWriter output=response.getWriter();

        output.println("<html>");
        output.println("<head>");
        output.println("<title> home</title>");
        output.println("</head>");
        output.println("<body>");
        output.println("<h1>");
        output.println("Globle File: "+GlobalFile);
        output.println("<br/>");
        output.println( "Local File: "+LocalFile);
        output.println("</h1>");
        output.println("</body>");
        output.println("</html>");
        output.close();
    } // end of method

    public void destroy()
    {
        System.out.println("destroy method of home called");
    }
}
```

FIGURE 8.8. *home.java*

FIGURE 8.9. Screen of browser—home.java

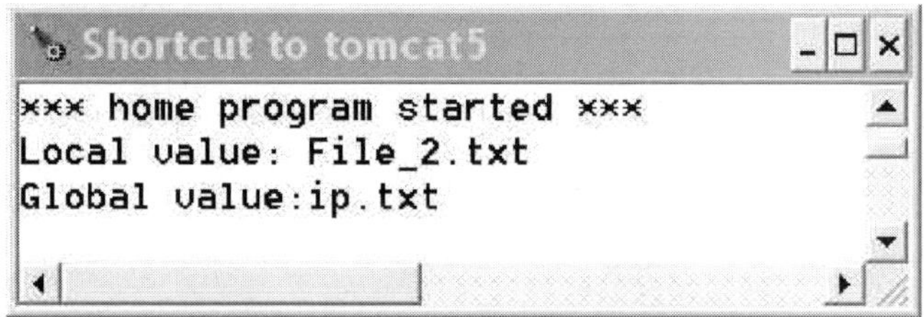

FIGURE 8.10. Screen of server—home.java

8.4 Synchronization

A web server creates a thread of the servlet to handle a browser's request. Multiple threads can be created at the same time. The advantage is that the creation of threads is handled automatically by the server. We do not need to code it in the servlet. On the other hand, this feature could be a problem for some applications.

Let us consider the following examples:

- A client sends a number to the servlet.
- The servlet adds the number to the variable 'sum'.

The value of 'sum' might not be correct if we allow multiple threads to update the variable 'sum' at the same time. Locking mechanism is required, and it can be achieved by synchronization.

Syntax of the synchronization is:

```
public class ExampleServelt  extends HttpServlet
{
      Declare your variable here (e.g. sum)
      .................
      public void init() throws ServletException
```

```
    {
        initialise your variable here (e.g. sum=0;)
        ...................
    }

    public void doGet(HttpServletRequest request,
                              HttpServletResponse response)
                   throws ServletException, IOException
    {
        do something here
        ...................
        synchronized (this)
        {
            obtain input
            update your variable here (e.g. sum=sum+newNumber;)
        }
        ...........................
        assemble a web page for the client
    } // end of doGet method

    public void destroy()
    {
        write the variable to disk, if necessary
    }
}
```

A variable is initialized in the init() method. The ***synchronized*** keyword restricts multiple accesses to the block in the doGet method. In other words, only one thread is allowed at a time to access selected statements in a servlet.

There are three ways to synchronize a servlet:

- Synchronization of a block.

```
    synchronized (this)
    {
     ...............
     ...............
    }
```

- Synchronization of a method.

```
public synchronized void NameOfMethod(....)
{
    do something here
    ...................
}
```

- Synchronization of a servlet.

```
public class NameOfServelt extends HttpServlet implement SingleThreadModel
{
            do something here
            .....................
}
```

Locking mechanisms must be implemented with care. They might cause the following problems if synchronization is not designed properly:

1. It might become a bottleneck in the system. The performance of the network will be degraded.
2. It might cause deadlock which is extremely difficult to debug in a distributed system with a large number of computers.

8.5 Tips to Speed up Testing

If you are planning to develop a large project, you might consider the following suggestions:

- A good IDE will be a useful tool. Some of them are freeware and can be downloaded from various websites.
- Always try to use one computer to test your programs in the initial test, if possible. A computer can play the role of server and client simultaneously. If your computer has enough memory, you can even start several web servers and web browsers at the same time. In this way, you do not need to worry about cables, router problems, firewalls, *etc.*, in your first test. Of course, you still need to test it with two or more computers later if your first test is successful. You cannot test the performance of the network with one computer either.
- Even if all computers are installed in the same room, it is still troublesome to move from one keyboard to the others. An inexpensive switch box will allow you to control several computers with one single set of monitor, mouse and keyboard.
- A switch box is good for a small number of computers. Your room will be full of cables if you have many computers. It is also a very time-consuming exercise if you want to move computers to a new place after the installation. 'Remote control' function is a better alternative if the operation systems of your computers (*e.g.*, Microsoft XP) support this function. Note that 'telnet' allows users to login remotely to Unix or Linux machines. There are some public domain software packages (*e.g.*, UltraVNC), which can perform similar functions. Certainly there is a trade-off for this method. The speed is slower as the remote computer needs to transfer its screen image to your control computer. It might distort

the experiment results if you are testing the performance of the programs or settings.

- Use a network drive to store your programs if all computers are on the same network. It saves a lot of time when copying programs among computers.
- You need a lot of screen space if you are using the 'remote control' to test programs on many computers. It is worthwhile to buy display cards that can support dual monitors. That will definitely speed up your testing processes. Buying two high-resolution monitors is a good investment as it will save a lot of time in the testing phase.

8.6 Troubleshooting

We provide a checklist of common problems and actions as follows:

- Compile problems
  - ◦ Check classpath.
  - ◦ Make sure that directories of all jar files are in the classpath definition.
  - ◦ Make sure that all jar and class files are in the right directories.
- Problem in invoking servlet
  - ◦ Check port number.
  - ◦ Check mappings in the web.xml.
  - ◦ Make sure that the web server is running.
  - ◦ Make sure that the compiled version of the servlet (*i.e.*, the class file) is in the right directory (*i.e.*, WEB-INF\classes of the application directory).
  - ◦ Check the typing of URL.
- New changes are not in effect
  - ◦ Make sure that the 'servlet reloading' is on.
  - ◦ Close and restart the server, if necessary.
  - ◦ It will be useful to include a print statement in the init() and destroy() methods, even if they are not required in your system. These statements can provide additional information so you can be sure that the reloading is in effect.
  - ◦ Click the 'reload' icon (for Netscape users) or 'refresh' icon (for Internet Explorer users) on your browser.
  - ◦ Make sure that the new version of the class is in the right directory.
- Display problem in the browser
  - ◦ Check html pages with the following methods:
    - ▪ For Internet Explorer users,
      1. click *view.*
      2. click *source.*
    - ▪ For Netscape users,
      1. click *view.*
      2. click *page source.*

- Web server is not working (or not working properly)
  - Check the correctness of configuration files.

Note that it is very easy to make mistakes in changing the settings in the configuration files. Before you make any changes, prepare a backup copy. Tomcat is very sensitive for errors (*i.e.*, even error with only one single character) in the configuration files. If anything goes wrong, you can recover from a previous version.

9
Power Server: Model 1

9.1 Introduction

We will present the detailed operations of the power server model in this chapter. After reading this chapter, readers will be able to install a power server P2P network to solve their problems. In order to demonstrate the operations, we need the following two components:

- The model itself
- A problem that we want to solve.

A toy problem (*i.e.*, a very simple problem without any practical value) is used instead of a real life complex problem as an example in this book. There are several advantages in using the toy problem:

- The programs can be kept as simple (with minimum number of lines) as possible. It is easier for readers to understand small programs than large programs.
- Readers can concentrate on learning how to set up the power model and do not need to spend time in learning the problem itself.
- Readers can verify the correctness of the computer output easily when they conduct their own experiments using the program codes in this book.
- Reader can modify the programs for their applications. It is easier to modify a simple program than a complex program. The program files can be obtained from the website of this book.

We have discussed the example of adding a large amount of numbers in Section 3.4. We will use this example again as our application. To make it even simpler, we will add sequential integers from 1 to n, where n is an integer greater than 1. The equation is:

$$\text{Sum} = \sum_{1}^{n} i \tag{9.1}$$

Although it has no practical value—it is of course easier to get the answer with a pocket calculator—we choose it as our example because

- everyone can understand the calculation easily. It can consume some computer time if the computer adds the values one by one. If n is big enough, then we can compare efficiencies of different configurations.
- the reader can verify the correctness of the answer provided by the computers. The formula for the answer is:

$$\text{Sum} = \frac{n\,(a+l)}{2} \tag{9.2}$$

where a is the smallest number in the series and l is the largest number in the series.

9.2 Model Without Web Server—Model 1

We start with the simplest model which can achieve parallel programming without web server in this section. In the subsequent sections, we will improve the model bit by bit until it can handle real-life applications.

Naturally, there are two parts in the model—the client and server programs. Let us start with the server program first.

9.2.1 Server Program

The server program consists of three components as described in Fig. 9.1. The server program waits until it receives a request from the client. It then creates a thread, which communicates with the client. The thread will get a sub-task (*i.e.*, a range of numbers in this case) from the client. The thread invokes the 'add'

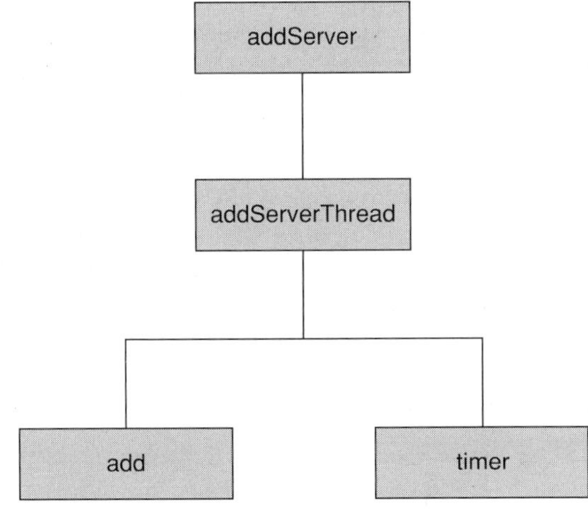

FIGURE 9.1. Structure of server program.

module to perform the actual calculation. The answer is then transmitted to the client.

9.2.1.1 addServer Module

Figure 9.2 shows the codes of addServer module. The following line listens to the port 3333. This port number can be modified if 3333 is being used in the computer.

Once a request for connection is received, it passes the control to the following block:

```
while (listening)
{
    .............
}
```

Inside this block, a new thread is created to handle the request by the following statement:

new addServerThread(serverSocket.accept()).start();

The variable 'Thread_id' is used to record the number of requests received from the client. It is increased by 1 every time a thread is created. This number provides more information to the users for debugging purposes.

This module does not need to wait for the completion of the first thread before it invokes a new one. In other words, it is possible to entertain requests from several clients simultaneously. That is the advantage of using threads in this program. A schematic diagram of this operation is shown on Fig. 9.3.

9.2.1.2 addServerThread

Figure 9.4 shows the code of this module. Its function is to get the sub-task from the server. It then calculates and passes back the result to the client.

9.2.1.2.1 First 'Try' Block

In the first 'try' block, the program uses the following two statements to establish the socket connection for input (*in*) and output (*out*).

out = new PrintWriter(addSocket.getOutputStream(), true);

in = new BufferedReader(new InputStreamReader(addSocket.getInputStream()));

9.2.1.2.2 Second 'Try' Block

The server receives four input messages from the client. For example, the user wants to get the sum of the numbers from 1 to 10 with two servers. The client will

```
import java.io.*;
import java.net.*;
import java.util.*;
public class addServer

{
    public addServer() {
        try {
            jbInit();
        } catch (Exception ex) {
            ex.printStackTrace();
        }
    }

    public static void main (String[] args)
                    throws IOException
    {
        ServerSocket serverSocket = null;
        boolean listening = true;

        int Thread_id=0;
        Socket addSocket= null;

System.out.println("*******************************************************");

        Date start_date=new Date();
        System.out.println( start_date);
        try
        {
            serverSocket = new ServerSocket(3333);
        }
        catch (IOException e)
        {
            System.err.println("Could not listen on port: 3333.");
            System.exit(-1);
        }
        while (listening)
        {
            try
            {
            System.out.println("waiting for Thread : " + Thread_id+" ******");
            new addServerThread(serverSocket.accept()).start();
            Thread_id =Thread_id + 1;
            }
            catch (IOException e)
            {
            System.err.println("accept failed");
            }
        } // end of while
    } // end of method

    private void jbInit() throws Exception {
    }
}
```

FIGURE 9.2. addServer.java

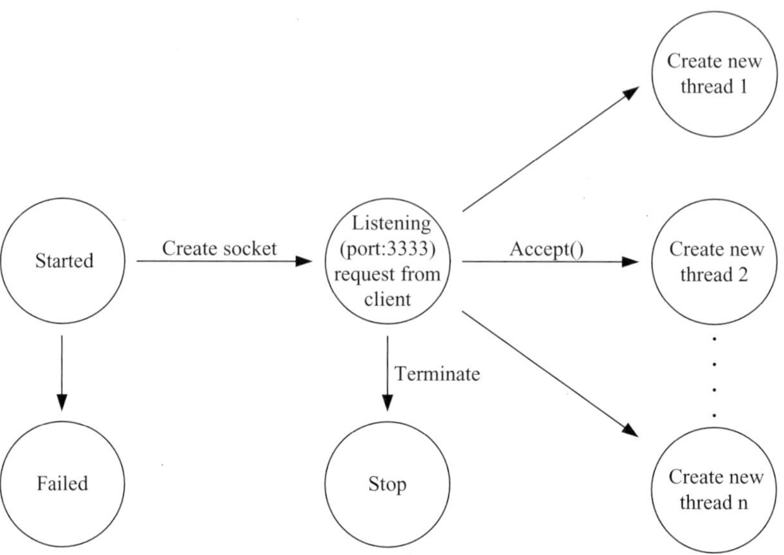

FIGURE 9.3. Operations of the addServer module.

divide the interval into two sub-tasks (*i.e.*, 1 to 5 and 6 to 10). A server will get the following messages:

1. Starting value and ending value of the numbers (1 and 5 in this case).
2. Since there are many servers in the network, the client will allocate an ID number to each server (ID is 1 in this case).
3. The whole internal of the problem (10 in this case).
4. The total number of servers in the system (2 in this case).

Items 2 to 4 are not required for this calculation. However, it will be useful for calculations of a more complex problem. It will provide information for debugging in the development phase.

In the second 'try' block, the program gets these messages with the following statement:

```
fromRemote = in.readLine();
```

The first message is somehow more complicated than others as it consists of two numbers—the beginning value and the ending value. These two values are transmitted as a string. Functions of StringTokenizer are used to extract the numbers and convert them back to numerical values. The statements for this operation are

```
StringTokenizer tokens = new StringTokenizer(fromRemote);
startPosition= Double.valueOf(tokens.nextToken()).doubleValue();
endPosition= Double.valueOf(tokens.nextToken()).doubleValue();
```

The sequence of messages between server and client is presented in Fig. 9.5.

```
import java.io.*;
import java.net.*;
import java.util.*;
import java.net.*;
public class addServerThread   extends Thread
{
      Socket addSocket=null;
      public addServerThread (Socket addSocket)
                   throws IOException
      {
            this.addSocket=addSocket;
            String fromRemote= " ";
            String fromUser= "initial value";
            double startPosition=0.0,endPosition=0.0;
            int interval=0;
            int totalProcessor=0;
            int Thread_id=0;
            Date start_date=new Date();
            System.out.println(start_date +"    Calculation Started");
            PrintWriter out =null;
            BufferedReader in=null;
            try
            {
            out = new PrintWriter(addSocket.getOutputStream(), true);
            in = new BufferedReader(new InputStreamReader(
                                   addSocket.getInputStream()));
            } // END TRY
            catch (IOException e)
                  {
                        System.out.print ("io exception in input/output");
                  }
            //------------------------------------ get data --------------
            try
            {
            fromRemote = in.readLine();
            StringTokenizer tokens = new StringTokenizer(fromRemote);
            startPosition= Double.valueOf(tokens.nextToken()).doubleValue();
            System.out.println("start position :"+ startPosition);
            endPosition= Double.valueOf(tokens.nextToken()).doubleValue();
            System.out.println("end position :"+ endPosition);

            // *********************** send information to client *****************
            fromUser = Double.toString(startPosition);
            out.println(fromUser);
            fromUser = Double.toString(endPosition);
            out.println(fromUser);
            // get ID
            if ((fromRemote = in.readLine()) != null)
                        System.out.print("number of remote thread: "+ fromRemote);

            Thread_id = Integer.parseInt(fromRemote);
```

FIGURE 9.4. addServerThread

```
        if ((fromRemote = in.readLine()) != null)
                {
                interval=Integer.parseInt(fromRemote);
                System.out.print(" interval: "+interval); // get interval
                }
        if ((fromRemote = in.readLine()) != null)
                {
                totalProcessor = Integer.parseInt(fromRemote);
                System.out.println(" total no. of processor: "+ totalProcessor);
                // get no of processor
                }
        } // END TRY
        catch (IOException e)
                {
                System.out.print ("io exception in socket input/output");
                }
      // ************************add operations ***********
      try
      {
        System.out.print("waiting for 'go ahead' signal from Client ");
        // get go ahead signal
        if ( (fromRemote = in.readLine()) != null)
          {
            timer t =new timer();
            t.start();
            add getSum= new add((long) startPosition, (long) endPosition);
            long sum=getSum.adding();
            t.elasp("It take : ");
            fromUser=Long.toString(sum);
            out.println(fromUser);
          }
        }
        catch (IOException e)
        {
            System.out.print("Exception in reading from Server");
        }
    try
        {
            out.close();
            in.close();
            addSocket.close();
        }
        catch (IOException e)
        {
            System.out.print ("io exception in CLOSING");
        }
    } // end of method
}
```

FIGURE 9.4. (*Continued*)

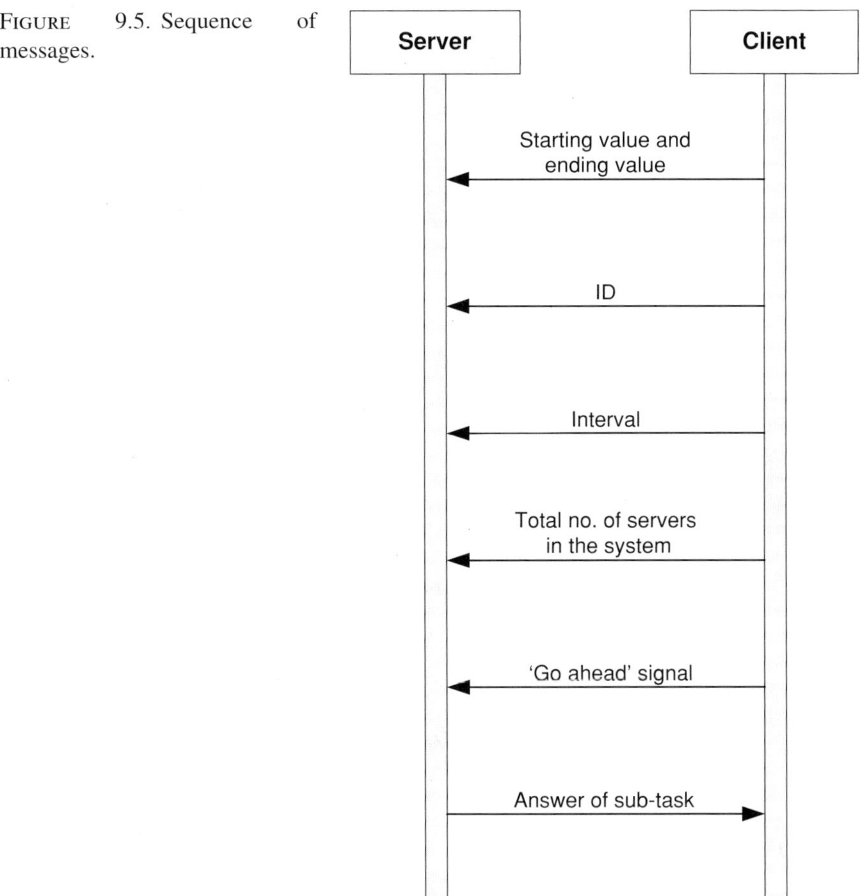

FIGURE 9.5. Sequence of messages.

9.2.1.2.3 Third 'Try' Block

The first statement in the block is:

if ((fromRemote = in.readLine()) != null)

It waits for a 'go ahead' signal from the client. The client issues this signal when all servers receive the sub-tasks. This signal will synchronize the calculation process of servers and enable us to measure the time of calculation only. In other words, servers will start calculation only when all servers get a sub-task from the client. If such measurement is not required, this synchronization can be removed from this program.

The actual calculation is performed in add.java class (Fig. 9.6).

```
/*
adding numbers
*/
class add
{
long startPosition,endPosition;
add(long start,long end)
{
            startPosition=start;
            endPosition=end;
}

long adding()
{
      long sum=0;
      System.out.println("start="+startPosition+" end="+endPosition);
      for(long i=startPosition ; i<= endPosition ;i++)
            {
                  for (int j=0;j<100000;j++) {int temp=j*j;}; // this is a delay loop
                  sum=sum+i;
            }
      System.out.println("\nsum="+sum );
      return sum;
}

}
// end of class
```

FIGURE 9.6. add.java

The following statements are used to invoke this module and get back the answer.

```
add getSum= new add((long) startPosition, (long) endPosition)
long sum=getSum.adding();
```

In order to measure the time of this process, a class timer is used. The code of this class is presented in Fig. 9.7. Inside the program, it can be invoked using the following statements:

```
timer t =new timer();
t.start();

............ Something you want to measure here

t.elasp("It take : ");
```

```
//------------ timer to handle time -----------
// require java.util.Date to run
//   additional varible start_time and end time is used so that it will be easier
//   to be understood
import java.util.Date;
class timer
{
            long start_time,end_time;
            float differn;
            Date start, end;

   timer()
            {
            start = new Date();
            start_time=(System.currentTimeMillis() );
            }

   void start()
            {
            start_time=System.currentTimeMillis() ;
            }

   void mark()
   {
               end_time=System.currentTimeMillis() ;
   }

   void cal_diff()
   {

            mark();
            differn =(float) (end_time - start_time)/1000;
   }

   void elasp()
            {
             cal_diff();
             System.out.print("elsaped second : "+differn+"sec.\n");
            }

void elasp(String msg)
            {
             cal_diff();
             System.out.print( msg +" "+ differn + "sec.\n");
            }

}
```

FIGURE 9.7. timer.java

The first statement of this block creates an object t from a class timer. The second statement calls the function start() and the clock will start to tick. The last statement will invoke the function elasp() and stop the recording. The computer then prints 'It take xxx seconds'.

9.2.1.2.4 Last 'Try' Block

The statements in this block close the socket, input and output streams. The thread will then be terminated.

9.2.1.2.5 Sequence of Operations

The operations are presented in Fig. 9.8.

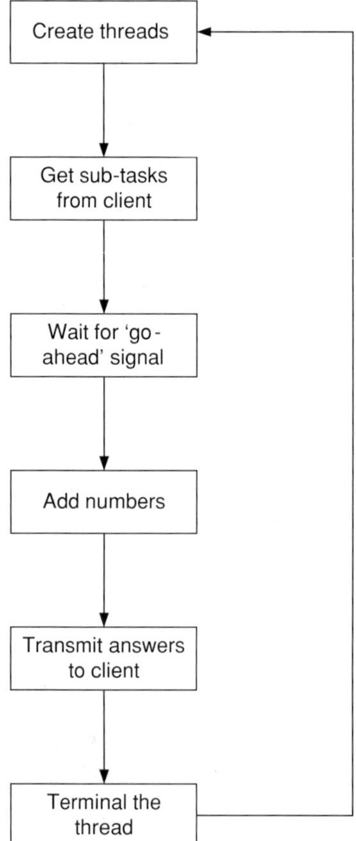

FIGURE 9.8. Operations of the server.

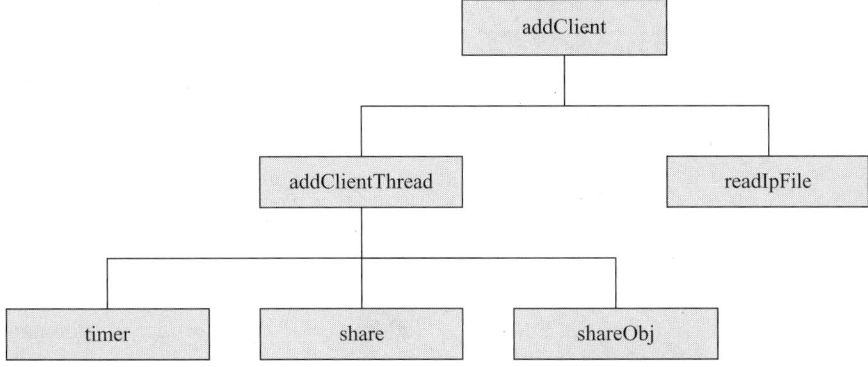

FIGURE 9.9. Overall structure of the client program.

9.2.2 *Client Program*

The client receives input data from the user. It picks up the IP addresses of the servers from a local file. A job from the user is divided into sub-tasks. One thread is created to handle one sub-task. Each thread passes a sub-task to one server and collects the answer from it. The overall structure is shown in Fig. 9.9.

9.2.2.1 addClient Module

This module accepts the following four parameters from the user:

- Number of severs in the systems (*e.g.*, two).
- Interval of the series (*e.g.*, 10 if the user wants to add the numbers from 1 to 10).
- File name which holds the IP address of the severs (*e.g.*, ip.txt).
- Debug indicator. The value is 1 if the user wants to turn on this mode. The program will print out more messages useful for debugging. This field is optional.

If a user forgets the parameter, he can type 'java addClient' and the system will print an instruction on the screen to remind user the position of each parameter as in Fig. 9.10.

For example, the user wants to get the sum of the numbers from 1 to 10 with two servers. The command is 'java 2 10 ip.txt', where ip.txt is a file name.

The ip.txt is a text file. The lines shown in Fig. 9.11 are the contents of an example file with two IP addresses.

```
c:\uq\servlets\add>java addClient
 number of processor, number of interval
 , name of IP_file, debug indicator
```

FIGURE 9.10. Output of addClient to remind user.

```
2
192.168.1.3
192.168.1.2
```

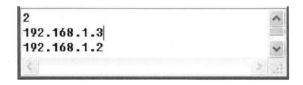

FIGURE 9.11. Contents of ip.txt file.

In Fig. 9.11, two is the number of IP addresses in the files. The IP addresses are in lines 2 and 3. The user can edit this file according to his/her configuration with any text editor. If you do not know the IP addresses of your computers, you can type 'ipconfig' in DOS. Figure 9.12 is the response from computer.

The client divides the job into sub-tasks according to number of servers in the system. The sub-tasks are stored in an array. For example, we need to calculate the sum of 1 to 10 using two servers. The sub-task array is presented in Fig. 9.13.

The creation of sub-tasks is handled by the following block:

```
for (int i=0;i< x.length;i=i+2)
    {
        if (i==0)
            x[i]=1;
        else
            x[i]= x[i-1]+1;
        if ((i+2)==x.length)
            x[i+1]=endPosition;
        else
            x[i+1]=x[i]+width-1;
    }
```

We create two objects to control the synchronization of threads with the following statements:

```
Share answer = new Share(totalProc,debug); // control answer update
ShareObj mToken = new ShareObj(totalProc,debug);
```

Each thread collects the answer of a sub-task from one server and updates the total. As it is possible that two threads need to update simultaneously, the object

```
Windows IP Configuration

Ethernet adapter Local Area Connection:

        Connection-specific DNS Suffix  . : ln.edu.hk
        IP Address. . . . . . . . . . . . : 202.40.197.69
        Subnet Mask . . . . . . . . . . . : 255.255.255.0
        Default Gateway . . . . . . . . . : 202.40.197.1
```

FIGURE 9.12. IP address.

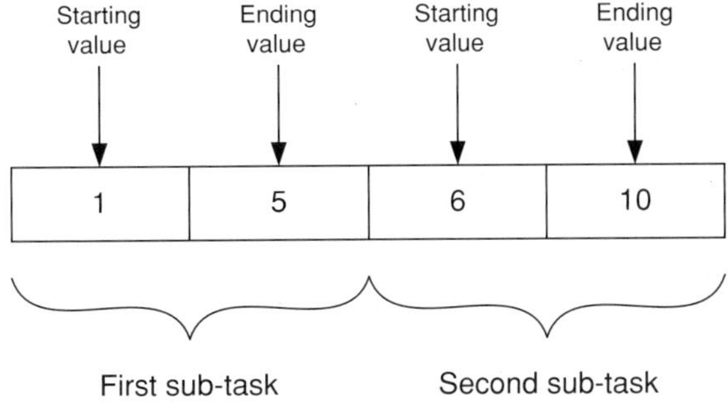

FIGURE 9.13. Array of sub-tasks.

'*answer*' is used to control the synchronization. Only one thread is allowed to update.

We want to know the exact time for transmission and calculation. The object 'mToken' is used to count the number of connections. The actual connections are done by the threads. When the number of connection equals the number of servers, a 'go ahead' signal will be sent to all servers. Although there are many threads in the system, the 'answer' and 'mToken' objects can be shared by all of them.

The following two lines read the IP file and store it in an array ip[].

```
String ip[]=new String[50];
readIpFile reader= new readIpFile(ipFile,ip);
```

A thread is created by the following statement:

```
for (int i=1;i<=totalProc;i++)
new addClientThread(ip[i-1],x, ,i,totalProc,answer,mToken,debug).start() ;
```

The following two statements control the synchronization.

```
mToken.allConnected(); // transmission to all computers completed
answer.setGoAhead();    // send a go ahead signal to all thread
```

The source codes of the addClient module are presented in Fig. 9.14.

9.2.2.2 addClientThread Module

The source codes of this module are presented in Fig. 9.15. This module establishes connection with servers. It then sends the sub-task and related information to the server as described in Fig. 9.5. It collects the answer from the server and updates the total.

The first 'try' block creates the socket connection and prepares for input and output. Port 3333 is used for communication. If you modify the port number

```
import java.net.*;
import java.io.*;
public class addClient {
    public static void main(String[] args) throws IOException {
        int Thread_id=1;
        int totalProc =0;
        timer t = new timer();
        // ************ get parameter from command argument *******
        if (args.length >= 1)
            {
                totalProc = Integer.parseInt(args[0]);
                System.out.println("number of processor :" + totalProc);
            }
        else
        {
                System.out.println(" number of processor, number of interval");
                System.out.println(" , name of IP_file, debug indicator");
                System.exit(-1);
        }
        long n= Integer.parseInt(args[1]);    // no. of interval
        boolean debug = false;
        String ipFile= "ip.txt";
        String hostIp="localhost";
        if (args.length >=3)      ipFile= args[2];
        if (args.length >=4)
            if (Integer.parseInt(args[3])==1)      debug=true;
        long startPosition =0;
        long endPosition =n;
        double x[]= new double[totalProc*2];
        long width=endPosition/totalProc;
        // ****** dividing job into sub-tasks ****************
        for (int i=0;i< x.length;i=i+2)
            {
                if (i==0)
                    x[i]=1;
                else
                    x[i]= x[i-1]+1;
                if ((i+2)==x.length)
                    x[i+1]=endPosition;
                else
                    x[i+1]=x[i]+width-1;
            }

        if (debug) System.out.print(" x[i]=");
        for (int j=0;j< x.length;j++)
            {
                    if (debug) System.out.print (" "+x[j]);
            }
```

FIGURE 9.14. addClient.java

```
            if (debug) System.out.println("    size of array = " + x.length);
            // ****************** Create object for synchronization ********
            Share answer = new Share(totalProc,debug); // control answer update
            ShareObj mToken = new ShareObj(totalProc,debug);
            String ip[]=new String[50];
            readIpFile reader= new readIpFile(ipFile,ip);
            timer total =new timer(); // timer for transmission + calculation
            total.start();
            // *************************** create Threads    ***************
            for (int i=1;i<=totalProc;i++)
                  new addClientThread(ip[i-1],x,
n,i,totalProc,answer,mToken,debug).start() ;
            if (debug) System.out.println("wait for connection to complete ");
            mToken.allConnected(); // transmission to all computers completed
            if (debug) System.out.print("start to call setGoAhead");
            answer.setGoAhead();   // send a go ahead signal to all thread
            timer t1= new timer(); // timer for calculation only
            t1.start();
            System.out.println("********* Answer: "+(long)answer.getAnswer()+
"*********");
            total.elasp("total time calculation + transmission :");
            t1.elasp("Total calculation takes : ");
            System.out.println("program terminated");
      } // end of main method
}
```

FIGURE 9.14. *(Continued)*

in the server program, you must also modify the port number in this module accordingly.

```
try
{
      powerSocket = new Socket(site, 3333);
      System.out.println("connecting site "+Thread_id+" : "+ site);
      out = new PrintStream(powerSocket.getOutputStream());
      in = new DataInputStream(powerSocket.getInputStream());
}
```

A sub-task is extracted from the task array and converted to a string. The string is distributed to the server. This process is performed by the following statements:

```
for (int i=first; i < last;i++)
      {
         arrayBuffer.append(x[i]+" ");
      }
out.println(arrayBuffer);
```

```
import java.net.*;
import java.io.*;
import java.util.*;
public class addClientThread extends Thread {
    private Socket socket = null;
    double x[];
    int Thread_id;
    int totalProcessor;
    boolean debug;
    String msg;
    Share answer;
    ShareObj mToken;
    long interval;
    boolean Done= false;
    PrintStream out=null ;
    BufferedReader in =null;
    Socket powerSocket;
    public addClientThread(String site, double[] y, long interval,
                                    int id, int totalProc,Share answer,
                                    ShareObj mToken,boolean debug )
    {
        super("ClientThread");
        if (debug) System.out.println("add Client Theard");
        this.Thread_id =id;
        this.x =y;
        this.totalProcessor = totalProc;
        this.mToken = mToken;
        this.answer=answer;
        this.debug=debug;
        this.interval= interval;
        // ********************** try to connect now    *************
        try
        {
            powerSocket = new Socket(site, 3333);
            System.out.println("connecting site "+Thread_id+" : "+ site);
            out = new PrintStream(powerSocket.getOutputStream());
            in = new BufferedReader(new InputStreamReader(
                            powerSocket.getInputStream()));
        }
        catch (UnknownHostException e)
        {
            System.err.println("Don't know about host: "+site);
            System.exit(1);
        }
        catch (IOException e) {
            System.err.println("Couldn't get I/O for the connection to: "+site);
            System.err.println(" shutting down");
            return;
        }
```

FIGURE 9.15. addClientThread class

```
        if (debug) System.out.println("connection ok");
    }
    public void run()
    {
    timer t = new timer();
    try
      {
      String inputLine, outputLine;
             int first = (Thread_id -1 ) * (x.length /totalProcessor);
             if (debug) System.out.print( "*************** first=" +first);
             int last = (Thread_id ) * (x.length /totalProcessor);
             if (Thread_id > totalProcessor)
             {
                   System.out.println("conection not created");
                   System.exit(1);
             }
             if (debug) System.out.print("connection to site " + Thread_id);
             if (debug) t.elasp(" takes:");
             if (debug) System.out.println("Start to transfer for " + Thread_id);
             t.start();
             StringBuffer arrayBuffer = new StringBuffer(last*8);
             if (debug) System.out.print("buffer created " );
             for (int i=first; i < last;i++)
             {
                arrayBuffer.append(x[i]+" ");
             }
             out.println(arrayBuffer); // transmit to power server
             if (debug) System.out.print("Transmission of site " + Thread_id);
             if (debug) t.elasp(" takes:");
             timer t2= new timer();
             t2.start();
             if (debug) System.out.println("T_id="+Thread_id+ " done=    " +Done);
             //
             // ***************** get back information ********************
             //                      make sure power server get the right data
             String localMin="                           ";
             String localMax="                           ";
             if (debug) System.out.println("wait for server's first transmission");
             if ((inputLine = in.readLine()) != null)
                   localMin = inputLine;
             if (debug) System.out.println("wait for server's seond transmission");
             if ((inputLine = in.readLine()) != null)
                   localMax = inputLine;
             System.out.println("site:"+Thread_id+ " Min= " +localMin+" Max=
" +localMax);
             // ****** send other information to server *************
             mToken.increaseConnection(); // increase number of connection
             outputLine = String.valueOf(Thread_id);
             out.println(outputLine);
```

FIGURE 9.15. (*Continued*)

```
                outputLine = String.valueOf(interval);
                out.println(outputLine);
                if (debug) System.out.println("interval="+interval);
                outputLine = String.valueOf(totalProcessor);
                out.println(outputLine);
                double subAnswer=0.0;
                if (debug) System.out.println("id="+Thread_id+ "go ahead" );
                out.println("go ahead");
                if (debug) System.out.println("id="+Thread_id+ "wait for answer" );
                 // get the answer from server **********************
                if ((inputLine = in.readLine()) != null)
                      subAnswer= Double.valueOf(inputLine).doubleValue();
                t2.elasp("id="+Thread_id +" time for cal+tran =" );
                // update total Answer ********
                if (debug) System.out.println("id="+Thread_id+ "get answer" );
                answer.updateAnswer(subAnswer);
                System.out.println("*** id="+Thread_id+ " sub-task answer=    "
                                              +(long)subAnswer);
                if (debug) System.out.println("id="+Thread_id+ " done3=    " +Done);
        out.close();
        in.close();
        powerSocket.close();
          } // end of try
   catch (IOException e)
          {
                e.printStackTrace();
          }
       }
}
```

FIGURE 9.15. (*Continued*)

The following lines receive the feedback information from the server so that the user can verify the correctness of the transmission.

```
//
// ***************** get back information ********************
//                          make sure power server get the right data
String localMin="                    ";
String localMax="                    ";
if (debug) System.out.println("wait for server's first transmission");
if ((inputLine = in.readLine()) != null)
       localMin = inputLine;
if (debug) System.out.println("wait for server's seond transmission");
if ((inputLine = in.readLine()) != null)
       localMax = inputLine;
System.out.println("site:"+Thread_id+ " Min= " +localMin+" Max=
" +localMax);
```

The following statement increases the number of connections in the object mToken:

```
mToken.increaseConnection();        // increase number of connection
```

The following lines send other messages to the server according to Fig. 9.5:

```
outputLine = String.valueOf(Thread_id);
out.println(outputLine);
outputLine = String.valueOf(interval);
out.println(outputLine);
if (debug) System.out.println("interval="+interval);
outputLine = String.valueOf(totalProcessor);
out.println(outputLine);
double subAnswer=0.0;
if (debug) System.out.println("id="+Thread_id+ "go ahead " );
out.println("go ahead");
if (debug) System.out.println("id="+Thread_id+ "wait for answer " );
 // get the answer from server ***********************
if ((inputLine = in.readLine()) != null)
```

The following statements get the answer from server:

```
if ((inputLine = in.readLine()) != null)
    subAnswer= Double.valueOf(inputLine).doubleValue();
```

Finally the total will be updated by calling the method 'updateAnswer' with the following statement:

```
answer.updateAnswer(subAnswer);
```

A schematic diagram of the communications between server and client is displayed in Fig. 9.16.

9.2.2.3 readIpFile Module

The source codes of this module are presented in Fig. 9.17. The logic of this module is quite simple. It reads all addresses in the address file and stores them in an array. It then returns the control to the calling module.

9.2.2.4 Share Module

The coding list of this class is presented in Fig. 9.18. In addition to the construction method, there are three other methods:

- setGoAhead—It informs all threads which are waiting to go ahead by invoking the notifyAll() statement.

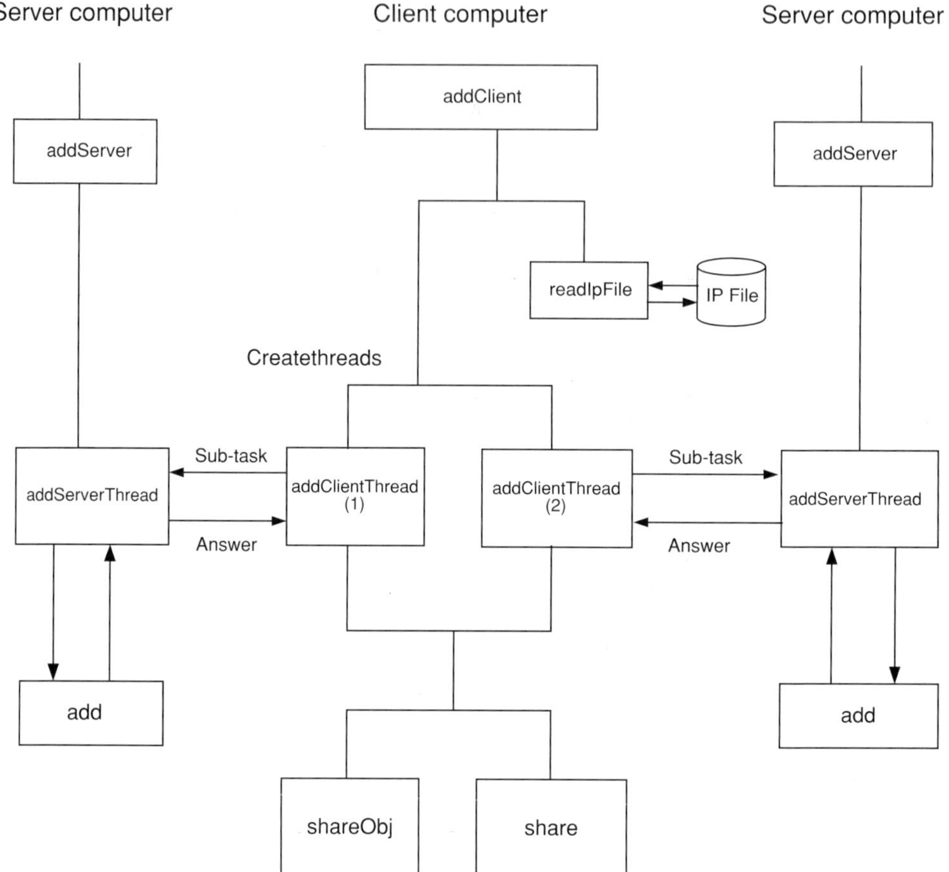

FIGURE 9.16. Schematic diagram of the communication.

- updateAnswer—It updates the total. Only one thread is allowed to update at one time.
- GetAnswer—It returns the grand total to the calling program.

9.2.2.5 ShareObj Module

The source code of this module is presented in Fig. 9.19. There are only two methods (excluding the constructor) in this class.

- increaseConnection—It increases the internal counter by 1 if the connection and transmission of a thread is successful. This function is for synchronization as discussed in previous sections.
- allConnected—It remains in a 'wait' state until the number of connection equals to the number of servers in the system.

```
import java.io.*;
public class readIpFile
{
    String ipFile;
    String ip[];
    String hostIp;
    int rec_no=0;
    public readIpFile(String ipFile, String ip[])
    {
        this.ipFile=ipFile;
        this.ip=ip;
        try
        {
        BufferedReader in = new BufferedReader (
                    new InputStreamReader (new FileInputStream(ipFile)));
        rec_no = Integer.parseInt(in.readLine());
        for (int i=0 ; i<=rec_no-1 ; i++ )
           {
           ip[i] = in.readLine();
           }
        in.close();
        } // end of try
        catch (EOFException e)
        {
            System.out.println (" error");
        }
        catch (FileNotFoundException e)
        {
              System.out.println("file not found ");
              return;
              // System.exit(-1);
        }
        catch (IOException e)
        {
            System.out.println(" IO errors ");
        }
        boolean connected = false;
    }   // end of invoke method
    public int getNumServer()
    {
          return rec_no;
    }
}
```

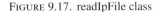

FIGURE 9.17. readIpFile class

```
class Share {
    private boolean go = true;
    boolean debug = false;
    int totalProcessor=0;
    int doneProcessor=0;
    double answer=0.0;
    public Share(int totalProcessor,boolean debug)
    {
        this.debug= debug;
        this.totalProcessor = totalProcessor;
    }

    public synchronized void setGoAhead( )
    {
        if (debug) System.out.println( "Share called        go: " + go);

        while ( !go )
        {
            try
            {
                wait();
            }
            catch ( InterruptedException e )
            {
                System.err.println( "Exception: " + e.toString() );
            }
        }
        if (debug) System.out.println( "Share setGoAhead go: " + go);
        go = false;
        notifyAll();
    }

     public synchronized void updateAnswer(double ans)
    {
        answer =answer+ans;
        doneProcessor++;
        notifyAll();
    }
     public synchronized double getAnswer()
    {
     if (debug) System.out.println("waiting for answer by Server");
     while ( doneProcessor != totalProcessor )
        {
            try
            {
                wait();
            }
            catch ( InterruptedException e )
            {
                System.err.println( "Exception: " + e.toString() );
            }
        }
    return answer;
    }
}
```

FIGURE 9.18. share.java

```
class ShareObj
{
      boolean Done = false;
      private int totalProcessor;
      private int totalAccess;
      private boolean free =true;
      boolean debug;
      boolean connected=false;
      public ShareObj(int i,boolean debug)
      {
            totalProcessor=i;
            this.debug=debug;
            totalAccess= 0;
      }
      public synchronized void increaseConnection()
      {
            if (debug) System.out.println( "Share obj       free: " + free
                                                        +" no. of Processor: "+
totalProcessor);
            while ( !free )
            {
                  try
                  {
                        wait();
                  }
                  catch ( InterruptedException e ) {
                        System.err.println( "Exception: " + e.toString() );
                  }
            }
            free = false;
            Done = true;
            totalAccess++;
            if (totalAccess == totalProcessor)
                  {
                  totalAccess =0;
                  connected=true;
                  if (debug) System.out.println( "Share obj " + "access:"+totalAccess);
                  }
            free = true;
            notify();
      }

      public synchronized void allConnected()
      {
            while ( !connected)
            {
                  try
                  {
                        wait();
                  }
                  catch ( InterruptedException e )
                  {
                        System.err.println( "Exception: " + e.toString() );
                  }
            }
      }
}
```

FIGURE 9.19. shareObj.java

```
***********************************************************
Sun Nov 06 14:03:29 GMT+08:00 2005
waiting for Thread : 0 ******
```

FIGURE 9.20. Screen of the server in waiting state.

9.3 First Test

You can use only one computer to run your first test. If you are not familiar with client-server programming, I will recommend you to use one computer for the first test. A computer can be both server and client concurrently. You must start the server program first before you run the client program.

1. You start the server program by typing the following command in DOS:

   java addServer

   The computer will be in a wait state as in Fig. 9.20.
2. Start the client program by typing the following command in anther DOS session.

   java addClient 1 10 local.txt

   The first parameter '1' indicates that there is only one server in the system. The system will add the number from 1 to 10. There are only 2 lines in the 'local.txt' file:

1
localhost

The '1' in the first line indicates there is only one address in the whole file. 'localhost' is the synonym of the IP address of your local computer.

The local.txt file enables you to access your own local computer without specifying its IP address. You can see the result in both windows: Fig. 9.21 is the screen of the server window, while Fig. 9.22 is the screen of the client window.

```
c:\vq\servlets\add>java addServer
********************************************************
Sun Nov 06 15:12:06 GMT+08:00 2005
waiting for Thread : 0 ******
Sun Nov 06 15:12:25 GMT+08:00 2005   Calculation Started
start position :1.0
end   position :10.0
number of remote thread: 1  interval: 10  total no. of processor
waiting for 'go ahead' signal from Client  start=1  end=10

sum=55
It take :  0.04sec.
waiting for Thread : 1 ******
```

FIGURE 9.21. Screen of server window.

```
c:\vq\servlets\add>java addClient 1 10 local.txt
number of processor :1
connecting site 1 : localhost
site:1 Min= 1.0 Max=  10.0
id=1 time for cal+tran = 0.14sec.
*** id=1 sub-task answer=   55.0
********* Answer: 55.0 *********
Total processing time : 0.531sec.
Total calculation takes :  0.1sec.
program terminated
```

FIGURE 9.22. Screen of client window.

After the successful computation, the server's thread will be ready for another request from the client as displayed in Fig. 9.21.

9.4 Second Test

If the first test is successful, you are ready to start the second test with two or more computers.

1. Copy all programs to both computers.
2. Type 'java addServer' in DOS in both computers.
3. Obtain the IP addresses of both computers.
4. You can use a third computer or use one of the two computers as client.
   - Edit the ip.txt and replace the IP addresses with your server computers.
   - Type 'java addClient 2 1000 ip.txt'.
     where 2 is total number of servers and 1000 is the range 1 to 1000.

The screen of the client is displayed in Fig. 9.23.

```
c:\vq\servlets\add>java addClient 2 1000 ip.txt
number of processor :2
connecting site 1 : 192.168.1.3
site:1 Min= 1.0 Max=  500.0
id=1 time for cal+tran = 0.46sec.
*** id=1 sub-task answer=   125250.0
connecting site 2 : 192.168.1.2
site:2 Min= 501.0 Max=  1000.0
id=2 time for cal+tran = 0.952sec.
*** id=2 sub-task answer=   375250.0
********* Answer: 500500.0 *********
Total processing time : 5.548sec.
Total calculation takes :  0.391sec.
program terminated
```

FIGURE 9.23. Screen from client of test 2.

```
c:\vq\servlets\add>ping 192.168.1.2

Pinging 192.168.1.2 with 32 bytes of data:

Reply from 192.168.1.2: bytes=32 time=22ms TTL=128
Reply from 192.168.1.2: bytes=32 time<1ms TTL=128
Reply from 192.168.1.2: bytes=32 time<1ms TTL=128
Reply from 192.168.1.2: bytes=32 time<1ms TTL=128

Ping statistics for 192.168.1.2:
    Packets: Sent = 4, Received = 4, Lost = 0 (0% loss),
Approximate round trip times in milli-seconds:
    Minimum = 0ms, Maximum = 22ms, Average = 5ms
```

FIGURE 9.24. Normal ping test.

The answer for the sub-task from first server is 125250, while the answer from second server is 375250. You can verify the final 500500 with the formula in Eq. (9.2).

9.5 Troubleshooting

If you have problems, try to fix the problems with the following methods:

1. Make sure that the connection is fine by typing 'ping xxxxxxx' in DOS, where xxxxxxx is the IP of the remote computer.

   e.g., ping 192.168.1.3

   You will get the following messages (Fig. 9.24) if the connection is fine.
   You will get the timeout messages as in Fig. 9.25 if there are problems in the connection. You need to check the cable connection and configuration of your computer system before you proceed any further.
2. If the connection is fine in the 'ping' test and the programs still do not work, it is possible that port 3333 is being used by some other program in your system.

```
c:\vq\servlets\add>ping 192.168.1.4

Pinging 192.168.1.4 with 32 bytes of data:

Request timed out.
Request timed out.
Request timed out.
Request timed out.
```

FIGURE 9.25. Connection problems.

Change the port number in the addClient and addServer program from 3333 to other number.

3. If you are using any firewall, it will block the port 3333. You should invoke the firewall and release the port 3333 (TCP).

9.6 Further Tests

If the second test is fine, you can try further tests, adding more computers, and using different combinations until you understand the operations. You will then be able to modify the programs to solve your real-life problems.

10
Power Server: Model 2

10.1 Introduction

The major advantage of the model in Chapter 9 is its ease of implementation. All you need is a JDK in the computer. Additional software packages are not required. This model is perfect for small-scale networks and where every computer is under your control. It is easy to debug the system in the development phase so it is good for beginner.

However, there is a major drawback in this model—you need to invoke a server program in each computer manually. If there are a large number of computers inside the system, it will be very time consuming. A simple and inexpensive way to invoke a program in remote computers is required. Although there are a large number of methods (such as RMI, COBRA, *etc.*) for this purpose, they are difficult to use for programmers without much networking experience. In some cases, additional expensive software packages are required.

Web servers will be able to solve this problem easily. Remote servlet programs can be invoked easily by an HTTP message. This method provides the following advantages:

- There is a large number of web servers. Most of them are free and small (in terms of memory and disk space required). Owners of peer computers will be happy to install this piece of additional software.
- The interface methods of web server and servlets are standards. That means each owner of a peer computer can choose different web server. Owners of peer computers do not need to trust any single party. The P2P will work nicely with heterogeneous web servers inside the network.
- The life cycle is well defined. It will be easy for programmers to develop and maintain the servlet.
- The web server will automatically pick up the new servlet on the hard disk whenever there is any update. The user does not need to close down and restart the web server.

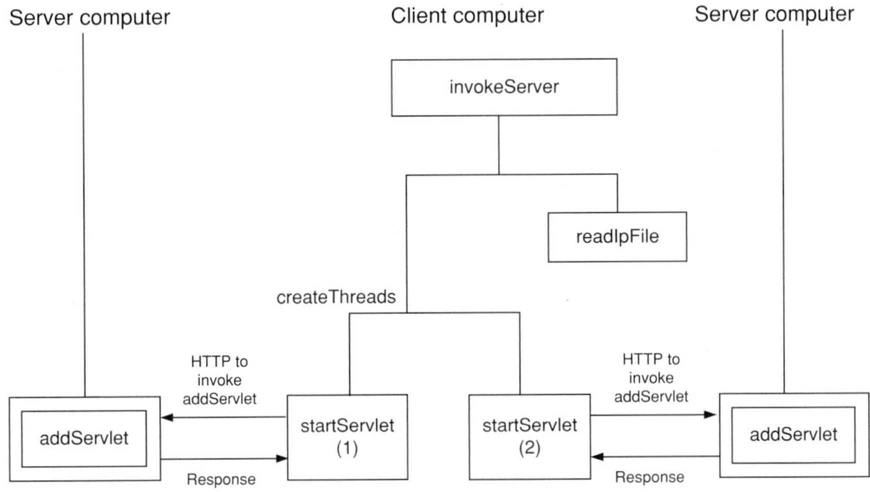

FIGURE 10.1. Invoking the servlet of remote computer.

10.2 Power Server with Web Server—Model 2

The model can be modified easily to work with any web server. A new program for the client is written to send HTTP messages to invoke servlets in server computers. A schematic diagram is presented in Fig. 10.1. This program reads the IP addresses in a local file. It then creates a thread to invoke servlets from remote servers by sending them HTTP messages.

10.2.1 invokeServer Module

The source codes of this module are presented in Fig. 10.2. The operations of this module are quite straightforward. It accepts the following two parameters from the user:

- Number of server computers.
- Name of the file which stores the IP addresses—default value is ip.txt.

It reads IP addresses from the file and stores them in an array. It then creates startServlet threads according to the first parameter with the following statements:

```
for (int i=0;i<totalProc;i++)
{
new startServlet(ip[i]).run();
}
```

```
import java.net.*;
import java.io.*;

public class invokeServer {
    public static void main(String[] args) throws IOException {
        int Thread_id=1;
        int totalProc =0;
        timer t = new timer();
        // ************ get parameter from command argument *******
        if (args.length >= 1)
            {
                totalProc = Integer.parseInt(args[0]);
                System.out.println("number of servers :" + totalProc);
            }
        else
        {       System.out.println(" number of servers");
                System.out.println(" , name of IP_file ");
                System.exit(-1);
        }
        String ipFile= "ip.txt";
        // default file name
        if (args.length >=2)       ipFile= args[1];
        String ip[]=new String[totalProc+1];
        readIpFile reader= new readIpFile(ipFile,ip);
        System.out.println("invoked " + Thread_id);
        // ************************** ending operation ***************
        timer t1= new timer();
        t1.start();
        for (int i=0;i<totalProc;i++)
            {
            new startServlet(ip[i]).run();
            }
        t1.elasp("********************************* It takes : ");
        System.out.println("program terminated");
    } // end of main method
}
```

FIGURE 10.2. invokeServer.java

Threads are used because each one of them can invoke a remote servlet independently. They do not need to wait for the completion of other threads to begin their tasks.

10.2.2 startServlet Module

This module calls the URL_connect module to send the HTTP message to the server. It will get a true value if the connection is normal, otherwise it will get a

```
import java.net.*;
public class startServlet extends Thread
{
      String ip;
      InetAddress hostIp;
      public startServlet(String ip)
      {
            super ("invokeServer");
            this.ip=ip;
            this.hostIp=hostIp;
      }
      public void run()
      {
        boolean connected = false;
              try
              {
                    InetAddress address = InetAddress.getLocalHost();
                    System.out.println("try to connect "+ip);
                    String urlString ="http://"
+ip+":8080/servlet/addServlet?site="+address;
                    connected =new URL_connect(urlString).go();
                    if (connected)
                             System.out.println("connected :"+ ip);
                    else
                       System.out.println("failed to connect "+ip);
              }
              catch (Exception e)
              {
                    System.err.println("get error: " + e);

                 }
      }  // end of run method
}
```

FIGURE 10.3. startServlet.java

false value from the URL_connect module. The complete coding list is shown in Fig. 10.3.

The name and IP address of the client computer are obtained by the following line:

InetAddress address = InetAddress.getLocalHost();

The information of the client computer is sent to the server for debugging purposes. It is embedded in the following line:

String urlString ="http://" +ip+":8080/servlet/addServlet?site="+address;

```
import java.awt.*;
import java.io.*;
import java.net.*;

public class URL_connect
{
String site;
boolean connected;

public URL_connect(String site)
{
   this.site=site;
}

public boolean go()
{
      URL powerURL;
      InputStream powerInputStream;
      try
        {
              powerURL = new URL(site);
           powerInputStream = powerURL.openStream();
        }
        catch (Exception e)
        {
           System.out.println("get error: "+ e);
           return false;
        }
        return true;
} // runn

} //class   URL_connect
```

FIGURE 10.4. URL-connect.java

10.2.3 URL_connect Module

This module (Fig. 10.4) takes the HTTP message from the calling module (*i.e.*, startServlet).

It returns a true value to the calling module if the connection is fine. The actual connection is carried out by the following block:

```
try
{
     powerURL = new URL(site);
     powerInputStream = powerURL.openStream();
}
```

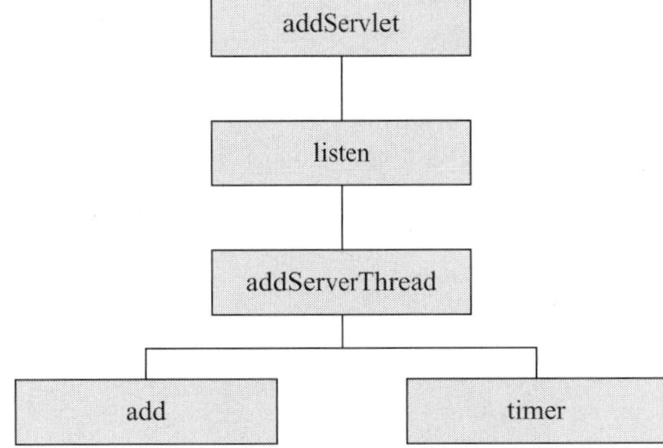

FIGURE 10.5. Structure of addServlet.

10.3 Server Side Programs

This servlet enables the user to invoke the addServer program (in Chapter 9) with an HTTP message. The structure of this servlet is presented in Fig. 10.5.

10.3.1 addServlet

The constructor of this module invokes the listen module with the following block:

```
listenSocket= new listen();
listenSocket.setPriority(Thread.MIN_PRIORITY);
listenSocket.start();
```

The constructor is executed only once even the client sends several HTTP messages to the server. However, the doGet() records the number of messages and returns it to the client for future debugging purposes. The coding list is presented in Fig. 10.6.

10.3.2 Listen Module

The listen module establishes a socket (in port 3333). Whenever it receives a request from the client, an addServer thread will be invoked by the following statements:

```
while (listening)
{
      try
      {
      System.out.println("tring to connect Thread : " + Thread_id);
      new addServerThread(serverSocket.accept()).start();
      System.out.println("connected Thread : " + Thread_id);
      Thread_id =Thread_id + 1;
      }
```

```
import java.io.*;
import java.net.*;
import java.util.*;
import javax.servlet.*;
import javax.servlet.http.*;
public class addServlet   extends HttpServlet
{
      int Thread_id=0;
      int count =1;
      listen listenSocket;
      public void init(ServletConfig config) throws ServletException
      {
            super.init(config);

System.out.println("**************************************************");
            Date start_date=new Date();
            System.out.print( start_date);
            listenSocket= new listen();
            listenSocket.start();
            System.out.println("*****list socket
called*************************");
      }
      public void doGet(HttpServletRequest req, HttpServletResponse res)
                  throws ServletException, IOException
      {
            PrintWriter out=res.getWriter();
            System.out.println("addServlet count="+count);
            out.flush();
            String line="request accepted";
            out.println(line);   //ending message
            count++;
            out.close();
      } // end of method
      public void destroy()
      {
            System.out.println("destroy method called");
      }
}
```

FIGURE 10.6. addServlet.java

```
      catch (IOException e)
      {
      System.err.println("accept failed");
      }
} // end of while
```

The server side programs in Chapter 9 are modified. The addServerThread, add and timer module do not need any further modification. The coding list is presented in Fig. 10.7.

10.4 Phase 1 Testing—invokeServer Program

You need a web server to test this module. If you have one server running on your computer and it supports servlets, all you need to do is to install the servlet classes in the appropriate folder. Again it is simpler to use one computer in the first test even you have several computers.

10.4.1 Test 1

You can test the program by following these steps:

1. Copy the programs to the default servlet path.
2. Invoke the web server.
3. Type 'java invokeServer 1 local.txt' in DOS. The first parameter '1' is the number of servers in the system. One computer is used as both client and server in this test. The results are displayed in Figs. 10.8 and 10.9. Figure 10.8 is the screen of the server window, while Fig. 10.9 is the client window.

10.4.2 Troubleshooting

Check the following if you have any problems:

- Make sure that the web server is running.
- Check the port number of your web server. The default port is 8080 for Tomcat. This number could be different if you are using other servers. Type http://localhost:8080 to test this port.
- If you are not sure whether it is a server side or client side problem, you can also test the servlet by typing the URL http://localhost:8080/servlet/addServlet on your browser.

You will get the screen as shown in Fig. 10.10 on your browser if the server side is working properly.

10.4.3 Test 2

In this test, you use several computers to test the programs in this chapter with the following steps:

1. Install the addServlet programs in two computers (refer to step 1–5 of the Section 10.4.2). Note that alternatively you can share the folder with other computers; it will save a lot of time.

```
import java.io.*;
import java.net.*;
import java.util.*;
public class listen    extends Thread
{
      Socket addSocket= null;
      ServerSocket serverSocket = null;
      boolean listening = true;
      int count =1;
      int Thread_id;
      int portNumber= 3333;
      public listen()
      {
            System.out.println("listening started");
      }
      public void run()
      {
            Date start_date=new Date();
            System.out.print( start_date);

            try{
                     serverSocket = new ServerSocket(portNumber);
                     System.out.println("Add servlet init, started");
                  }
            catch (IOException e)
                  {
                     System.err.println("Could not listen on port: "+ portNumber);
                     System.exit(-1);
                  }
            while (listening)
            {
                  try
                  {
                  System.out.println("trying to connect Thread : " + Thread_id);
                  new addServerThread(serverSocket.accept()).start();
                  System.out.println("connected Thread : " + Thread_id);
                  Thread_id =Thread_id + 1;
                  }
                  catch (IOException e)
                  {
                  System.err.println("accept failed");
                  }
            } // end of while
      } // end of method
}
```

FIGURE 10.7. listen.java

```
************************************************
Fri Jan 13 20:14:01 CST 2006listening started
*****list socket called*************************
addServlet count=1
Fri Jan 13 20:14:01 CST 2006Add servlet init, started
trying to connect Thread : 0
```

FIGURE 10.8. Server window.

```
c:\vq\servlets\add>java invokeServer 1 local.txt
number of servers :1
invoked 1
try to connect localhost
connected :localhost
******************************** It takes :  0.14sec.
program terminated
```

FIGURE 10.9. Client window.

```
request accepted
```

FIGURE 10.10. Screen of the browser.

2. Start the Tomcat.
3. Check the IP addresses of your two servers.
4. Modify the ip.txt file with the IP addresses/.
5. Type 'java invokeServer 2 ip.txt' in DOS on a third computer. The second parameter ('2') means two servers.

The contents of the ip.txt file in this test are

2
192.168.1.2
192.168.1.3

The window shown in Fig. 10.11 is the result of client side program. The screen of both servers is presented in Fig. 10.12.

10.5 Phase 2 Testing

The advantage of this model is that client program can invoke the server side program automatically. It will save a lot of time. A schematic diagram of the operations is presented in Fig. 10.13.

```
c:\Tomcat 5.5\webapps\root\web-inf\classes>java invokeServer 2 ip.txt
number of servers :2
invoked 1
try to connect 192.168.1.2
connected :192.168.1.2
try to connect 192.168.1.3
connected :192.168.1.3
********************************* It takes :  0.861sec.
program terminated
```

FIGURE 10.11. Screen of client (with two servers).

```
*************************************************
Tue Jan 17 17:19:39 GMT+08:00 2006listening started
*****list socket called*************************
Tue Jan 17 17:19:39 GMT+08:00 2006addServlet count=1
Add servlet init, started
trying to connect Thread : 0
```

FIGURE 10.12. Screen of both servers.

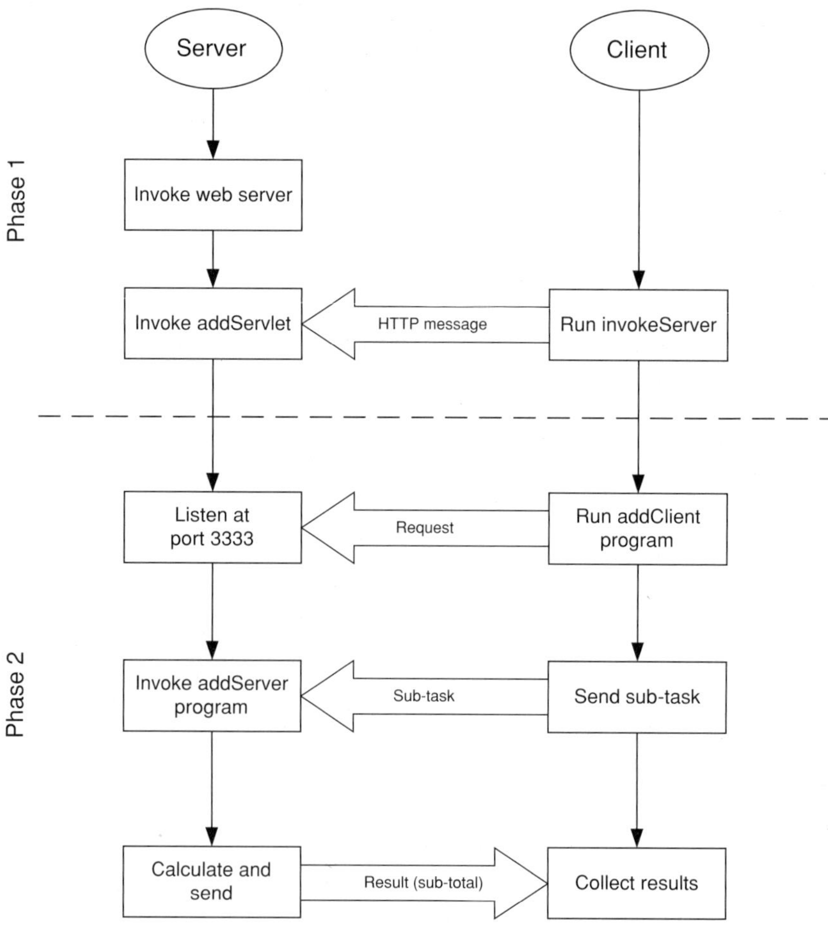

FIGURE 10.13. Sequence of operations.

```
C:\add>java addClient 2 100 ip.txt
number of processor :2
connecting site 1 : 192.168.1.2
site:1 Min= 1.0 Max=  50.0
id=1 time for cal+tran = 2.624sec.
*** id=1 sub-task answer=   1275
connecting site 2 : 192.168.1.3
site:2 Min= 51.0 Max=  100.0
id=2 time for cal+tran = 0.55sec.
*** id=2 sub-task answer=   3775
********* Answer: 5050*********
total time calculation + transmission : 5.317sec.
Total calculation takes :  0.28sec.
program terminated
```

FIGURE 10.14. Screen of client (phase 2).

```
*************************************************
Tue Jan 17 19:04:20 GMT+08:00 2006listening started
*****list socket called**************************
Tue Jan 17 19:04:20 GMT+08:00 2006Add servlet init, started
trying to connect Thread : 0
addServlet count=1
Tue Jan 17 19:07:10 GMT+08:00 2006   Calculation Started
start position :1.0
end   position :50.0
number of remote thread: 1  interval: 100  total no. of processor: 2
waiting for 'go ahead' signal from Client  start:1  end=50

sum=1275
It take :  0.1sec.
connected Thread : 0
trying to connect Thread : 1
```

FIGURE 10.15. Screen of the first server (phase 2).

```
c:\Tomcat 5.5\webapps\root\web-inf\classes>java invokeServer 2 ip.txt
number of servers :2
invoked 1
try to connect 192.168.1.2
connected :192.168.1.2
try to connect 192.168.1.3
connected :192.168.1.3
********************************* It takes :  0.861sec.
program terminated
```

FIGURE 10.16. Screen of the second server (phase 2).

10.5.1 Further Testing

If the test in Section 10.4.3 is successful, you are ready to start the phase 2 test. Type the following command in your client computer:

java addClient 2 100 ip.txt

The grand total (5050) is displayed in the client computer as shown in Fig. 10.14. The two sub-totals (1275 and 3775) are displayed in the servers' screens (Figs. 10.15 and 10.16).

11
Power Server: Model 3

11.1 Introduction

The models in Chapters 9 and 10 divide a task into n sub-tasks for a system with n servers so we can maintain 'load balance'. In other words, each server receives one sub-task. The programs for these models are also simpler so they are good for readers who do not have related experience in building these kinds of systems. These designs are based on two assumptions:

- Every server has similar computing power. One computer is not much faster than the others.
- Each server is reliable. A computer will not be shut down for a prolonged period.

These models are perfect if these assumptions are true as the overall completion time is minimized. However, sometimes these assumptions are not true. For example, as hardware cost decreases rapidly, newly purchased computers will be much faster than those purchased two years ago for the same amount of money even in the same department. A faster computer will complete the sub-task much earlier than a slower one and become idle while other computers are still working on the sub-tasks. In other words, we cannot maximize the utilization of computer powers inside the network. Thus, such designs are efficient only for homogeneous systems with similar computers, and not for heterogeneous systems.

Computers connected by Internet are heterogeneous in terms of platforms, CPU speed, communication speed, primary memory and disk spaces. Furthermore, we cannot impose any centralized control to ensure that all servers are working properly. A new model is required if we are working on an application on the Intranet.

11.2 Power Server—Model 3

We will modify the programs in Chapter 9 in this model as it is easier to test. The programs in Chapter 10 will be modified in later sections. The major differences between this model and the counterpart in Chapter 9 are as follows:

- A task will be divided into m sub-tasks in the systems with n servers. 'm' is an integer much bigger than n (*i.e.*, $m >> n$, where m and n are both integers).
- More error-checking procedures are built into the programs so they will detect whether a server is working normally. Sub-tasks will not be distributed to servers not working properly. For example, the server might get shut down by the owner. The programs are more robust at the cost of more complicated logic and bigger size (in term of number of coding lines).
- Synchronizations are removed as different servers will get sub-tasks at different times. Some time measurements are removed as they are not meaningful any more. Note that in Chapters 9 and 10, the servers wait until every server gets a sub-task before they start calculation.
- The communication costs of this model will be higher as the number of communication messages is greater in this new model. In addition to the actual exchanges of sub-task and answer between server and client, we need to consider the overhead in establishing the communication socket which might be extremely time consuming, particularly when these computers are in different countries.
- Some communication messages in Chapter 9, which are not absolutely necessary (but good for debugging) for the calculation, are removed.

11.3 Server Program of Model 3

There are minor modifications in the server program. The overall structure is presented in Fig. 11.1. Communication messages are minimized to only two following messages:

- Sub-task (*i.e.*, starting value and ending value) from client to server.
- Answer (*i.e.*, the sub-total) from server to client after the calculation.

There are no changes in both add.java and timer.java modules. The source codes of addServer2.java and addServerThread2.java are presented in Figs. 11.2 and 11.3.

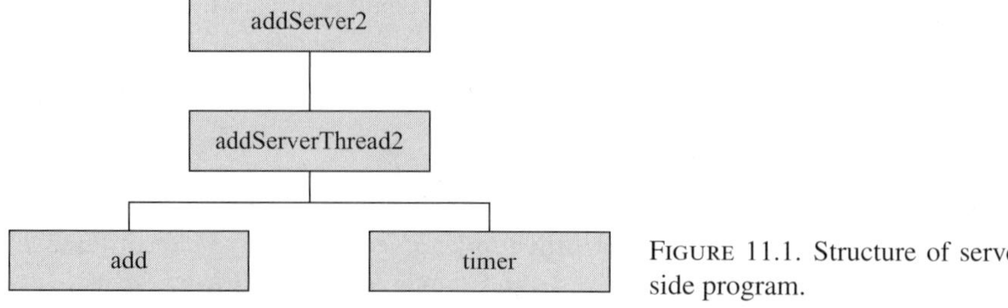

FIGURE 11.1. Structure of server side program.

```
import java.io.*;
import java.net.*;
import java.util.*;
public class addServer2
{
      public static void main (String[] args)
                  throws IOException
      {
            ServerSocket serverSocket = null;
            boolean listening = true;
            boolean debug=false;
            int Thread_id=0;

System.out.println("****************************************************
*******");
            if (args.length ==1) debug = true;
            Date start_date=new Date();
            System.out.println( start_date);
            try
            {
                  serverSocket = new ServerSocket(3333);
            }
            catch (IOException e)
            {
                  System.err.println("Could not listen on port: 3333.");
                  System.exit(-1);
            }
            while (listening)
            {
                  try
                  {
                  System.out.println("waiting for Thread : " + Thread_id+" ******");
                  new addServerThread2(serverSocket.accept(),debug).start();
                  Thread_id =Thread_id + 1;
                  }
                  catch (IOException e)
                  {
                  System.err.println("accept failed");
                  }
            } // end of while
      } // end of method
}
```

FIGURE 11.2. addServer2.java

```
import java.io.*;
import java.net.*;
import java.util.*;
import java.net.*;
public class addServerThread2    extends Thread
{
    Socket addSocket=null;
    boolean debug=false;
    public addServerThread2 (Socket addSocket, boolean debug)
                throws IOException
    {
        this.addSocket=addSocket;
        this.debug=debug;
        String fromRemote= " ";
        String fromUser= "initial value";
        double startPosition=0.0,endPosition=0.0;
        Date start_date=new Date();
        System.out.println(start_date +"    Calculation Started");
        PrintWriter out =null;
        BufferedReader in=null;
        try
        {
        out = new PrintWriter(addSocket.getOutputStream(), true);
        in = new BufferedReader(new InputStreamReader(
                                addSocket.getInputStream()));
        } // END TRY
        catch (IOException e)
            {
                System.out.print ("io exception in input/output");
                return;
            }
        //------------------------------------ get data --------------
        try
        {
        fromRemote = in.readLine();
        if (debug) System.out.println("remote input:"+ fromRemote+"********");
        StringTokenizer tokens = new StringTokenizer(fromRemote);
        startPosition= Double.valueOf(tokens.nextToken()).doubleValue();
        endPosition= Double.valueOf(tokens.nextToken()).doubleValue();
        if (debug)
            {
                System.out.println("start position :" + startPosition);
                System.out.println("end position :" + endPosition);
            }
        } // END TRY
```

FIGURE 11.3. addServerThread2.java

```
        catch (IOException e)
        {
                System.out.print ("io exception in socket input/output");
        }
    // ************************add operations ***********
            timer t =new timer();
            t.start();
            add getSum= new add((long) startPosition, (long) endPosition);
            long sum=getSum.adding();
            t.elasp("It take : ");
            fromUser=Long.toString(sum);
            out.println(fromUser);
    try
        {
            out.close();
            in.close();
            addSocket.close();
        }
        catch (IOException e)
        {
                        System.out.print ("io exception in CLOSING");
        }
    } // end of method
}
```

FIGURE 11.3. (*Continued*)

11.4 Client Program of Model 3

The structure of this program is presented in Fig. 11.4. The followings are the differences between Models 1 and 3:

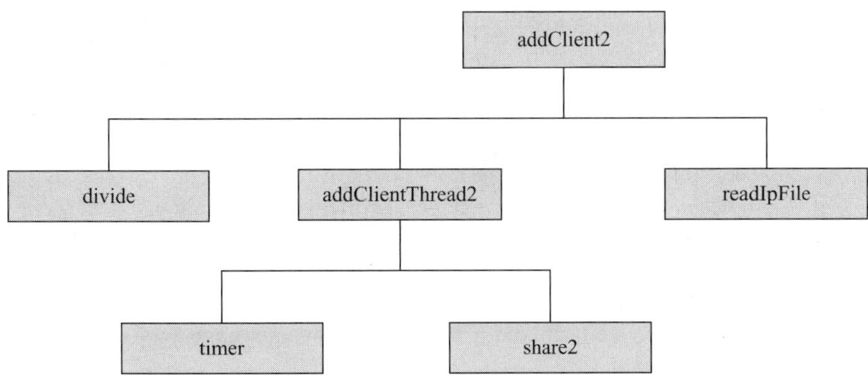

FIGURE 11.4. Structure of the client side program.

- There are three new modules *i.e.*, addClient2.java (modified from addClient .java), addClientThread2.java (modified from addClientThread.java) and share2 .java (share.java) and divide.java (extracted from addClient.java so readers).
- The module ShareObj module has been removed.

This module accepts the following four parameters from the user:

- Number of sub-tasks, *e.g.*, 2 if the user divides the task into 2 sub-tasks.
- Interval of the series, *e.g.*, 10 if the user wants to add the numbers from 1 to 10.
- File name which holds the IP address of the servers, *e.g.* ip.txt.
- Debug indicator—The value is 1 if the user wants to turn on this mode. The program will print out more messages, which are useful for debugging. This field is optional.

If a user forgets the parameter, he/she can type 'java addClient2' and the system will print an instruction on the screen to remind the user the position of each parameter as follows:

```
C:\vq\servlets\add>java addClient2
 number of sub-tasks, number of interval
 , name of IP_file, debug indicator
```

11.4.1 addClient2.java

This module provides the following functions:

- Accept input parameters from users.
- Invoke addClientThread2 according to the IP address file.
- Assign a sub-task to each thread.
- Update the grand total through the share2.java module.

The source codes of this module are presented in Fig. 11.5.

11.4.2 addClientThread2.java

This module differs from addClientThread.java (Chapter 9) in the following ways:

- It will check whether a sub-task is available in the beginning of both constructor method and run() method. It will terminate itself if no more sub-tasks are available.
- A sub-task will not be assigned to a thread until the connection is successful. This design is more fault tolerant as servers on the websites might not be reliable. Servers in the network will be racing for the sub-tasks.
- After the completion of calculation and before the termination of this thread, it will check whether there are still any sub-tasks in the system. A new thread will be generated before the termination if there are any unassigned sub-tasks.

The logic of this module is presented in Fig. 11.6, and the source codes of this module are presented in Fig. 11.7.

```
import java.net.*;
import java.io.*;
public class addClient2 {
    public static void main(String[] args) throws IOException {
        int Thread_id=1;
        int totalTasks =0;
        timer t = new timer();
        // ************ get parameter from command argument *******
        if (args.length >= 1)
            {
                totalTasks = Integer.parseInt(args[0]);
                System.out.println("number of sub-tasks :" + totalTasks);
            }
        else
        {       System.out.println(" number of sub-tasks, number of interval");
                System.out.println(" , name of IP_file, debug indicator");
                System.exit(-1);
        }
        long n= Integer.parseInt(args[1]);   // no. of interval
        boolean debug = false;
        String ipFile= "ip.txt";
        String hostIp="localhost";
        if (args.length >=3)     ipFile= args[2];
        if (args.length >=4)
            if (Integer.parseInt(args[3])==1)     debug=true;
        long startPosition =0;
        long endPosition =n;
        double x[]= new double[totalTasks*2];
        divide subTaskArray = new divide(x,endPosition,totalTasks,debug);
        subTaskArray.go();
        Share2 answer = new Share2(totalTasks,debug); // control answer update
        String ip[]=new String[50];
        readIpFile reader= new readIpFile(ipFile,ip);
        int numServer = reader.getNumServer();
        if (debug) System.out.println("number of servers: "+ numServer);
        timer total =new timer(); // timer for transmission + calculation
        total.start();
        // *************************** create Threads    ***************
        for (int i=1;i<=numServer;i++)
            new addClientThread2(ip[i-1],x, i,totalTasks,answer,debug).start() ;
        if (debug) System.out.println("wait for connection to complete ");
        System.out.println("********* Answer: "+(long) answer.getAnswer()+ "
*********");
        total.elasp("total time calculation + transmission :");
        System.out.println("program terminated");
    } // end of main method
}
```

FIGURE 11.5. addClient2.java

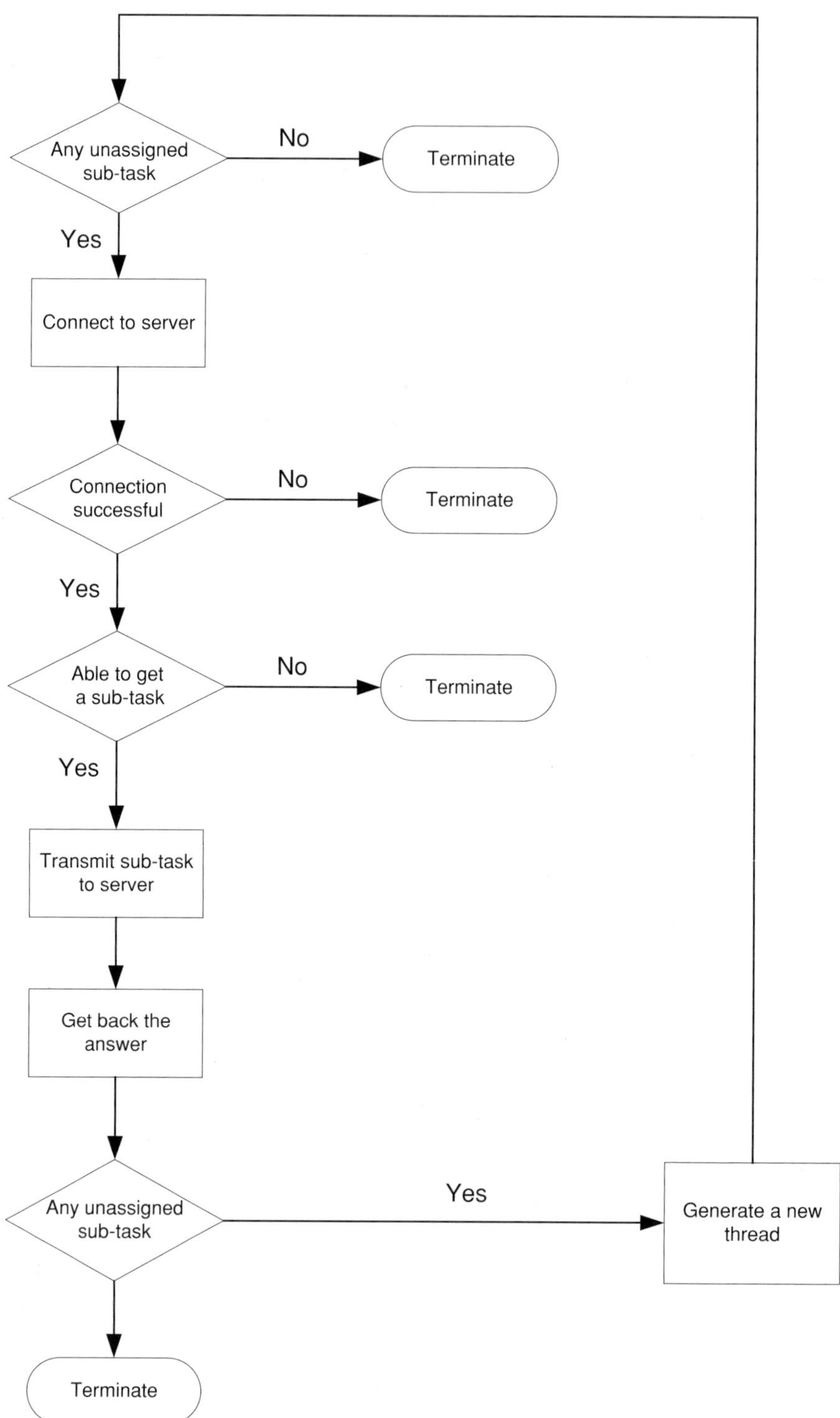

FIGURE 11.6. Logic of addClientThread2

```
import java.net.*;
import java.io.*;
import java.util.*;
public class addClientThread2 extends Thread
{
	private Socket socket = null;
	double x[];
	int Thread_id;
	int totalTasks;
	boolean debug;
	Share2 answer;
	boolean Done= false;
	PrintStream out=null ;
	Socket powerSocket;
	BufferedReader in=null;
	String site;
	boolean connected=false;
	long interval;
	int subTask;
	public addClientThread2(String site, double[] y,
					int id, int totalTasks,Share2 answer,
					boolean debug )
	{
		super("ClientThread");
		if (debug) System.out.println("add Client Theard");
		this.Thread_id =id;
		this.x =y;
		this.totalTasks = totalTasks;
		this.answer=answer;
		this.debug=debug;
		this.site=site;
		this.interval=interval;
		// ********************** try to connect now    *************
		subTask = answer.getTaskNumber();
		if (debug) System.out.println("subTask number="+subTask);
		if (subTask >0)
		{
			try
			{
			powerSocket = new Socket(site, 3333);
			if (debug) System.out.println("connecting "+Thread_id+" : "+ site);
			out = new PrintStream(powerSocket.getOutputStream());
			in = new BufferedReader(new InputStreamReader(
						powerSocket.getInputStream()));
			connected= true;
			if (debug) System.out.println("connection ok");
			}
```

FIGURE 11.7. addClientThread2.java

```
            catch (UnknownHostException e)
            {
            System.err.println("unknown host: "+site);
            }
            catch (IOException e)
            {
            System.err.println("I/O connection problem to: "+site);
            System.err.println(" close this thread:"+Thread_id);
            }
        }
}
public void run()
{
if (!connected) return; // do not continue if it is not connected
// *************** send data to server *********************
timer t = new timer();
subTask=answer.getNextTask();
if (debug) System.out.println("subTask="+subTask);
if (subTask>0)
   {
      if (debug) System.out.println("subTask="+subTask);
      StringBuffer arrayBuffer = new StringBuffer(totalTasks*8);
      try
      {
            String inputLine, outputLine;
            int first = (subTask -1 ) * (x.length /totalTasks);
            if (debug) System.out.print( "*************** first=" +first);
            int last = (subTask ) * (x.length /totalTasks);
            if (Thread_id > totalTasks)
            {
                  System.out.println("conection not created");
                  System.exit(1);
            }
            if (debug) t.elasp(" takes:");
            if (debug) System.out.println("Start to transfer for " + Thread_id);
            t.start();

            if (debug) System.out.println("buffer created " );
            for (int i=first; i < last;i++)
            {
               arrayBuffer.append(x[i]+" ");
            }
            if (debug) System.out.println("array: " + arrayBuffer);
            out.println(arrayBuffer); // transmit to power server
            if (debug) System.out.println("Transmission of site " + Thread_id);
            if (debug) t.elasp(" takes:");
            timer t2= new timer();
```

FIGURE 11.7. (*Continued*)

```
                t2.start();
                double subAnswer=0.0;
                if (debug) System.out.println("id="+Thread_id+ "wait for answer" );
                 // get the answer from server *********************
                if ((inputLine = in.readLine()) != null)
                   subAnswer= Double.valueOf(inputLine).doubleValue();
                t2.elasp("id="+Thread_id +" time for cal+tran =" );
                // update total Answer ********
                if (debug) System.out.println("id="+Thread_id+ " sub total:
"+subAnswer );
                answer.updateAnswer(subAnswer);
                System.out.println("*** id="+Thread_id+ " sub-task answer= "
                                              + (long) subAnswer);
                if (debug) System.out.println("subTask="+subTask);
             }// end of try
             catch (IOException e)
             {
                e.printStackTrace();
             }
          } // end of if
      try
      {
      out.close();
      in.close();
      powerSocket.close();
      } // end of try
      catch (IOException e)
      {
      e.printStackTrace();
      }
      int nextSubTask = answer.getTaskNumber();
      if (debug) System.out.println(" ************next subTask="+nextSubTask);
      if (nextSubTask <= totalTasks)
            new addClientThread2(site,x,Thread_id,totalTasks,answer,debug).start() ;
   }// end of run method
}
```

FIGURE 11.7. (*Continued*)

11.4.2.1 Constructor

In the constructor method, the program checks the availability of sub-tasks with the following statements:

subtask = answer.getTaskNumber();

where answer is an object of the share2 class.

Note that it is important to distinguish the differences between getNextNumber() and getTaskNumber() methods. The getNextNumber() returns the number of next available sub-task *but* the sub-task is not assigned to the thread yet. On the other hand, the getNextTask() method returns the number next available sub-task *and* assigns it to the thread. The sub-task is assigned only when the server is ready to process it.

11.4.2.2 run() Method

In the run() method, the connection is checked by the following statement:

```
if (!connected) return;
```

The sub-task is assigned by the following statement:

```
subTask=answer.getNextTask();
```

The source codes of the addClientThread2 module are presented in Fig. 11.7.

11.5 divide.java Module

This module divides the task into sub-tasks and returns the task array to the calling module. The source codes are presented in Fig. 11.8.

11.6 share2.java

This module differs from the share.java (in Chapter 9) in the following ways:

- Two new methods are added, *i.e.*, getTaskNumber and getNextTask.
- The setGoAhead method is removed as this synchronization is not required.

The following are the functions of the new methods:

getTaskNumber—return the next available task number to the calling thread.
getNextTask—*assign and* return the next available sub-task number to the calling thread.

The source codes of this module are presented in Fig. 11.9.

11.7 Testing

Programs can be tested in a similar way to Sections 6.5 and 6.6. Again I would recommend that you start with one computer even if you have several computers in front of you.

```
import java.io.*;
import java.util.*;
public class divide
{
      double x[];
      long endPosition;
      long totalTasks;
      boolean debug;
      public divide(double[] x, long endPosition, long totalTasks, boolean debug )
      {
            if (debug) System.out.println("divide    module");
            this.x = x;
            this.endPosition=endPosition;
            this.totalTasks = totalTasks;
            this.debug = debug;
      }
      public void go()
      {
            long width = endPosition / totalTasks;
            // ****** dividing job into sub-tasks ****************
            for (int i = 0; i < x.length; i = i + 2) {
                  if (i == 0)
                        x[i] = 1;
                  else
                        x[i] = x[i - 1] + 1;
                  if ((i + 2) == x.length)
                        x[i + 1] = endPosition;
                  else
                        x[i + 1] = x[i] + width - 1;
            }
            if (debug)
            {
                  System.out.print(" x[i]=");
                  for (int j = 0; j < x.length; j++)
                  {
                        System.out.print(" " + x[j]);
                  }
                  System.out.println("    size of array = " + x.length);
            }
      }
}
```

FIGURE 11.8. divide.java

```
class Share2
{
	boolean debug = false;
	int subTask =0;
	int totalTask=0;
	int doneTask=0;
	double answer=0.0;
	public Share2(int totalTask,boolean debug)
	{
		this.debug= debug;
		this.totalTask = totalTask;
	}
	public synchronized int getTaskNumber()
	{
		int nextTaskNumber = subTask +1;
		return nextTaskNumber; // return the number of the next available sub-task
	}
	public synchronized int getNextTask()
	{
		if (subTask == totalTask)
			return 0;
		else
		{
			subTask++; // assign the task
			return subTask; // return the number of this sub-task
		}
	}

	 public synchronized void updateAnswer(double ans)
	{
		answer =answer+ans;
		doneTask++;
		notifyAll();
	}
	 public synchronized double getAnswer()
	{
	 if (debug) System.out.println("waiting for answer by Server");
	 while ( doneTask != totalTask )
		{
			try
			{
				wait();
			}
			catch ( InterruptedException e )
			{
				System.err.println( "Exception: " + e.toString() );
			}
		}
	return answer;
	}
}
```

FIGURE 11.9. share2.java

11.7.1 First Test

1. Start the server program by typing the following command in DOS:

   java addServer2

   Remember to type '2' at the end of this command.
   More information can be displayed if you turn on the debug indicator. This indicator can be turned on by appending '1' in the command.

   e.g., java addServer2 1

2. Start the client program by typing the following command in DOS:

   e.g., java addClient2 4 100 local.txt

   where 4 is the total number of sub-tasks, 100 is the range from 1 to 100 and local.txt is the IP file (refer to Section 6.5 for the content of this file).

You can obtain more information by turning on the debug indicator. You can turn it by adding appendix '1' in the above command. Refer to Section 11.3 for the description of the parameters.

11.7.2 Server and Client Screens

Figure 11.10 shows the server screen. Four sub-totals are displayed. Figure 11.11 shows the client screen. In addition to showing the grand totals, the four sub-totals are also displayed.

11.7.3 Troubleshooting

Make sure that you are using the right version of programs (*i.e.*, addClient2 and addServer2). It is very easy to forget typing '2' in either one of them, particularly if you have done a lot of tests using the models in Chapters 9 and 10.

11.7.4 Second Test

If the first test is successful, you are ready to start the second test with two or more computers.

1. Copy all programs to all computers.
2. Type 'java addServer' in DOS of both server computers.
3. Obtain the IP addresses of both computers.
4. You can use a third computer or use one of the two computers as client.
   - Edit the ip.txt and replace the IP addresses with your server computers.
   - Type 'java addClient2 4 1000 ip.txt', where 4 is total number of sub-tasks and 1000 is the range 1 to 1000.

The screen of the client is displayed in Fig. 11.12.

```
*********************************************************
Tue Nov 29 11:18:24 GMT+08:00 2005
waiting for Thread : 0 ******
Tue Nov 29 11:18:35 GMT+08:00 2005   Calculation Started
start=1  end=25

sum=325
It take :  0.04sec.
waiting for Thread : 1 ******
Tue Nov 29 11:18:35 GMT+08:00 2005   Calculation Started
start=26  end=50

sum=950
It take :  0.03sec.
waiting for Thread : 2 ******
Tue Nov 29 11:18:35 GMT+08:00 2005   Calculation Started
start=51  end=75

sum=1575
It take :  0.03sec.
waiting for Thread : 3 ******
Tue Nov 29 11:18:35 GMT+08:00 2005   Calculation Started
start=76  end=100

sum=2200
It take :  0.031sec.
waiting for Thread : 4 ******
```

FIGURE 11.10. Server screen

```
c:\vq\servlets\add>java addClient2 4 100 local.txt
number of sub-tasks :4
id=1 time for cal+tran = 0.05sec.
*** id=1 sub-task answer= 325
id=1 time for cal+tran = 0.04sec.
*** id=1 sub-task answer= 950
id=1 time for cal+tran = 0.04sec.
*** id=1 sub-task answer= 1575
id=1 time for cal+tran = 0.041sec.
*** id=1 sub-task answer= 2200
********* Answer: 5050 *********
total time calculation + transmission : 0.481sec.
program terminated
```

FIGURE 11.11. Screen of client

```
c:\vq\servlets\add>java addClient2 4 100 ip.txt
number of sub-tasks :4
id=2 time for cal+tran = 0.0sec.
*** id=2 sub-task answer= 950
id=2 time for cal+tran = 0.0sec.
*** id=2 sub-task answer= 1575
id=1 time for cal+tran = 0.33sec.
*** id=1 sub-task answer= 325
id=2 time for cal+tran = 0.101sec.
*** id=2 sub-task answer= 2200
********* Answer: 5050 *********
total time calculation + transmission : 5.138sec.
program terminated
```

FIGURE 11.12. Screen from client of test2 (with two servers)

11.7.5 Further Tests

If the second test is fine, you can try further tests, adding more computers, and using different combinations until you understand the operations.

11.8 Comparison with Model 1

The overall structure of model 3 is presented in Fig. 11.13. The model in this chapter has the following advantages and disadvantages compared with model 1:

Advantages

- It is more robust and fault tolerant.
- It can maintain 'load balance' in both homogeneous and heterogeneous systems. Thus completion time can be reduced in different systems.

Disadvantage

- The programming logic is more complex. It will take longer time to develop and debug the programs.
- The overall communication cost is much higher, especially if the servers are deployed in different countries.
- Users need to specify the number of sub-tasks for the system. However, it is not easy to find out the number that can ensure the shortest time of completion. A lot of factors can affect this number. Such factors include:
  - ◦ CPU speed of each server.
  - ◦ Communication speed (establishment of socket) and transmission of sub-task and sub-total.
  - ◦ Overhead in generating threads within the server.

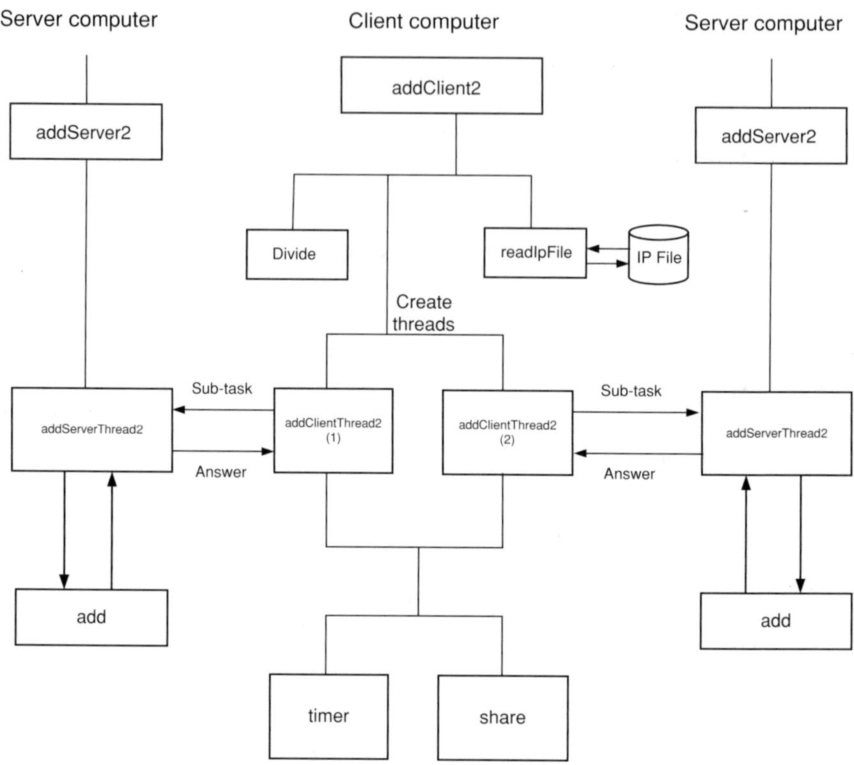

FIGURE 11.13. Overall structure of model 3

Note that you can test the system with different numbers of sub-tasks with the same configuration and problem size. Such experiments will help you to understand the aforementioned factors.

12
Power Server: Model 4

12.1 Introduction

In model 3, you need to type a command to invoke the server side program. It is good for systems with the following characteristics:

- There is a small number of servers in the network.
- There are only one or two applications in the network, and these applications are frequently used. Thus, users can simply invoke the program and await the request from the client. Users do not need to interface anymore after the unitization.

If these characteristics are not true, model 3 can be modified to run under a web server using a similar method in Chapter 11.

12.2 Power Server with Web Server—Model 4

Model 3 can easily be modified to work with any web server. A program 'invoke-Server2' for the client is written to send HTTP messages to invoke servlets in server computers. A schematic diagram is presented in Fig. 12.1. This program reads the IP addresses in a local file. It then creates a thread to invoke servlets from remote servers by sending them HTTP messages.

12.2.1 invokeServer2 Module

The source codes of this module are presented in Fig. 12.2. The operations of this module are similar to invokeServer.java. This module differs from invoke-Server.java in the following way:

- A module startServlet2 is invoked instead of startServlet.

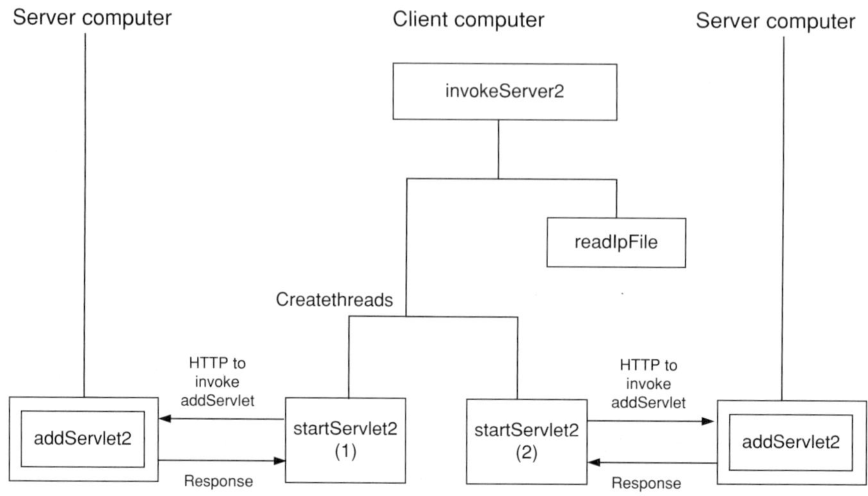

FIGURE 12.1. Invoking the servlet of remote computer.

12.2.2 startServlet2 Module

This module calls the URL_connect module to send the HTTP message to the server. It will get a true value if the connection is normal, otherwise it will get a false value from the URL_connect module. The complete coding list is given in Fig. 12.3.

The name and IP address of the client computer are obtained by the following line:

InetAddress address = InetAddress.getLocalHost();

The information of the client computer is sent to the server for debugging purposes. It is embedded in the following line:

String urlString ="http://" +ip+":8080/servlet/addServlet2?site="+address;

12.3 Server Side Program

This servlet enables the user to invoke the addServerThread2 program (Chapter 11) with an HTTP message. The structure of this servlet is presented in Fig. 12.4.

12.3.1 listen2 Module

The listen Module establishes a socket (in port 3333). Whenever it receives a request from the client, an addServer2 thread will be invoked by the following statements:

```
import java.net.*;
import java.io.*;

    public class invokeServer2 {
        public static void main(String[] args) throws IOException {
            int Thread_id=1;
            int totalProc =0;
            timer t = new timer();
            //************ get parameter from command argument *******
            if (args.length >= 1)
          {
            totalProc = Integer.parseInt(args[0]);
            System.out.println("number of servers :" + totalProc);
          }
      else
      {      System.out.println(" number of servers");
             System.out.println(" , name of IP_file ");
             System.exit(-1);
      }
      String ipFile= "ip.txt";
      // default file name
      if (args.length >=2) ipFile= args[1];
      String ip[]=new String[totalProc+1];
      readIpFile reader= new readIpFile(ipFile,ip);
      System.out.println("invoked " + Thread_id);
      // ************************** ending operation ***************
      timer t1= new timer();
      t1.start();
      for (int i=0;i<totalProc;i++)
        {
        new startServlet2(ip[i]).run();
        }
      t1.elasp("********************************** It takes : ");
      System.out.println("program terminated");
    }// end of main method
}
```

FIGURE 12.2. invokeServer2.java

```
while (listening)
{
    try
    {
    System.out.println("tring to connect Thread : " + Thread_id);
    new addServerThread2(serverSocket.accept()).start();
```

```
import java.net.*;
public class startServlet2 extends Thread
{
      String ip;
      InetAddress hostIp;
      public startServlet2(String ip)
      {
            super ("invokeServer");
            this.ip=ip;
            this.hostIp=hostIp;
      }
      public void run()
      {
      boolean connected = false;
            try
            {
                  InetAddress address = InetAddress.getLocalHost();
                  System.out.println("try to connect "+ip);
                  String urlString ="http://"
      +ip+":8080/servlet/addServlet2?site="+address;
                  connected =new URL_connect(urlString).go();
                  if (connected)
                  System.out.println("connected :"+ ip);
                  else
                                    System.out.println("failed to connect "+ip);
            }
            catch (Exception e)
            {
                  System.err.println("get error: " + e);
            }
      }  // end of run method
}
```

FIGURE 12.3. startServlet2.java

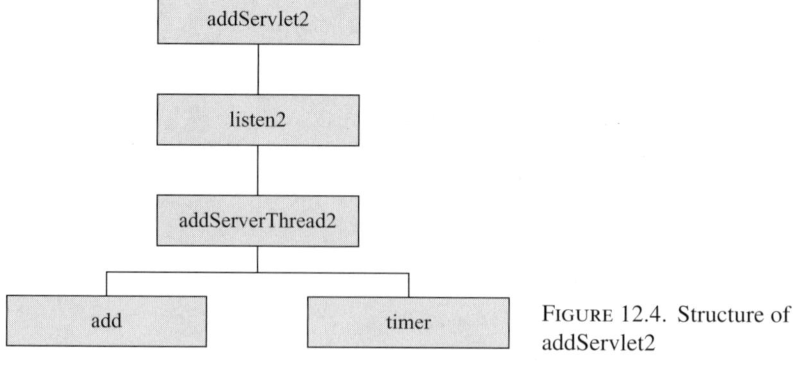

FIGURE 12.4. Structure of addServlet2

```
    System.out.println("connected Thread : " + Thread_id);
    Thread_id =Thread_id + 1;
    }
    catch (IOException e)
    {
    System.err.println("accept failed");
    }
}// end of while
```

The server side programs in Chapter 11 are modified. The addServerThread, add and timer modules do not need any further modification. The coding list is presented in Fig. 12.5.

12.4 Testing the invokeServer2 Program

You need a web server to test this module. Again it is simpler to use one computer in the first test even if you have several computers.

12.4.1 Test 1

You can test the program by following these steps:

1. Copy the server side programs to the default servlet path of your web server.
2. Start your web server.
3. Type 'java invokeServer2 1 local.txt' in DOS. The first parameter '1' is the number of servers in the system. One computer is used as both client and server in this test. The results are displayed in Figs. 12.6 and 12.7. Fig. 12.6 shows the screen of the server window, while Fig. 12.7 shows the client window.

12.4.2 Troubleshooting

Check the following if you have any problems:

- Make sure that the web server is running.
- Make sure that you are using correct versions of programs as there are several models.
- Check the port number of your web server. The default port is 8080 for Tomcat. This number could be different if you are using other servers. Type http://localhost:8080 to test this port.
- If you are not sure whether it is a server side or client side problem, you can also test the servlet by typing the URL http://localhost:8080/servlet/addServlet2 on your browser

You will get the screen as shown in Fig. 12.8 on your browser if the server side is working properly.

```
import java.io.*;
import java.net.*;
import java.util.*;
public class listen2    extends Thread
{
      Socket addSocket= null;
      ServerSocket serverSocket = null;
      boolean listening = true;
      int count =1;
      int Thread_id;
      int portNumber= 3333;
      public listen2()
      {
            System.out.println("listening started");
      }
      public void run()
      {
            Date start_date=new Date();
            System.out.print( start_date);

            try{
                  serverSocket = new ServerSocket(portNumber);
                  System.out.println("Add servlet2 init, started");
              }
            catch (IOException e)
                  {
                     System.err.println("Could not listen on port: "+ portNumber);
                     System.exit(-1);
                  }
            while (listening)
            {
                  try
                  {
                  System.out.println("trying to connect Thread : " + Thread_id);
                  new addServerThread2(serverSocket.accept(),true).start();
                  System.out.println("connected Thread : " + Thread_id);
                  Thread_id =Thread_id + 1;
                  }
                  catch (IOException e)
                  {
                  System.err.println("accept failed");
                  }
            }// end of while
      }// end of method
}
```

FIGURE 12.5. listen2.java

```
*************************************************
Sat Jan 14 14:03:40 GMT+08:00 2006listening started
addServlet2 count=1
Sat Jan 14 14:03:40 GMT+08:00 2006Add servlet2 init, started
trying to connect Thread : 0
```

FIGURE 12.6. Server window

```
c:\vq\servlets\add>java invokeServer2 1 local.txt
number of servers :1
invoked 1
try to connect localhost
connected :localhost
******************************** It takes :  12.197sec.
program terminated
```

FIGURE 12.7. Client window

```
request accepted
```

FIGURE 12.8. Screen of the browser

12.4.3 Test 2

In this test, you use several computers to test the programs in this chapter with the following steps:

1. Install the addServlet2 programs in three computers.Nnote that alternatively you can share the folder with other computers, it will save a lot of time.
2. Start the Tomcat.
3. Check the IP addresses of your three servers.
4. Create an office.txt file with the IP addresses of your computers.
5. Type 'java invokeServer2 2 office.txt' in DOS on a third computer. The second parameter ('2') means two servers.

The contents of the office.txt file in this example are:

3
202.40.197.26
202.40.197.173
202.40.197.69

The following figures show the screens of client side program (Fig. 12.9) and server side programs (Fig. 12.10).

```
C:\add>java invokeServer2 3 office.txt
number of servers :3
invoked 1
try to connect 202.40.197.26
connected :202.40.197.26
try to connect 202.40.197.173
connected :202.40.197.173
try to connect 202.40.197.69
connected :202.40.197.69
******************************** It takes :  0.703sec.
program terminated
```

FIGURE 12.9. Client screen (with three servers in the network)

```
**************************************************
Wed Jan 18 18:42:45 GMT+08:00 2006listening started
addServlet2 count=1
Wed Jan 18 18:42:46 GMT+08:00 2006Add servlet2 init, started
trying to connect Thread : 0
```

FIGURE 12.10. Server screen (with three servers in the network)

12.5 Testing the System

You can test the system by following the same instructions in Section 11.7.4. The operations on the client are almost identical to those on Chapter 11.

12.5.1 Experiment with Three Servers

If the testing in Section 12.4.2 is successful, you can start the following experiment with three servers. Type the following command in your client computer:

java addClient2 5 100 office.txt

```
C:\add>java addClient2 5 100 office.txt
number of sub-tasks :5
id=1 time for cal+tran = 0.094sec.
*** id=1 sub-task answer= 210
id=1 time for cal+tran = 0.015sec.
*** id=1 sub-task answer= 1410
id=1 time for cal+tran = 0.0sec.
*** id=1 sub-task answer= 1810
id=3 time for cal+tran = 0.328sec.
*** id=3 sub-task answer= 1010
id=2 time for cal+tran = 1.641sec.
********* Answer: 5050 *********
*** id=2 sub-task answer= 610
total time calculation + transmission : 1.797sec.
program terminated
```

FIGURE 12.11. Client screen (with three servers)

```
Wed Jan 18 18:49:01 CST 2006   Calculation Started
remote input:1.0 20.0 ********
start position :1.0
end   position :20.0
start=1  end=20

sum=210
It take :  0.031sec.
connected Thread : 0
trying to connect Thread : 1
Wed Jan 18 18:49:02 CST 2006   Calculation Started
remote input:61.0 80.0 ********
start position :61.0
end   position :80.0
start=61  end=80

sum=1410
It take :  0.015sec.
connected Thread : 1
trying to connect Thread : 2
Wed Jan 18 18:49:02 CST 2006   Calculation Started
remote input:81.0 100.0 ********
start position :81.0
end   position :100.0
start=81  end=100

sum=1810
It take :  0.0sec.
connected Thread : 2
trying to connect Thread : 3
```

FIGURE 12.12. Screen of first server (with three servers)

The job is divided into five sub-tasks. They are distributed to three servers. As you can see from the following figures, server 1 is much faster than the other two computers. It gets three sub-tasks, while the other two computers get only one. Figure 12.11 shows the screen of the client computer, while Figs. 12.12 to 12.14 show the screens of three different servers.

```
Wed Jan 18 18:49:29 GMT+08:00 2006   Calculation Started
remote input:41.0 60.0 ********
start position :41.0
end   position :60.0
start=41  end=60

sum=1010
It take :  0.08sec.
connected Thread : 0
trying to connect Thread : 1
```

FIGURE 12.13. Screen of second server (with three servers)

```
Wed Jan 18 18:48:58 GMT+08:00 2006   Calculation Started
remote input:21.0 40.0 ********
start position :21.0
end   position :40.0
start=21  end=40

sum=610
It take :  0.38sec.
connected Thread : 0
trying to connect Thread : 1
```

FIGURE 12.14. Screen of third server (with three servers)

12.5.2 Further Testing

As the server side program is running on the servers, you do not need to type anything on the server. Try different configurations until you understand the operations of this model.

13
Power Server: Model 5

13.1 Introduction

In models 2 and 4, the servlet programs and client programs communicate with each other using a special port (*i.e.*, 3333 in our example). These designs have the following advantages and disadvantages:

Advantages
- The communication process is faster as there is a dedicated port for the socket.
- The default port 8080 (or 80) is used only in the initiation process, thus it will not overload this port, particularly if there are other applications in the system.

Disadvantages
- Many computers are behind a firewall. We need to reconfigure the firewall so it can release the port 3333 (or any other port which the user wants to employ). If we have a large number of servers with similar problems, it will be a time-consuming process.
- Many organizations might not be comfortable releasing ports for these purposes.

Model 4 can be modified to overcome the firewall problem. Client computers will only send messages to the server using HTTP. This new model, model 5, will be discussed in the subsequent sections in this chapter.

13.2 Power Server—Model 5

As discussed in Chapter 6, servlets can get input data from client computers with the doGet method. This model differs from model 4 in the following ways:

- All sub-tasks will be sent to the power server with HTTP message.
- Servers will not listen in port 3333.
- Client computers will not use sockets for communication.

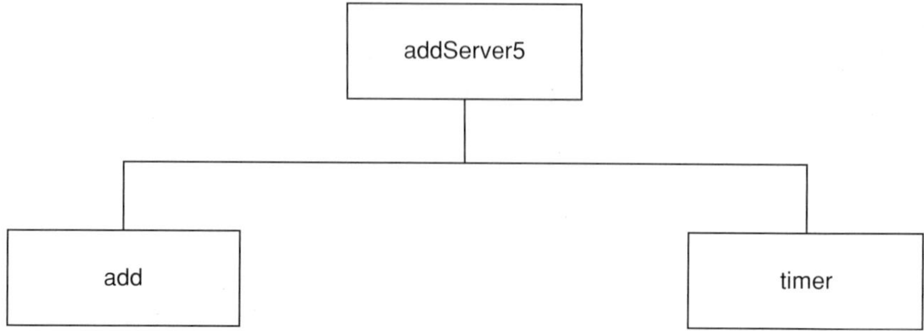

FIGURE 13.1. Structure of server program.

13.3 Server Side Program

The logic of this program is simpler as the actual communications will be handled by the web server. The overall structure of this program is presented in Fig. 13.1.

This module provides the following functions:

- Accept input data from the client (through the HTTP message) with the following statements:

```
fromRemote = in.readLine();
if (debug) System.out.println("remote input:"+ fromRemote+"********");
StringTokenizer tokens = new StringTokenizer(fromRemote);
startPosition = Double.valueOf(tokens.nextToken()).doubleValue();
endPosition = Double.valueOf(tokens.nextToken()).doubleValue();
```

- Pass the input data to the add.java class for calculation with the following statement:

```
add getSum = new add((long) startPosition, (long) endPosition);
long sum = getSum.adding();
```

- Send the sub-total back to the client with the following statement:

```
out.println(line);
```

All major functions are performed by the doGet() method. The init() method provides information for debugging only. The complete source codes of this module are presented in Fig. 13.2.

13.4 Client Side Program

The program differs from that of model 4 in the following ways:

- The data are embedded in an HTTP message.

```
import java.io.*;
import java.util.*;
import javax.servlet.*;
import javax.servlet.http.*;
public class addServlet5 extends HttpServlet
{
        int count = 1;
        boolean debug = true;
        public void init(ServletConfig config) throws ServletException
        {
System.out.println("**************************************************");
           Date start_date = new Date();
           System.out.println( start_date);
        }
        public void doGet(HttpServletRequest request, HttpServletResponse response)
                    throws ServletException, IOException
        {
           PrintWriter output = response.getWriter();
           String fromRemote = request.getParameter("input");
           if (debug) System.out.println("remote input:"+ fromRemote+"********");
           StringTokenizer tokens = new StringTokenizer(fromRemote);
           double startPosition = Double.valueOf(tokens.nextToken()).doubleValue();
           double endPosition = Double.valueOf(tokens.nextToken()).doubleValue();
           if (debug)
                {
                    System.out.println("start position :" + startPosition);
                    System.out.println("end position :" + endPosition);
                }
           //*************************add operations ***********
           timer t = new timer();
           t.start();
           add getSum = new add((long) startPosition, (long) endPosition);
           long sum = getSum.adding();
           t.elasp("It take :");
           String subTotal = Long.toString(sum);
           output.println(subTotal);
           System.out.println("addServlet count = "+count);
           System.out.println("addServlet count = "+count);
           count++;
           output.close();
        }// end of method
           public void destroy()
           {
                System.out.println("destroy method called");
           }
}
```

FIGURE 13.2. addServlet5.java

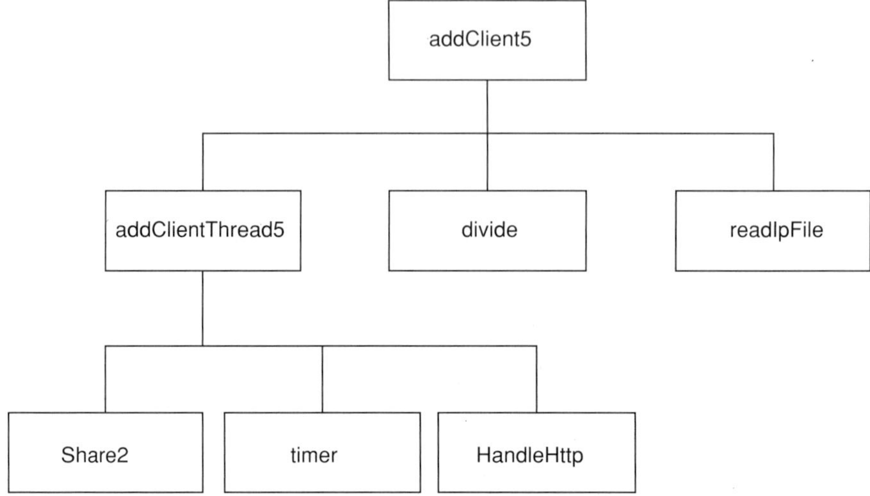

FIGURE 13.3. Structure of the client program.

- An HTTP message is sent to the servlet on the server.
- This program does not use sockets for communication.

The overall structure is presented in Fig. 13.3.

13.4.1 addClient5 Module

This module differs from addClient2 in only one statement:

new addClientThread5(ip[i-1],x, i,totalTasks,answer,debug).start() ;

The source codes of this module are presented in Fig. 13.4 for readers' easy reference.

13.4.2 addClientThread5 Module

This module differs from addClientThread2 in the following ways:

- All lines for socket communications are removed.
- It calls a new module html.java to handle the communications with the server.

The source codes are presented in Figs. 13.5 and 13.6.

13.4.3 handleHttp Module

This is a new module, and it provides the following functions:

- Accept input data from the calling module (*i.e.*, addClientThread5)

```
import java.net.*;
import java.io.*;
public class addClient5
{
    public static void main(String[] args) throws IOException
    {
        int totalTasks = 0;
        //************ get parameter from command argument *******
        if (args.length >= 1)
          {
                totalTasks = Integer.parseInt(args[0]);
                System.out.println("number of sub-tasks :" + totalTasks);
          }
          else
          {     System.out.println("number of sub-tasks, number of interval");
                System.out.println(", name of IP_file, debug indicator");
                System.exit(-1);
          }
          long n = Integer.parseInt(args[1]);       // no. of interval
          boolean debug = false;
          String ipFile = "ip.txt";
          if (args.length >= 3)      ipFile = args[2];
          if (args.length >= 4)
              if (Integer.parseInt(args[3]) == 1)      debug = true;
          long endPosition = n;
          double x[] = new double[totalTasks*2];
          divide subTaskArray = new divide(x,endPosition,totalTasks,debug);
          subTaskArray.go();
          Share2 answer = new Share2(totalTasks,debug); // control answer update
          String ip[] = new String[50];
          readIpFile reader = new readIpFile(ipFile,ip);
          int numServer = reader.getNumServer();
          if (debug) System.out.println("number of servers:"+ numServer);
          timer total = new timer(); // timer for transmission + calculation
          total.start();
          //************************* create Threads **************
          for (int i = 1;i<= numServer;i++)
              new addClientThread5(ip[i-1],x, i,totalTasks,answer,debug).start() ;
          if (debug) System.out.println("wait for connection to complete ");
          System.out.println("********* Answer:"+(long) answer.getAnswer()+ "
          *********");
          total.elasp("total time calculation + transmission :");
          System.out.println("program terminated");
    }// end of main method
}
```

FIGURE 13.4. addClient5.java

```
import java.io.*;
public class addClientThread5 extends Thread
{
      double x[];
      int Thread_id;
      int totalTasks;
      boolean debug;
      Share2 answer;
      PrintStream out = null;
      BufferedReader in = null;
      String site;
      int subTask;

      public addClientThread5(String site, double[] y,int id,
                                    int totalTasks,Share2 answer,boolean debug )
      {
            super("ClientThread");
            if (debug) System.out.println("add Client Theard");
            this.Thread_id = id;
            this.x = y;
            this.totalTasks = totalTasks;
            this.answer = answer;
            this.debug = debug;
            this.site = site;
            subTask = answer.getTaskNumber();
            if (debug) System.out.println("subTask number = "+subTask);
      }

      public void run()
      {
      //*************** send data to server ********************
      timer t = new timer();
      subTask = answer.getNextTask();
      if (debug) System.out.println("subTask = "+subTask);
      if (subTask>0)
        {
                  if (debug) System.out.println("subTask = "+subTask);
                  StringBuffer data = new StringBuffer(totalTasks*8);
                  String inputLine;
                  int first = (subTask -1 ) * (x.length /totalTasks);
                  if (debug) System.out.print( "*************** first = " +first);
                  int last = (subTask ) * (x.length /totalTasks);
                  if (Thread_id > totalTasks)
                  {
                        System.out.println("conection not created");
                        System.exit(1);
                  }
```

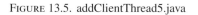

FIGURE 13.5. addClientThread5.java

```
            if (debug) t.elasp("takes:");
            if (debug) System.out.println("Start to transfer for" + Thread_id);
            t.start();
            if (debug) System.out.println("buffer created" );
            for (int i = first; i < last;i++)
            {
               data.append(x[i]+"+");
            }
            if (debug) System.out.println("array:" + data);
            timer t2 = new timer();
            t2.start();
            //********* send http message ******************************
            String input="http://" +site+":8080/servlet/addServlet5?input="+data;
            handleHttp handle = null;
            try
            {
               handle = new handleHttp(input, debug);
            }
            catch(Exception e)
            {
                  System.out.println(e);
                  System.out.print("Make sure that web server in" + site);
                  System.out.println("is running and the servlet is in the right path");
                  System.out.println("Start the job again when you are ready.");
                  System.exit(1);
            }
            inputLine = handle.getAnswer();
            if (debug) System.out.println("Transmission of site" + Thread_id);
            if (debug) t.elasp("takes:");
            double subAnswer = 0.0;
            if (debug) System.out.println("id = "+Thread_id+ "wait for answer" );
            //********* get the answer from server **********************
            subAnswer = Double.valueOf(inputLine).doubleValue();
            t2.elasp("id = "+Thread_id +"time for cal+tran = " );
            //************* update total Answer ********
            if (debug) System.out.println("id="+Thread_id+"sub total:"+subAnswer);
            answer.updateAnswer(subAnswer);
            System.out.println("*** id = "+Thread_id+ "sub-task answer = "
                                       + (long) subAnswer);
            if (debug) System.out.println("subTask = "+subTask);
      }//end of if
   int nextSubTask = answer.getTaskNumber();
   if (debug) System.out.println("************next subTask = "+nextSubTask);
   if (nextSubTask <= totalTasks)
            new addClientThread5(site,x,Thread_id,totalTasks,answer,debug).start();
   }//end of run method
}
```

FIGURE 13.5. *Continued*

```
import java.net.*;
import java.io.*;
public class handleHttp
{
    URL httpMessage;
    String answer;
    BufferedReader in = null;

    public handleHttp(String message, boolean debug) throws Exception
    {
        {
            if (debug)System.out.println("http called ********************");
            httpMessage = new URL(message);
            URLConnection connect = httpMessage.openConnection();
            in = new BufferedReader(new InputStreamReader(
                    connect.getInputStream()));
        }
    }
    public String getAnswer()
    {
        try
        {
            answer = in.readLine();
            in.close();
        }
        catch (IOException e)
        {
            System.out.println("io exception error in handleHttp");
            System.out.println(e);
        }
        return answer;
    }
}
```

FIGURE 13.6. handleHttp.java

- Send the following HTTP message to the server.

  String urlString = "http://" +ip+":8080/servlet/addServlet5?site = "+data;

- Receive the answer (*i.e.*, sub-total) and return it to the calling module.

  The source codes of this module are presented in Fig. 13.7.

13.5 Testing

Testing is simpler than previous models. As everything on the server computer is controlled by the web server, all we need is to type the command from the client.

1. Copy all programs to the default path of your servers.
2. Make sure that all web servers are running.
3. Edit the ip.txt files with the server's IP addresses.
4. Type the command to invoke the client side program. The parameters are identical to model 4. We present the four parameters here again for the readers' easy reference:
   - Number of sub-tasks, *e.g.*, 10 if the user divides the task into 10 sub-tasks.
   - Intervals of the series—50 if the user wants to add the numbers from 1 to 50.
   - File name which holds the IP address of the servers,—*e.g.*, ip.txt.
   - Debug indicator—the value is 1 if the user wants to turn on this mode. The program will print out more messages, which are useful for debugging. This field is optional.

The following line is an example of a command:

java addClient5 10 50 ip.txt

If a user forgets the parameters, he/she can type 'java addClient5' and the system will print an instruction on the screen to remind user the position of each parameter.

13.5.1 Experiment with One Server

Start the client program by typing the following command in a DOS session.

java addClient5 3 300 local.txt

Figure 13.8 shows the screen of the client, while Fig. 13.9 shows the screen of server.

13.5.2 Experiment with Two Servers

Start the client program by typing the following command in a DOS session.

java addClient5 5 500 local.txt

```
C:\add>java addClient5 3 300 local.txt
number of sub-tasks :3
id=1 time for cal+tran = 0.25sec.
*** id=1 sub-task answer= 5050
id=1 time for cal+tran = 0.161sec.
*** id=1 sub-task answer= 15050
id=1 time for cal+tran = 0.18sec.
*** id=1 sub-task answer= 25050
********* Answer: 45150 *********
total time calculation + transmission : 0.721sec.
program terminated
```

FIGURE 13.7. Screen of client (with one server)

```
addServlet count=7
remote input:1.0 100.0 ********
start position :1.0
end   position :100.0
start=1  end=100

sum=5050
It take :  0.11sec.
addServlet count=8
remote input:101.0 200.0 ********
start position :101.0
end   position :200.0
start=101  end=200

sum=15050
It take :  0.121sec.
addServlet count=9
remote input:201.0 300.0 ********
start position :201.0
end   position :300.0
start=201  end=300

sum=25050
It take :  0.11sec.
addServlet count=10
```

FIGURE 13.8. Screen of client (with one server)

Figure 13.10 shows the screen of the client, while Figs. 13.11 and 13.12 show the screens of server 1 and server 2.

```
C:\add>java addClient5 5 500 ip.txt
number of sub-tasks :5
id=1 time for cal+tran = 0.27sec.
*** id=1 sub-task answer= 5050
id=2 time for cal+tran = 0.34sec.
*** id=2 sub-task answer= 15050
id=1 time for cal+tran = 0.25sec.
*** id=1 sub-task answer= 25050
id=2 time for cal+tran = 0.301sec.
*** id=2 sub-task answer= 35050
id=1 time for cal+tran = 0.201sec.
*** id=1 sub-task answer= 45050
********* Answer: 125250 *********
total time calculation + transmission : 0.841sec.
program terminated
```

FIGURE 13.9. Screen of client (with two servers)

```
addServlet count=11
remote input:1.0 100.0 ********
start position :1.0
end   position :100.0
start=1  end=100

sum=5050
It take :  0.1sec.
addServlet count=12
remote input:201.0 300.0 ********
start position :201.0
end   position :300.0
start=201  end=300

sum=25050
It take :  0.1sec.
addServlet count=13
remote input:401.0 500.0 ********
start position :401.0
end   position :500.0
start=401  end=500

sum=45050
It take :  0.131sec.
addServlet count=14
```

FIGURE 13.10. Screen of server 1 (with two servers)

```
remote input:101.0 200.0 ********
start position :101.0
end   position :200.0
start=101  end=200

sum=15050
It take :  0.21sec.
addServlet count=28
remote input:301.0 400.0 ********
start position :301.0
end   position :400.0
start=301  end=400

sum=35050
It take :  0.231sec.
addServlet count=29
```

FIGURE 13.11. Screen of server 2 (with two servers)

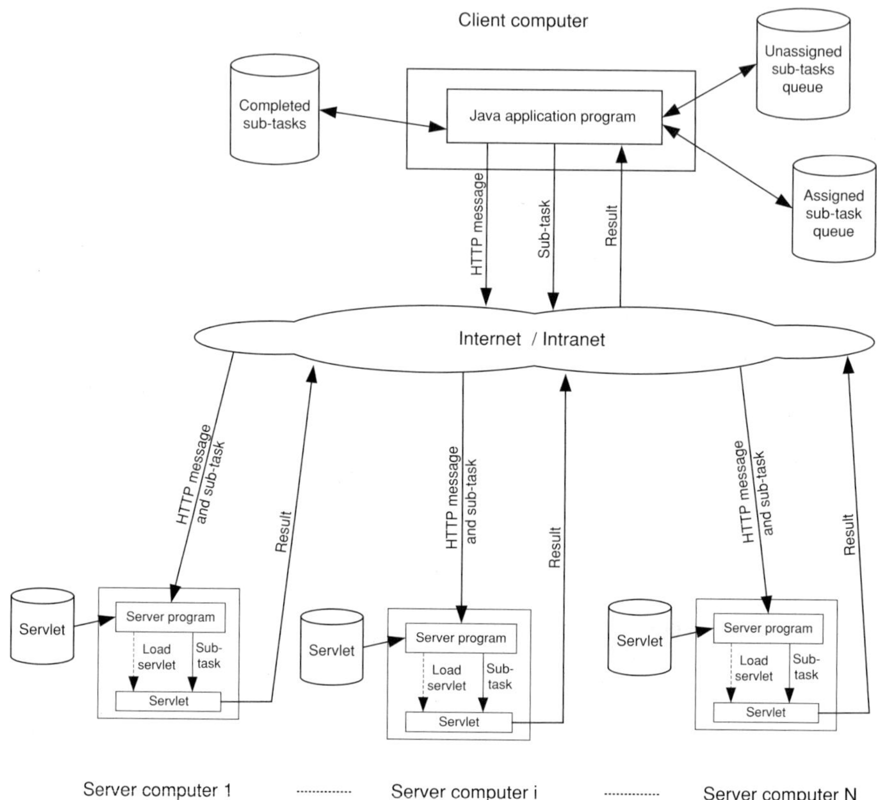

FIGURE 13.12. Robust power server model.

13.6 Comparison with Model 4

The model in this chapter provides the following advantages:

- The logic of the server program is simpler as the communications are handled by the web server. Thus it is easier to develop and debug. It will take a shorter time to develop the whole system.
- We do not need to worry about the communication port. It will be a time-consuming exercise to check and change (if necessary) the port number if we have a large number of servers. We will have problems under the following conditions:
  - Some other software packages are using the port.
  - The port is blocked by a firewall.

13.7 Further Tests

Five models have been introduced (from Chapters 9 to 12). Each model has its own advantages and disadvantages. I recommend you to carry out tests with different models using the same size of problem (*e.g.*, add 1 to 1,000,000 with different models and configurations) so you can compare the efficiencies of them.

13.8 Other Improvements

I have tried to keep the size of all programs as small as possible (in terms of number of coding lines) so they are easy to understand. If you develop mission critical applications in the future, you should consider incorporating some of the following improvements:

- More error-checking routines should be included.
- The sub-task queues and answers should be written to disk for applications which take a long time to complete (*e.g.*, months or even years). If the client computer crashes for any reason, it can recover from the disk and resume the process.
- It is possible that a server computer will crash after it accepts a sub-task from a client. The client computer will wait forever and the job will never be completed. For a time-consuming task, the client should be able to detect this problem. If the client does not receive the answer of a sub-task after a reasonable period, the sub-task should be assigned to a different server. Instead of maintaining one sub-task, three sub-task files should be maintained as in Fig. 13.13.
  - Unassigned sub-tasks queue.
  - Assigned sub-tasks queue.
  - Completed sub-tasks.

14
Wireless P2P System

14.1 Introduction

Traditional networks require cables to transmit messages. Wireless technologies enable devices to communicate without physical connections. Many people are already familiar with different kinds of wireless devices. Such devices include remote controls, cordless computer keyboards, mouse and stereo headsets using Infrared (IR) or radio transmission. The signals transmitted by these devices are very simple, and the distance between devices is quite short.

On the other hand, mobile phones allow people to transmit more complex signals over far greater distances. In addition to voice communication, nowadays many mobile phones are able to access the Internet using the Wireless Application Protocol (WAP) (Beaulieu, 2002; Cook, 2001) technology through the services of telephone companies.

Personal Digital Assistants (PDAs) are small computers, which can fit into a pocket or a purse. Such devices provide features such as address books, schedules, to-do lists, e-mail, *etc*. Early model PDAs could communicate with regular size computers via a special cable connection. Some of them employed IR ports for wireless communication. Although IR is more convenient than cable, there are some drawbacks to this type of communication. The communication distance between devices is very short (*i.e.*, usually within a few inches) and the users need to align the devices carefully. Later version of PDAs could communicate with networked PCs via a dial-up connection. PDAs with built-in modems are still relatively new. In order to meet the increasing demand for easier communication between mobile devices and wired PCs, there are many new wireless communications standards.

All these standards are different, and they all have security weaknesses. However, two of them are beginning to gain wide acceptance among mobile device vendors. They are the IEEE802.11b and Bluetooth technologies. Many new PDAs and mobile phones come with built-in IEEE802.11b and/or Bluetooth capabilities.

14.2 IEEE802 Standards

The IEEE802.11 standards were developed by the Institute of Electronic and Electrical Engineers (IEEE) Computer Society. The design began in 1990, and it took 7 years to complete the first standard. It uses the 2.4 GHz radio band for communication. Users do not need a license to use this band in most countries. This is one of the reasons that this standard has become so popular.

The standard specifies the communication between wireless client and the access points. It also defines the optional use of encryption. However, there are some well-known security weaknesses in this standard (Park et al., 1998), and the maximum speed is only 2 Mbps. IEEE workgroups have been developing many new IEEE802.11 standards to overcome these problems, and they differentiate these newer standards by appending a letter behind the 802.11. Although there are a large number of new standards, only three standards have products in the market now. They are IEEE802.11a, IEEE802.11b and IEEE802.11g.

The most popular standard is the IEEE802.11b. The data transfer rate is improved to 11 Mbps and the range to 100 meters while still using the 2.4 GHz radio band. Access points and network cards with this standard are inexpensive. Devices from different vendors are extremely compatible with each other. Installation is easy and there is wide-spread use in small offices and homes.

On the other hand, IEEE802.11a offers much higher speed (up to 54 Mbps). It uses the 5 GHz radio band so it avoids interference from electronic devices (such as microwave ovens, cordless phones, *etc*.). However, this radio band is not available for unlicensed use in many countries. Another problem is that IEEE802.11a devices are not backward compatible to the slower IEEE802.11b. This problem may be barrier for organizations, which already have IEEE802.11b devices to deploy 802.11a.

IEEE802.11g provides a higher speed (up to 54 Mbps), and it is backward compatible to 802.11b. Organizations do not need to replace existing 802.11b devices when they add new 802.11g technologies. The first product is available in January 2003, and it still uses the 2.4 GHz radio band.

14.3 Bluetooth

Bluetooth is named after the King Harald Bluetooth who united Denmark and Norway. The Bluetooth specification is a low-cost, low-power, wireless solution, which covers 10 m. The maximum speed is 700 Kbps. Bluetooth uses the 2.4 GHz radio frequency range, and it avoids interference from other electronic devices using frequency-hopping technologies.

This technology can be used to replace the inconvenient IR. It is easy to synchronize devices and transfer files. The inexpensive Bluetooth module can be built into printers, fax machines and other peripherals. It is not a competitor of IEEE802.11

standards as the low-power Bluetooth can operate only within a relatively short distance. It simply enables users to eliminate or minimize the number of cables between computers and peripherals. Devices with Bluetooth technologies can discover and talk to each other easily (Lamm et al., 2001).

14.4 Wireless LAN

Wireless LAN technologies provide the following advantages:

- You can move the computer to any place within the wireless signal coverage. Thus, a wireless network is more flexible in the long run.
- You can avoid the cost of installing network cables through walls or under floors.
- In many cases, a wireless network is easier and cheaper to extend than a wired network.

14.5 Wireless Routers

In addition to wireless applications, many people have installed wireless routers at home. Wireless routers became available several years ago, are very easy to install and mostly cost less than $100. They are convenient in the following ways:

- It is quite common that families have several computers, usually in different rooms. The installation of broadband cables to network those computers would be a time-consuming and expensive task. Wireless routers solve this problem easily.
- Users can move their computers easily around the home, as long as they remain within the coverage of the wireless signal. They do not need to rearrange network cables. For example, a notebook computer can be moved from the bedroom to the living room with ease at any time, always retaining its Internet connection.

14.6 Internet-Enabled Devices

The number of mobile phones has grown significantly in the past few years. There are 1.2 billion mobile phones, and these ubiquitous devices are changing the ways in which we conduct our daily lives. Mobile phones are becoming more powerful, and manufacturers are incorporating more functions into them. For example, many mobile phones have MP3 functions. Many can also take photos, play video, send e-mail messages and display and allow the editing of simple documents.

In addition to voice communication, many mobile phones are able to access the Internet using WAP technology. The owners of such phones can communicate with other users who are connected to the Internet via either wireless devices or wired connections, as shown in Fig. 14.1.

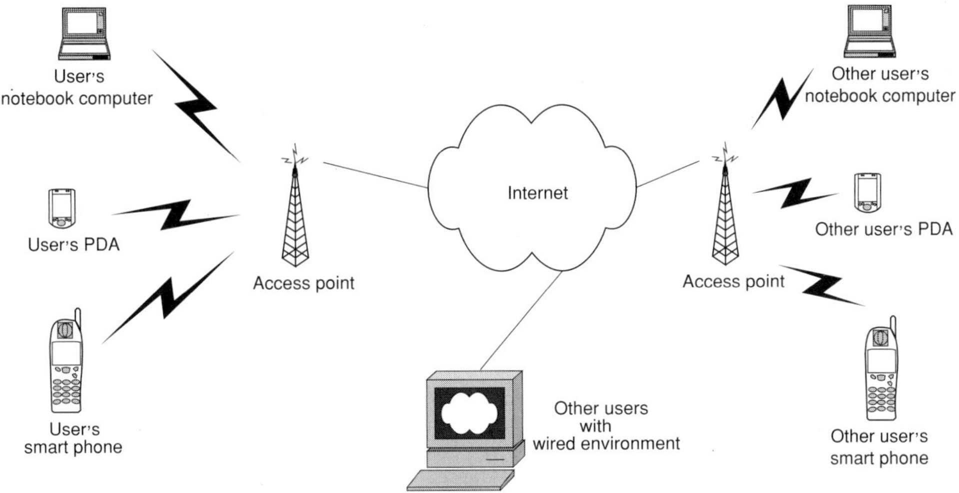

FIGURE 14.1. Internet with mobile devices.

14.7 Problems of Mobile Phones

We can consider high-end mobile phones as mobile computers because they have

- a processor,
- memory in the phone,
- a keyboard and
- the ability to connect to the Internet with one of the following services:
  - IEEE802.11 standards or Bluetooth or
  - services of telephone companies (*e.g.*, GPRS).

However, there are several problems in designing and developing software for mobile devices. These problems prevent mobile phones from participating with either clients or servers in our P2P models. Now let us discuss these:

- Speed of the CPU. The CPU speed on smart phones is much lower than that in regular PCs. However, the owners of these mobile devices operate in real time, and they expect quick responses. It is not possible to run a computationally intensive application on a mobile phone.
- Limited memory. Mobile phones have small amounts of memory, but many computer packages consume large amounts of memory. Hence, software for these devices must be carefully designed to reduce memory requirements.
- Screen size. The screen size on mobile phones is much smaller than regular monitors. Developers need to design the screen output carefully. Only essential information should be displayed.
- Time-consuming input method. Average phones have only 15 to 25 keys while regular computer keyboards have more than 102 keys. The keys on phones are

much smaller than those on the computers. One solution is to use a 'touch screen' as on the Sony Ericsson P910. However, this technology is still expensive, so only top model smart phones use it. Typing data into a phone is always unpleasant and time consuming. To make an application popular, designers need to reduce the amount of input needed.
- Lack of standards. We do not have common standards for mobile phones. They have different numbers of keys and functions and different capacities such as screen size. They also have different kinds of operating systems, such as Symbian, Windows CE, Palm, *etc*. Different manufacturers support different kinds of development tools. It is difficult to develop software that can be implemented on all platforms.
- Lack of standard Java support. Although many high-end mobile phones support Java, some do not. As mobile phones have only a small amount of memory, Java programs for normal computers are usually too large and must be modified. A special development kit, J2ME, must be used to compile the programs.

14.8 Extending the Power of Mobile Phones

Fortunately, there is a standard for connecting mobile phones to the Internet: WAP. WAP1.0 uses the wireless markup language (WML), but WAP2.0 can support both extensible markup language (XML) and html pages. A mobile phone accesses a WAP file by the following process (Fig. 14.2):

1. The mobile phone sends a GPRS signal.
2. The computer of the telephone company transforms the GPRS signal to a HTTP message and sends it to a remote server.

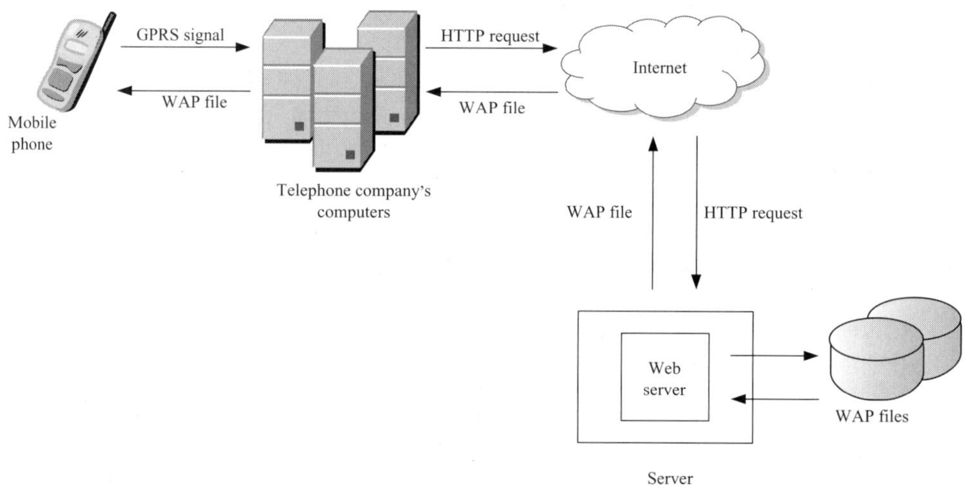

FIGURE 14.2. Accessing the Internet with WAP.

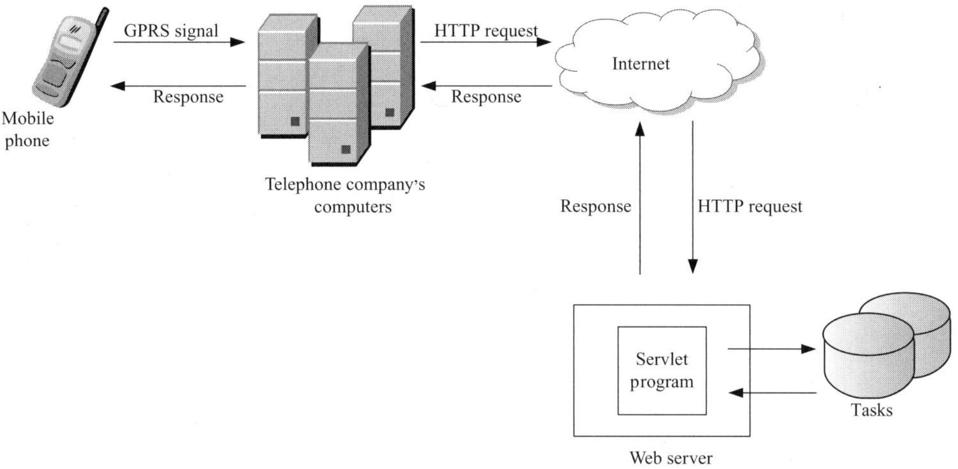

FIGURE 14.3. Invoking servlet with mobile phone.

3. The server retrieves the corresponding WAP file and sends it back to the telephone company's computer.
4. The telephone company's computer transforms the WAP file into a telephone signal and sends it to the phone.

It is possible to invoke a servlet with a GPRS signal. This ability enables the phone to handle some computationally intensive jobs. Instead of performing calculations with the phone's processor, the phone sends HTTP messages to invoke servlets in a remote computer. The servlets perform the calculations, assemble WAP files and send the answers back to the phone. The procedures are described in Fig. 14.3.

Some computationally intensive jobs can take several hours to complete, but we cannot expect a user to hold a phone for several hours. As an alternative, we can send the answer to the phone with SMS message, as in Fig. 14.4. If the answer is too long to fit on a single SMS message, then a server can store the answer. A URL address can then be embedded in the SMS message, and the user can click on it to access the answer on the server.

14.9 Wireless P2P Systems with Mobile Phones

The model in Figs. 14.3 and 14.4 can be further modified so that a mobile phone can access the power of a large P2P system. A mobile phone can only be a client (but not a server as it lacks computing power). The new model is presented in Fig. 14.5. The owner of a mobile phone requests a web page from a remote site by typing the URL (or using a bookmark in the memory of the phone). After obtaining the web page, the user can then type in the necessary data and send them to the

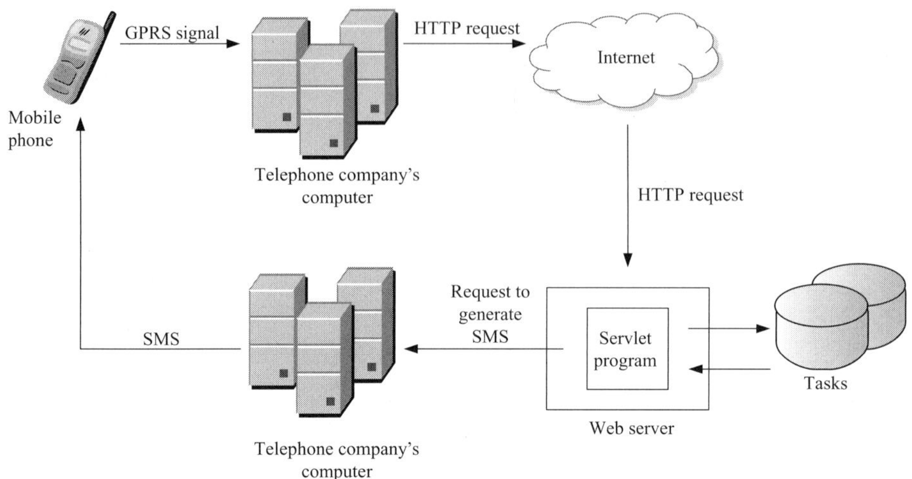

FIGURE 14.4. SMS with mobile phone.

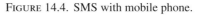

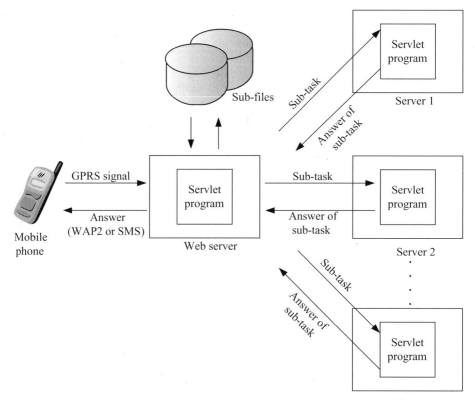

FIGURE 14.5. Wireless model.

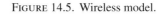

tier 1 web server. The tier 1 web server will invoke a servlet that will divide a single task into many small sub-tasks. These sub-tasks will then be stored as queues on the hard disk of the system.

The tier 1 server will send an HTTP message to a tier 2 server, which will then invoke another servlet. The tier 1 server will then transfer a sub-task to the tier 2 server for further computation. Note that there are many tier 2 servers in the system but only one tier 1 server as shown in Fig. 14.5.

After the computation, the tier 2 server will send the results to the tier 1 server. The tier 1 server will then send another sub-task to the tier 2 server if the sub-task queue is not empty. The tier 1 server computer will collect answers of sub-tasks from all tier 2 servers.

15
Implementation of Wireless P2P Systems

15.1 Introduction

In Chapter 14, we discussed methods of developing a wireless P2P model. We will present the actual implementation in this chapter. Wireless designs allow the users to access the P2P system with a mobile device such as mobile phone or PDA. They have the following advantages:

- It is easier to carry a mobile phone than a notebook computer.
- No training is required as almost everyone can use a phone.
- It can access computers behind a firewall.
- There is no need to buy additional equipment because most users have their own phones.

15.2 Client—Mobile Phone

As discussed in Chapter 14, the memory of a mobile phone is small compared with a desktop computer. Instead of running a program, users download a WAP page from the tier-1 server. This page allows the user to type in data for the operation. As it is more difficult to type in data with a mobile phone, the volume of typing is minimized in our model. Users need to type in only two items:

- The range of numbers to be added.
- The number of sub-tasks.

The source codes of the web page are presented in Fig. 15.1.

15.3 Tier 1 Server Program—phoneServlet.java

The structure of this program is presented in Fig. 15.2. There are three methods in the program:

- Init()
- doGet()
- destroy()

```
<?xml version="1.0"?>
<HTML>
  <HEAD>
        <TITLE>Add Numbers</TITLE>
  </HEAD>
  <BODY>
        <FORM ACTION="/servlet/phoneServlet" METHOD="get">

        Interval
        <INPUT TYPE="Text" NAME="interval" VALUE=" " size=9></INPUT>
                <BR>
            number of sub-tasks
        <INPUT TYPE="Text" NAME="tasks" VALUE=" "size=5></INPUT>
                <BR>
        <INPUT TYPE="Submit"></INPUT>
        </FORM>
  </BODY>
</HTML>
```

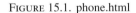

FIGURE 15.1. phone.html

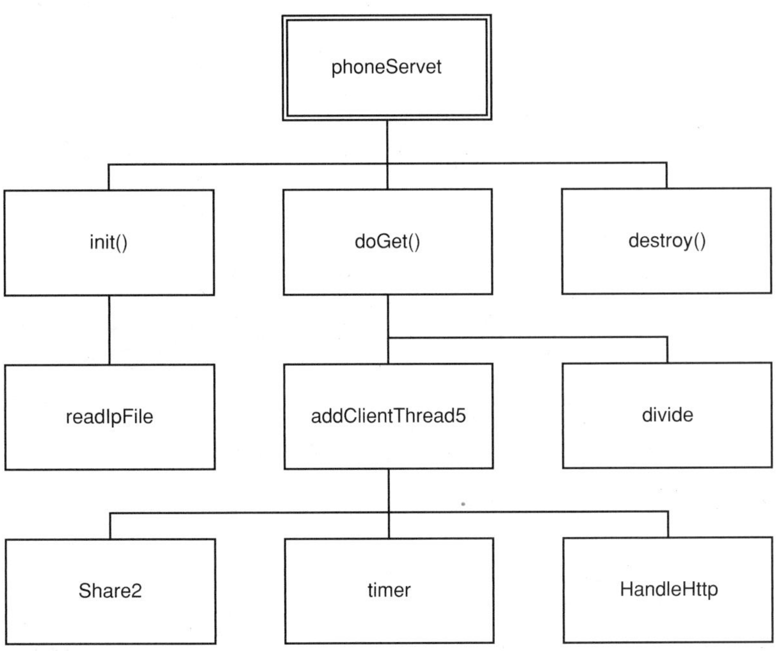

FIGURE 15.2. Structure of phoneServlet.java

The source codes of the java program are presented in Fig. 15.3.
This program has three methods:

1. init().This method reads the phone.txt, which stores the IP addresses of the available tier-2 computers in the system. The format of this file is similar to the ip.txt file in previous chapters. For example, the contents for a system with two tier-2 servers (*i.e.*, 192.168.1.2 and 192.168.1.3) are as follows:

   2
   192.168.1.2
   192.168.1.3

   The reading is performed by the following two lines:

   ```
   readIpFile reader= new readIpFile(ipFile,ip);
   numServer = reader.getNumServer();
   ```

   This file should be stored in the installation directory of the server (*e.g.*, c:\tomcat 5.5).
2. doGet(). This method performs the following jobs:
   - Read input data from the mobile phone (as in Fig. 14.4) with the following lines:

     ```
     String interval=request.getParameter ("interval");
     long endPosition= Integer.parseInt(interval);    // no. of interval
             String tasks=request.getParameter ("tasks");
             int totalTasks = Integer.parseInt(tasks);    // no. of sub tasks
     ```

   - Divide the task into sub-tasks (by calling the divide.java module).

     ```
     divide subTaskArray = new divide(x,endPosition,totalTasks,debug);
     ```

   - Distribute the sub-tasks to tier-2 server (by calling the addClientThread5.java) with the following lines:

     ```
     for (int i=1;i<=numServer;i++)
        new addClientThread5(ip[i-1], x, i,totalTasks,answer,debug).start() ;
     ```

   - Collect the answers of sub-tasks and get the grand total with the following call:

     ```
     (long) answer.getAnswer()
     ```

   - Assemble a WAP page and send it back to the mobile phone with the following lines:
     Note that if you are trying to send a special character " with the *out.print()* method, you need to add a \ *in front of* ".

```
import java.io.*;
import java.util.*;
import javax.servlet.*;
import javax.servlet.http.*;
public class phoneServlet extends HttpServlet
{
    boolean debug = false;
    String ipFile= "phone.txt";
    String ip[]=new String[50];
    int numServer=0;
    public void init() throws ServletException
    {
        System.out.println("***** phone servlet started ******");
        readIpFile reader= new readIpFile(ipFile,ip);
        numServer = reader.getNumServer();
        if (debug)
            System.out.println("number of servers: "+ numServer);
        if (debug) System.out.println("***** reading sucessful ******");
    }
    public void doGet(HttpServletRequest request, HttpServletResponse response)
        throws ServletException, IOException
    {
        String interval=request.getParameter ("interval");
        long endPosition= Integer.parseInt(interval);    // no. of interval
        String tasks=request.getParameter ("tasks");
        int totalTasks = Integer.parseInt(tasks);    // no. of sub tasks
        double x[]= new double[totalTasks*2];
        divide subTaskArray = new divide(x,endPosition,totalTasks,debug);
        subTaskArray.go();
        Share2 answer = new Share2(totalTasks,debug); // control answer update
        timer total =new timer(); // timer for transmission + calculation
        total.start();
        // ************************** create Threads ***************
        for (int i=1;i<=numServer;i++)
            new addClientThread5(ip[i-1],x, i,totalTasks,answer,debug).start() ;
        if (debug) System.out.println("wait for connection to complete ");
        System.out.println("********* Answer: "+ " *********");
        total.elasp("total time calculation + transmission :");
        System.out.println("program terminated");
        // send output to the phone
        PrintWriter out=response.getWriter();
        response.setContentType ("text/html");
    out.println(
        "<?xml version="1.0"?>"
    +       "<html xmlns=\"http://www.w3.org/1999/xhtml\" xml:lang=\"en\">"
    +       "<head>"
    +       "<title>Add Numbers</title>"
    +       "</head>"
    +       "<body>"
    +       "<h1>"
    +       "Answer: " +(long) answer.getAnswer()
    +       "</body>"
    +       "</html>");
    }
    public void destroy()
    {
        System.out.println("destroy method of PhoneServlet called");
    }
}
```

FIGURE 15.3. phoneServlet.java

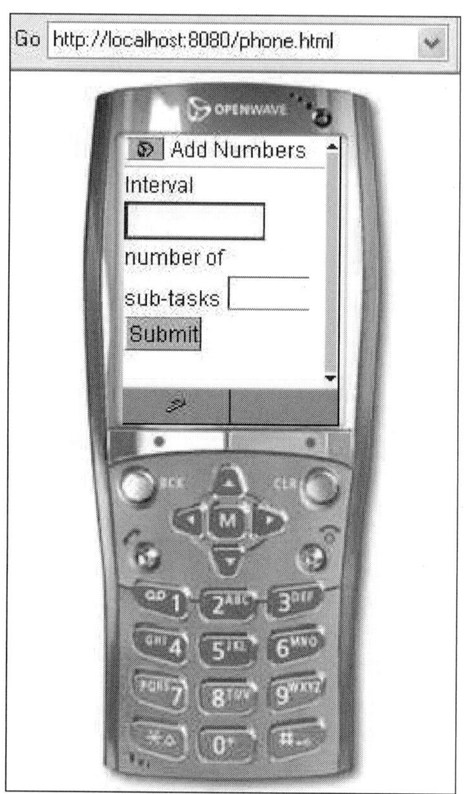

FIGURE 15.4. Screen of emulator.

```
PrintWriter out=response.getWriter();
response.setContentType ("text/html");
out.println(
      "<?xml version=\"1.0\"?>"
+     "<html xmlns=\"http://www.w3.org/1999/xhtml\" xml:lang=\"en\">"
+        "<head>"
+          "<title>Add Numbers</title>"
+        "</head>"
+        "<body>"
+          "<h1>"

+                  "Answer: " +(long) answer.getAnswer()

+        "</body>"
+     "</html>");
```

3. destroy() method—This method prints one message on the server's console for debugging and testing purposes.

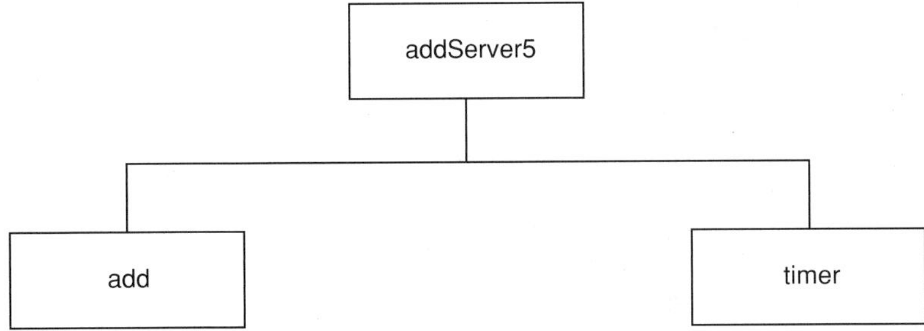

FIGURE 15.5. Structure of tier-2 server program.

15.4 Tier-2 Server Side Program

The structure of the tier-2 server side program is the same as model 5 in Chapter 13. The overall structure of this program has been presented in Fig. 15.5 for readers' easy reference.

15.5 Tools for Mobile Phone Development

It will be better to test the system with some software tools (phone emulators) than using your mobile phones in the initial testing phases. The advantages are:

- You can save a lot of money for the GPRS connections.
- It is easier and faster to type in data to the emulators than the real phones.
- You can test a lot of models with different emulators.

Emulators can be obtained from the websites of most phone manufacturers. You can also get a general-purpose emulator from www.openwave.com which is used in the examples in this book.

15.6 Testing the Wireless P2P

Testing is simpler than previous models. As everything on the server computer is controlled by the web server, all we need is to type the data into the phone emulator (or a real phone with GPRS connection).

1. Copy all programs to the default path of your servers.
2. Make sure that all web servers are running.
3. Edit the phone.txt files with the tier-2 server's IP addresses. The file should be stored in the installation directory of the tier-1 server (*e.g.*, c:\tomcat 5.5 for Tomcat).

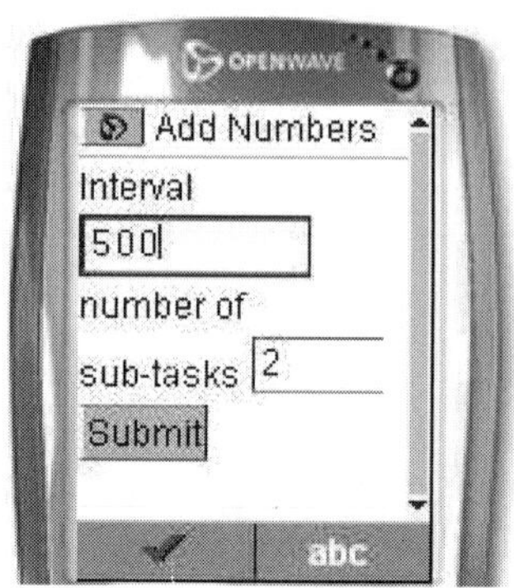

FIGURE 15.6. Screen of phone (with one server).

15.6.1 Experiment with One Computer

It is easier to start the testing with one computer. A single computer can play the role of client, tier-1 server and tier-2 server simultaneously.

1. Start the web server.
2. Start the phone emulator.
3. Type the following URL in the emulator as in Fig. 15.4:

   http://localhost:8080/phone.html
4. Type in interval and number of sub-tasks (Fig. 15.6).

   e.g.,
   Interval = 500
   number of sub-tasks = 2
   The system will add up all numbers from 1 to 500. This adding task will be divided into two sub-tasks.
5. Click the left button to move from one field to the other. After you type in both fields, click the left button to submit. Figure 15.7 shows the screen of the phone emulator. Figure 15.8 shows the screen of the server. The local computer plays the role of tier-1 and tier-2 server simultaneously.

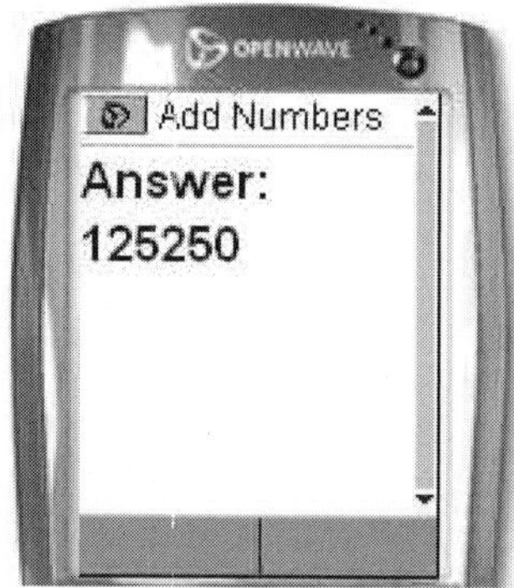

FIGURE 15.7. Screen of the phone (with one server).

```
***** phone servlet started ******
********* Answer:  *********
total time calculation + transmission : 0.0sec.
program terminated
*************************************************
Sun Jan 29 21:34:57 CST 2006
remote input:1.0 250.0 ********
start position :1.0
end   position :250.0
start=1  end=250

sum=31375
It take :  0.181sec.
addServlet count=1
id=1 time for cal+tran = 0.211sec.
*** id=1 sub-task answer= 31375
remote input:251.0 500.0 ********
start position :251.0
end   position :500.0
start=251  end=500

sum=93875
It take :  0.12sec.
addServlet count=2
id=1 time for cal+tran = 0.12sec.
*** id=1 sub-task answer= 93875
```

FIGURE 15.8. Screen of the server (tier 1 and 2).

15.6.2 Experiment with One Tier-1 Server and Two Tier-2 Servers

In this example, we use four computers (*i.e.*, one client with the phone emulator, one tier 1 server and two tier 2 servers).

1. Edit the contents of phone.txt file.

    e.g.,

    2
    192.168.1.2
    192.168.1.3

2. Type in http://website:8080/phone.html in the emulator.

    e.g.,

    http://192.168.1.4:8080/phone.html
    where 192.168.1.4 is the IP address of tier 1 server.

3. Type in data as in Fig. 15.9.
4. Click the left key of the phone to submit information to the tier-1 server.

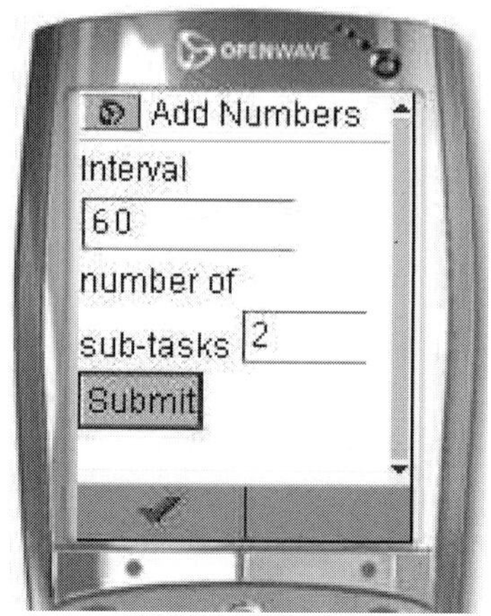

FIGURE 15.9. Screen of client (with two servers).

Figure 15.10 shows the screen of the phone. Figure 15.11 shows the screen of tier-1 server. The screen of the first tier-1 server is presented in Fig. 15.12, while the second tier-2 server is presented in Fig. 15.13.

15.7 Experiments with More Sub-tasks

In this example, we divide the task into four sub-tasks and two tier-2 servers. Each tier-2 server will get two sub-tasks. Edit the contents of phone.txt file.

1. Edit the contents of phone.txt file.

   e.g.,

   2
   192.168.1.2
   192.168.1.3

FIGURE 15.10. Screen of client (with two servers).

```
***** phone servlet started ******
********* Answer:  *********
total time calculation + transmission : 0.01sec.
program terminated
id=2 time for cal+tran = 0.121sec.
*** id=2 sub-task answer= 1365
id=1 time for cal+tran = 0.281sec.
*** id=1 sub-task answer= 465
```

FIGURE 15.11. Screen of tier-1 server.

```
It take :  0.11sec.
addServlet count=23
remote input:1.0 30.0 ********
start position :1.0
end   position :30.0
start=1  end=30

sum=465
It take :  0.11sec.
addServlet count=24
```

FIGURE 15.12. Screen of first tier-2 server.

```
It take :  0.04sec.
addServlet count=16
remote input:31.0 60.0 ********
start position :31.0
end   position :60.0
start=31  end=60

sum=1365
It take :  0.06sec.
addServlet count=17
```

FIGURE 15.13. Screen of second tier-2 server.

2. Type in http://website:8080/phone.html in the emulator.

   e.g.,

   http://192.168.1.4:8080/phone.html
   where 192.168.1.4 is the IP address of tier 1 server.

3. Type in data as in Fig. 15.14.
4. Submit data with the left button (Fig. 15.15).

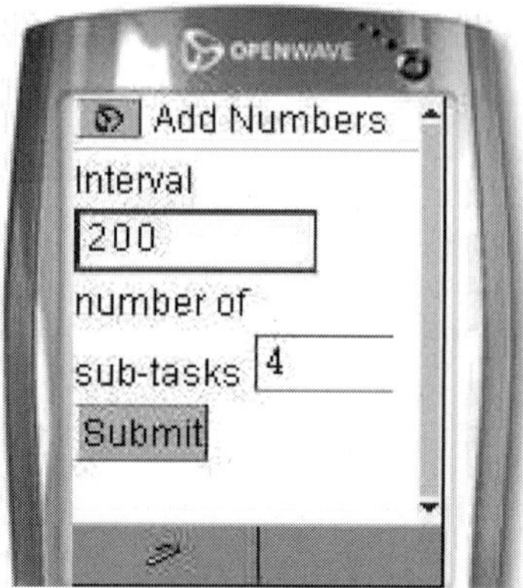

FIGURE 15.14. Input screen of phone.

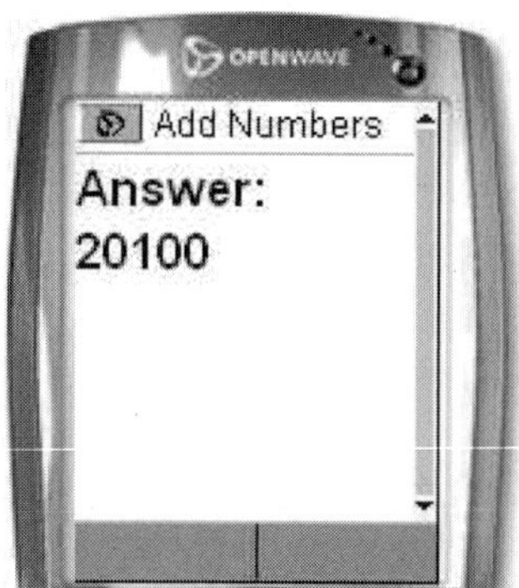

FIGURE 15.15. Input screen of phone.

```
id=2 time for cal+tran = 0.15sec.
*** id=2 sub-task answer= 3775
id=1 time for cal+tran = 0.17sec.
*** id=1 sub-task answer= 1275
id=2 time for cal+tran = 0.12sec.
*** id=2 sub-task answer= 6275
id=1 time for cal+tran = 0.15sec.
*** id=1 sub-task answer= 8775
```

FIGURE 15.16. Screen of tier-1 server.

```
remote input:1.0 50.0 ********
start position :1.0
end   position :50.0
start=1  end=50

sum=1275
It take :  0.1sec.
addServlet count=26
remote input:151.0 200.0 ********
start position :151.0
end   position :200.0
start=151  end=200

sum=8775
It take :  0.1sec.
addServlet count=27
```

FIGURE 15.17. Screen of first tier-2 server.

```
remote input:51.0 100.0 ********
start position :51.0
end   position :100.0
start=51  end=100

sum=3775
It take :  0.08sec.
addServlet count=19
remote input:101.0 150.0 ********
start position :101.0
end   position :150.0
start=101  end=150

sum=6275
It take :  0.08sec.
addServlet count=20
```

FIGURE 15.18. Screen of second tier-2 server.

The screen of the tier-1 server is presented in Fig. 15.16. This server collects four answers from tier-2 servers. The screens of two tier-2 servers are presented in Figs.15.17 and 15.18. Each server gets two sub-tasks so there are two answers on their screens. You can check the sequences of the operations according to Fig. 15.19.

15.8 Conclusions

Although this model is designed with mobile phones in mind, it can be easily modified so the mobile phone can be replaced with an ordinary computer. The

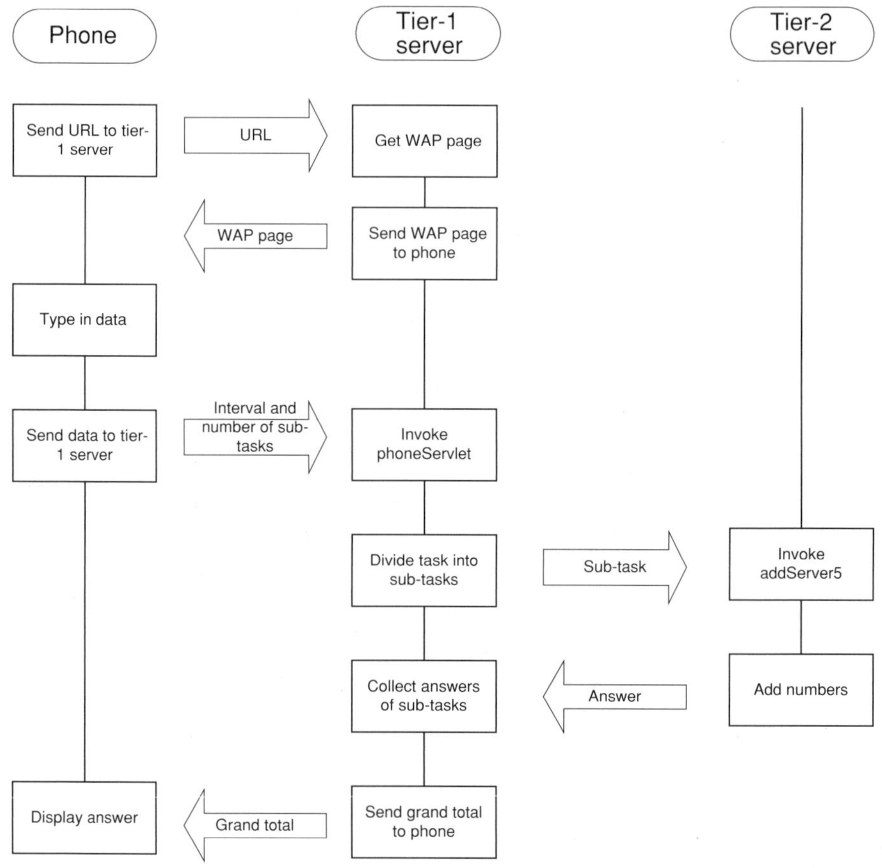

FIGURE 15.19. Sequences of operations.

advantage is that there is no need to install any program on the client devices (mobile phones or computers). It also saves a lot of maintenance work if we have a large number of clients.

16
Computer Architecture

16.1 Introduction

As discussed in Chapter 3, simply having a large amount of computers cannot make computation efficient. Good parallel algorithms are always required. Although we can design a new parallel algorithm each time, there is a better method. There are a large number of good parallel algorithms for different kind of parallel computers in research papers and books. P2P network can be considered as a special kind of parallel computer architecture. It is possible that we can modify some existing parallel algorithm for our particular problem. There is no need to start from scratch.

Since parallel algorithms are usually designed for a particular parallel computer architecture, knowledge of parallel computer architectures is important for the optimization of algorithm design. This chapter presents the major parallel computer architectures and discusses their classification, characteristics and performance metrics.

16.2 Classification of Computer Architectures

Several methods exist for classifying computer architectures. Flynn's method, first proposed in 1966, classifies architectures according to the number of instruction streams and data streams. His method has been extended by several researchers (Share, 1973; Treleaven et al., 1982; Hockney and Jesshope, 1998). Flynn's (1966, 1996) classification will be used for our discussion as it is the traditional way to classify architecture. It is also well known and used by many researchers in this field.

In Flynn's taxonomy, computer architectures can be classified according to the number of instruction and data streams they have and their ability to process single or multiple data streams simultaneously. There are four possible logical combinations:

- Single Instruction, single data stream (SISD).
- Multiple instruction, single data stream (MISD).

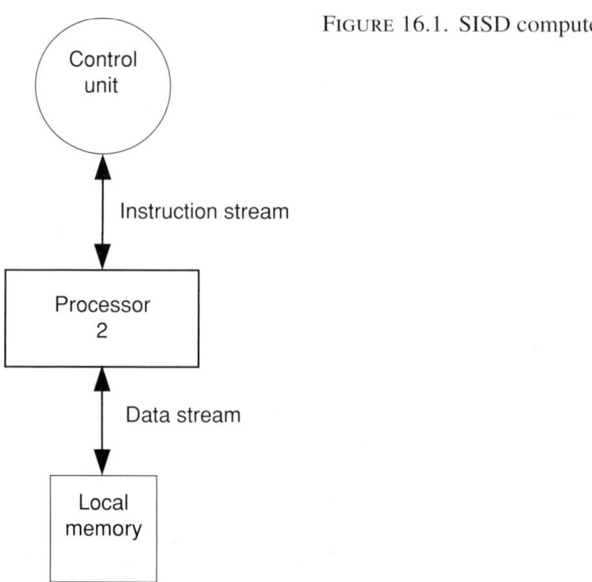

FIGURE 16.1. SISD computer

- Single instruction, multiple data stream (SIMD).
- Multiple instruction, multiple data stream (MIMD).

16.2.1 Single Instruction, Single Data Stream

All conventional von Neumann (Kumar, 1994) architecture computers can be classified as SISD computers as they have a single CPU (Fig. 16.1). It executes instructions from a single instruction stream to manipulate a single data stream. The CPU in such computers is a complex, contemporary processor.

All serial computers using the von Neumon architecture belong to this group, which will not be discussed further.

16.2.2 Single Instruction, Multiple Data Streams

SIMD architectures have multiple processors (Fig. 16.2). Each processor is responsible for computing a unique data stream. Only one instruction stream is present, and each processor executes the same instruction simultaneously. SIMD computers use a large number of simple custom-built processors, which are less powerful than contemporary microprocessors. For example, Connect Computer CM-2 used up to 65500 custom-built 4-bit processors. These processors can only execute a small set of instructions.

The master control unit of an SIMD computer broadcasts an identical instruction to all processors. They execute the same instruction simultaneously to their own data stream. Each processor has its own local memory.

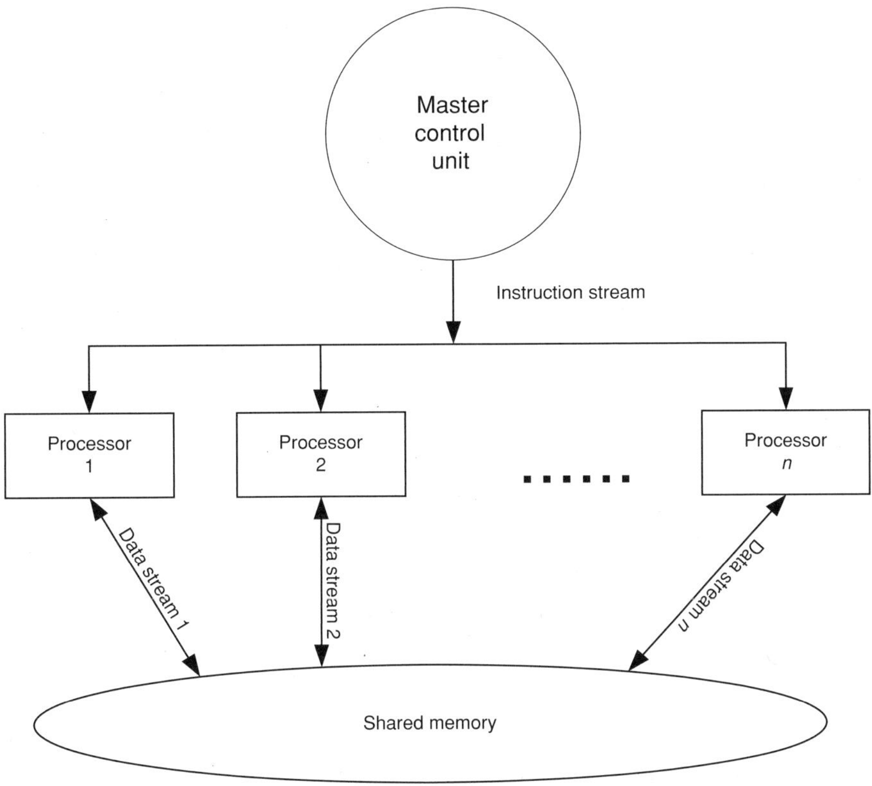

FIGURE 16.2. SIMD computer

16.2.3 Multiple Instruction, Single Data Stream

The MISD architecture consists of multiple processors. Each processor executes its own unique set of instructions (Fig. 16.3). However, all processors share a single common data stream. Different processors execute different instructions simultaneously to the same data stream. No practical example of a MISD has been identified to date, and this architecture remains entirely theoretical.

16.2.4 Multiple Instruction, Multiple Data Streams

The MIMD architecture consists of a number of processors. They can share and exchange data. Each processor has its own instruction and data stream, and all processors execute independently. The processors used in MIMD computers are usually complex contemporary microprocessors.

The MIMD architecture is becoming increasingly important as it is generally recognized as the most flexible form of parallel computer (Kumar, 1994). A collection of heterogeneous computers interconnected by a local network conforms to the MIMD architecture.

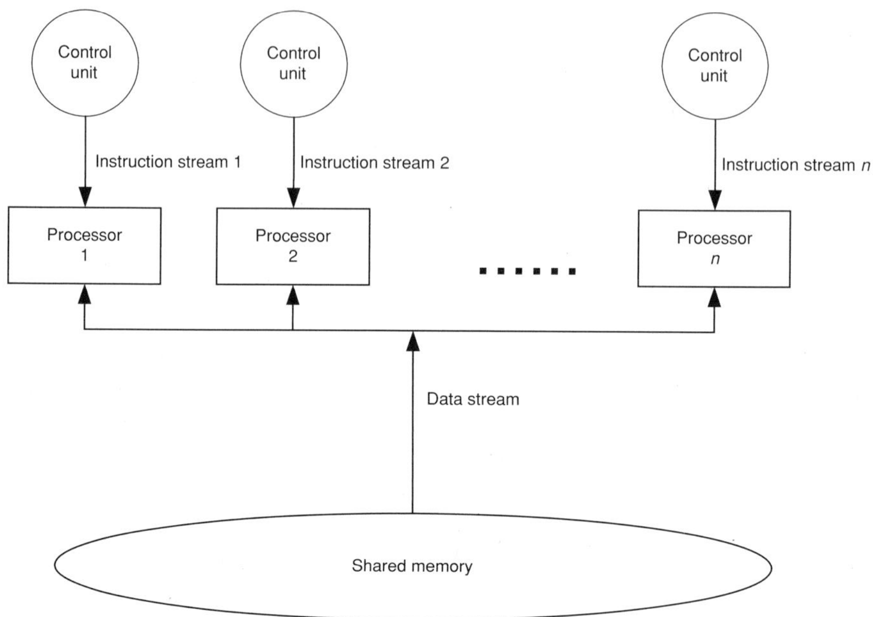

FIGURE 16.3. MISD computer

MIMD computers are significantly more difficult to program than traditional serial computers. Independent programs must be designed for each processor. The programmer needs to take care of communication, synchronization and resource allocation. MIMD architecture can be further divided into three categories according to the method of connection between memory and processors.

16.2.4.1 Multicomputer (Distributed Memory Multiprocessor)

There is no global memory in Multicompter. Each processor has its own local memory and works like a single-processor computer. A processor cannot read data from other processors' memory. However, it can read its own memory and pass that data to another processor.

Synchronization of processes is achieved through message passing. They can be scaled up to a large number of processors. Conceptually, there is little difference between the operation of a distributed memory multiprocessor and that of a collection of different computers operating over a local network or Internet/Intranet. Thus, P2P network can be considered as multicomputer (Fig. 16.4).

16.2.4.2 Loosely Coupled Multiprocessor (Distributed Shared Memory Multiprocessor)

A well-known example (Stone, 1980) of a loosely coupled multiprocessor is Cm* of Carnegie-Mellon University. Each processor has its own local memory, local

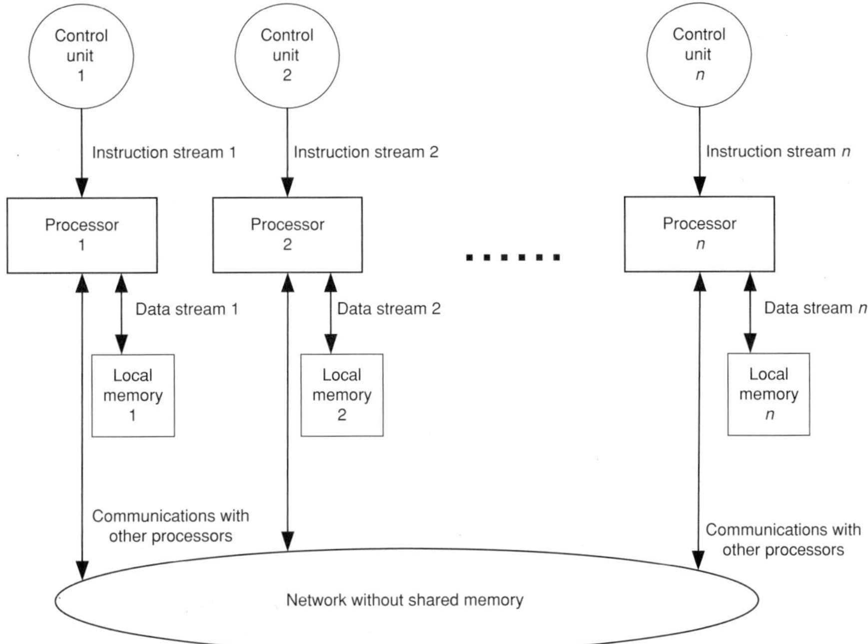

FIGURE 16.4. Multicomputer

I/O devices and a local switch connecting it to the other parts of the system. If the access is not local, then the reference is directed to search the memory of other processors. A large number of processors can be connected (Quinn, 1994) as there is no centralised switching mechanism.

16.2.4.3 Tightly Coupled Multiprocessor (Shared Memory Multiprocessor)

There is a global memory that can be accessed by all processors. Different processors use the global memory to communicate with each other (Fig. 16.5). Existing sequential computer programs can be modified easily (Morse, 1994) to run on this type of computer. However, locking mechanisms are required as memory is shared. A bus is required to interconnect processors and memory so scalability is limited by bus contention.

16.3 Granularity

Granularity is the amount of computation in a software process. One way to measure granularity is to count the number of instructions in a program. The parallel computers are classified as coarse grain and a fine grain computer.

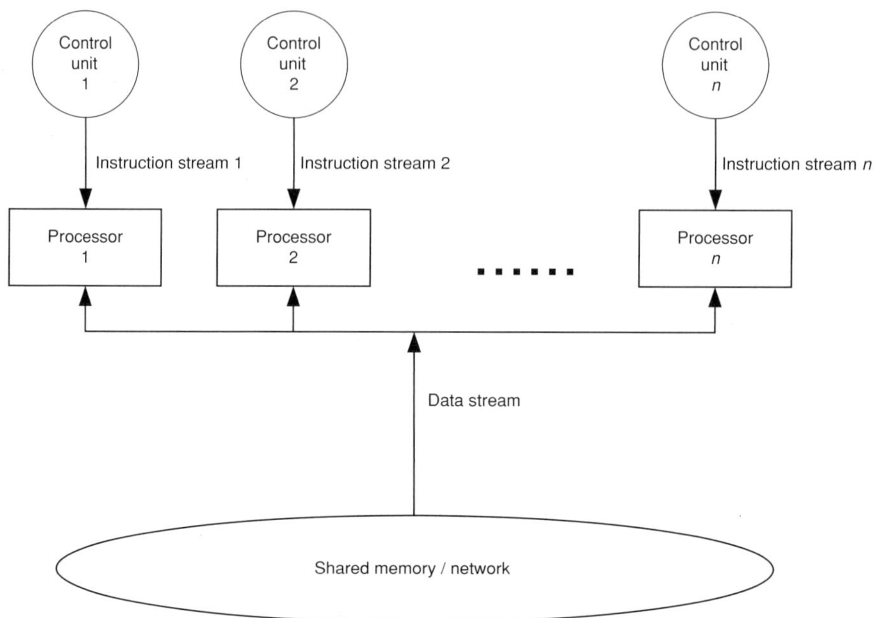

FIGURE 16.5. MIMD computer (tightly coupled multiprocessor).

16.3.1 Coarse Grain Computers

Coarse grain computers use small numbers of complex and powerful microprocessors, *e.g.*, the Intel iPSC which used a small number of Inteli860 microprocessors, and the Cray Computer which offers only a small number of processors. However, each processor can perform several Gflops (one G-flop = 10^9 floating point operations).

16.3.2 Fine Grain Computers

Another choice is to use relatively slow processors, but the number of processors is usually large, *e.g.*, over 10,000. Two SIMD computers, Mar MPP and CM-2, are typical examples of this design. They can use up to 16,384 and 65,536 processors. This kind of computer is classified as a fine grain computer.

16.3.3 Effect of Granularity and Mapping

Some algorithms are designed with a particular number of processors in mind. For example, one kind of algorithm maps one set of data to a processor.

Algorithms with independent computation parts can be mapped by another method. An algorithm with p independent parts can be mapped easily onto p processors. Each processor performs a single part of the algorithm. However, if fewer processors are used, then each processor needs to solve a bigger part of the problem and the granularity of computation on the processors is increased. Using fewer than the required processors for the algorithm is called 'scaling down' the parallel system. A naive method to scale down a parallel system is to use one processor to simulate several processors. However, the algorithm will not be efficient using this simple approach. The design of a good algorithm should include the mapping of data/computation steps onto processors and should include implementation on an arbitrary number of processors.

16.4 General or Specially Designed Processors

Some systems use off-the-shelf processors for their parallel operations. In other words, those processors are designed for ordinary serial computers. Sequent computer use general purpose serial processors (*e.g.*, Intel Pentium for PC) for their system. The cost is quite low compared with other special processors as these processors are produced in large volume. However, they are less efficient in terms of parallel processing when compared with specially designed processors such as transputers.

Some processors are designed with parallel processing in mind. The transputer is a typical example. The processors can handle concurrency efficiently and communicate with other processors (Hinton and Pinder, 1993) at high speed. However, the cost of this kind of processor is much higher than general-purpose processors as their production volume is much lower.

16.5 Processor Networks

To achieve good performance in solving a given problem, it is important to select an algorithm that maps well on to the topology used. One of the problems with parallel computing is that algorithms are usually designed for one particular architecture. A good algorithm on one topology may not maintain its efficiency on a different topology. Changing the topology often means changes to the algorithm.

The major networks are presented in this section and discussed using the following properties–diameter, bisection width and total number of links in the systems. The definitions of these properties are as follows:

- Diameter–If two processors want to communicate with each other and a direct link between them is not available, then the message must pass via one or more processors. These processors will forward the message to other processors until the message reaches the destination. The diameter is defined as the maximum number of intermediate processors that can be used in such communications. Performance of parallel algorithms will deteriorate for high diameters because it increases the amount of time spent in communications between processors. On the other hand, lower diameter will reduce communication overhead and will ensure good performance.

- Bisection width—Bisection width is the minimum number of links which must be removed so as to split a network into two halves. A high bisection width is better because more paths are still available between these sub-networks. Obviously, it is better to have more connection paths, which can improve the overall performance.
- Total number of links in the system—Communication between processors will usually be more efficient when there are more links in the system. The diameter will be reduced as the number of links grows. However, it is more expensive to build systems with more links.

A discussion of major processor networks is presented in Sections 16.5.1 to 16.5.6. The summary of the characteristics of these networks is presented in Section 16.5.7.

16.5.1 Linear Array

The processors are arranged in a line as shown in Fig. 16.6. The diameter is $p - 1$, and only two links are required for each processor. The transputer education kit is a typical example of this category. It is used for some low-cost education systems. It has only two links in each processor, and the cost is much lower than regular transputers which have four links (Hinton and Pinder, 1993). This kind of architecture is efficient when the tasks that make up the algorithm process data in a pipeline fashion.

- The advantage is that the architecture is easy to implement and inexpensive.
- The disadvantage is that the communication cost is high.

16.5.2 Ring

Processors are arranged as a ring as in Fig. 16.7. The connection is simple and easy to implement. The diameter may still be very large when there are a lot of processors in the ring. However, the performance of a ring is better than linear array for certain algorithms.

The advantage is that

- the architecture is easy to implement and
- the diameter is reduced to $p/2$ (compared with a linear array).

The disadvantage is that the communication cost is still high.

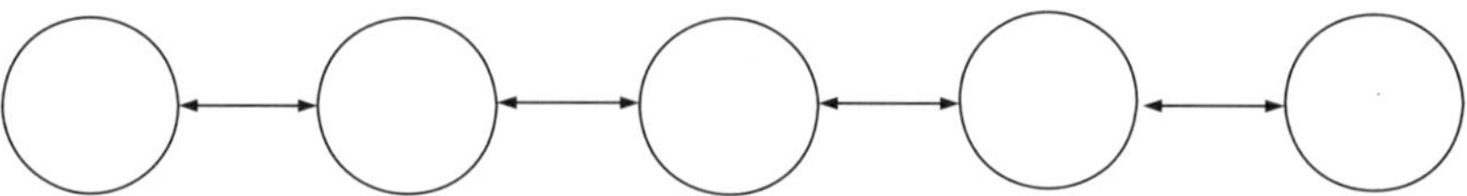

FIGURE 16.6. Linear array

FIGURE 16.7. Ring.

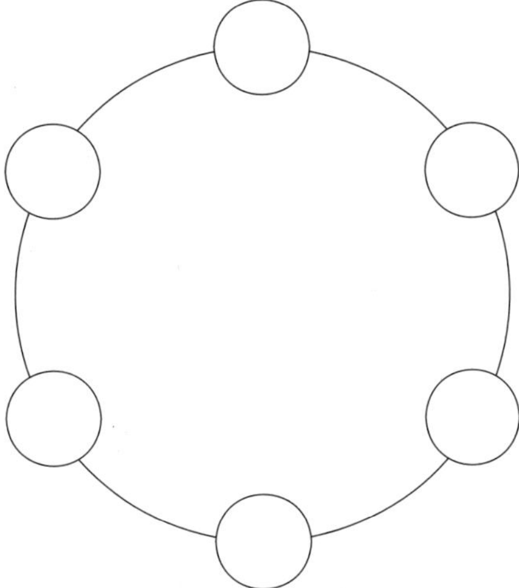

16.5.3 Binary Tree

Each processor of a binary tree has at most three links and can communicate with its two children and its parent. Figure 16.8 shows a binary tree with depth 3 and 15 processors. The binary tree has a low diameter but a poor bisection width. It suffers from the problem that a communication bottleneck will occur at the higher levels of the tree.

Advantages

- The architecture is easy to implement.
- The diameter is small (compared with a linear array and ring).

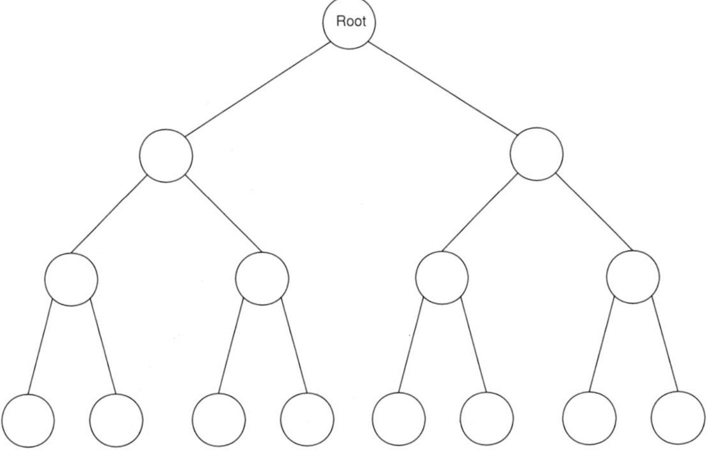

FIGURE 16.8. Binary tree with depth 3 and size 15.

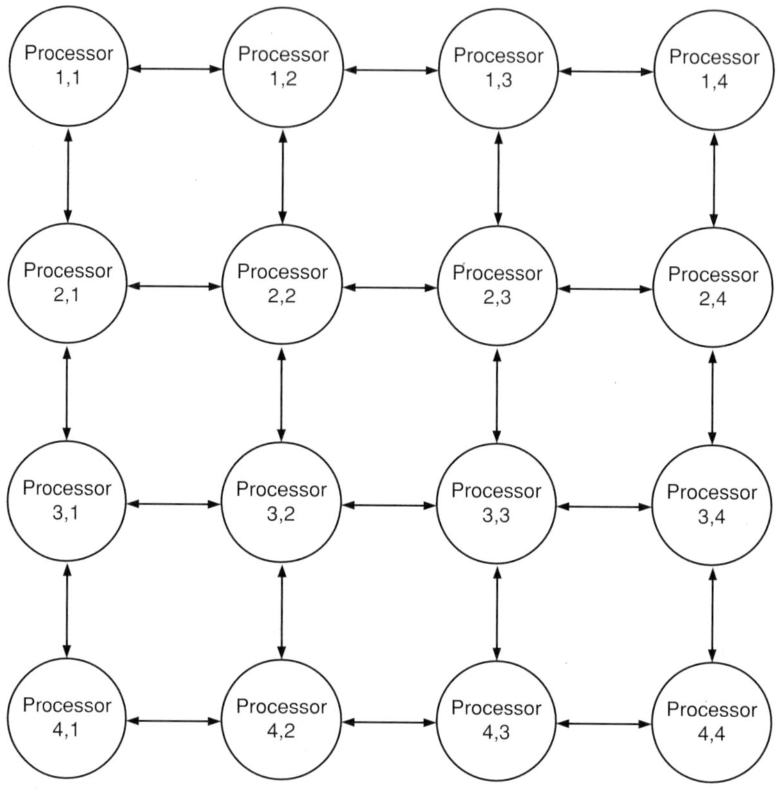

FIGURE 16.9. Two-dimensional mesh.

Disadvantages

- Bisection width is poor.
- It is thus difficult to maintain 'load balancing'.
- The number of links per processor is increased to three (*i.e.*, one more link than the linear array).

16.5.4 Mesh

Processors are arranged into a q-dimensional lattice. Communication is only allowed between adjacent processors. Figure 16.9 shows a two-dimensional mesh. A large number of processors can be connected using this method. It is a popular architecture for massively parallel systems. However, the diameter of a mesh could be very large.

There are variants of mesh. Figure 16.10 shows a wrap around model that allows processors on the edge to communicate with each other if they are in the same row or column. Figure 16.11 shows another variant that also allows processors on the edge to communicate if they are in an adjacent row or column. Figure 16.12 shows the X-net connection. Each processor can communicate with its eight nearest

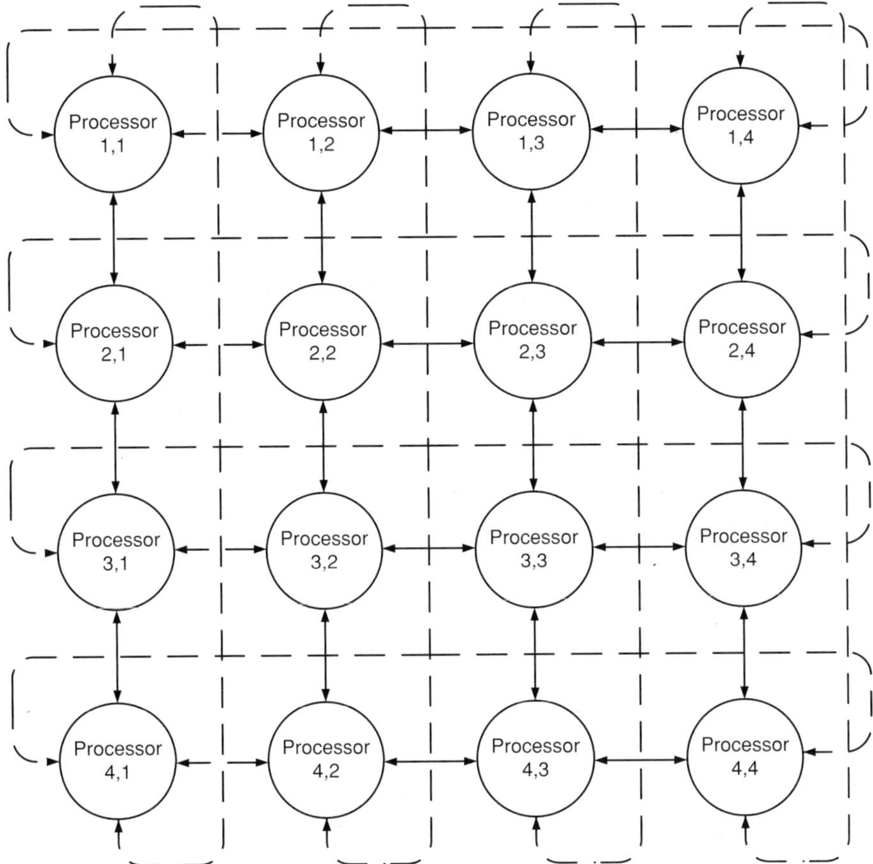

FIGURE 16.10. Mesh with wrap around connection on the same row.

neighbours instead of four in the original mesh design. It is obvious that the X-net has the smallest diameter, but additional links per processor are required to build the system. Mesh topologies are often used in SIMD architectures.

Advantages

- The bisection width is better than that of binary tree.
- A large number of processors can be connected.

Disadvantages

- It has high diameter.
- The number of links per processor is four (*i.e.*, one more link than the binary tree).

16.5.5 Hypercube

A hypercube is a d-dimensional mesh, which consists of 2^d processors. Figures 16.13 to 16.17 show hypercubes from 0 to 4 dimensions. A d-dimensional

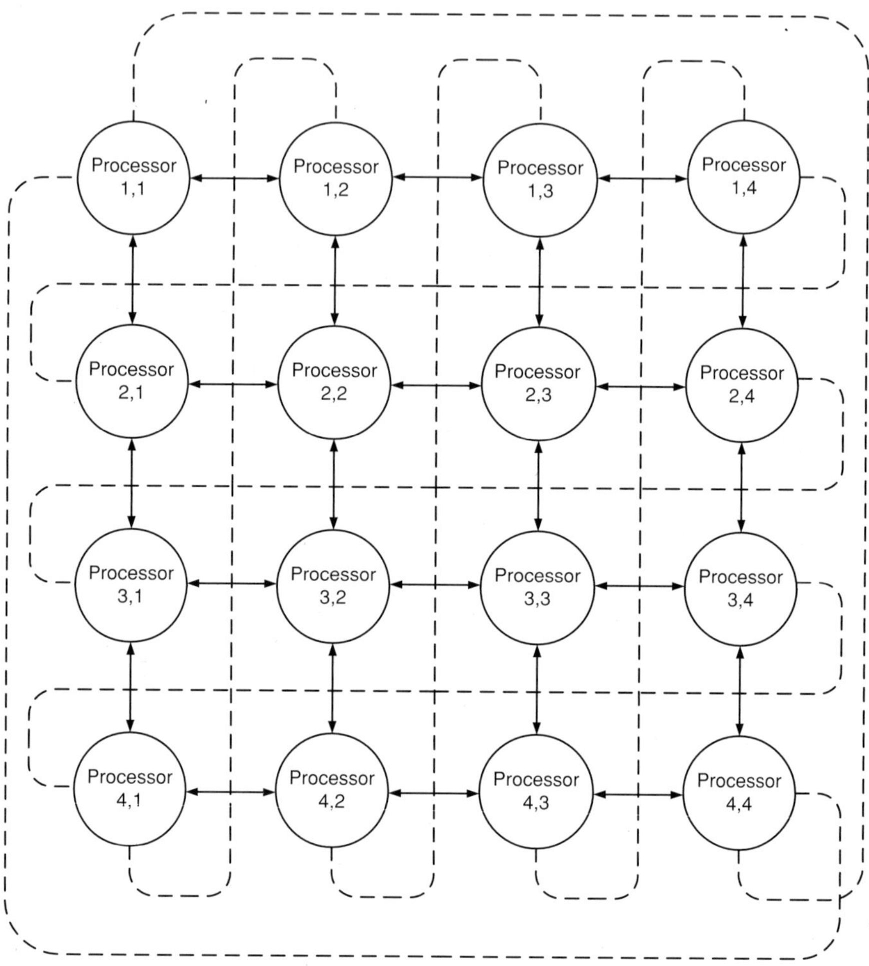

FIGURE 16.11. Mesh connection with wrap around for adjacent rows.

hypercube can be built by connecting two $d - 1$ dimensional hypercubes. The hypercube is the most popular (Moldovan, 1993) topology because it has the smallest diameter for any given number of processors and retains a high bisection width. A p-processor hypercube has a diameter of $\log_2 p$ and a bisection width of $p/2$ (Hwang and Briggs, 1984). A lot of research has been done on the hypercube.

Advantages

- The number of connections increases logarithmically as the number of processors increases.
- It is easy to build a large hypercube.
- A hypercube can be defined recursively.

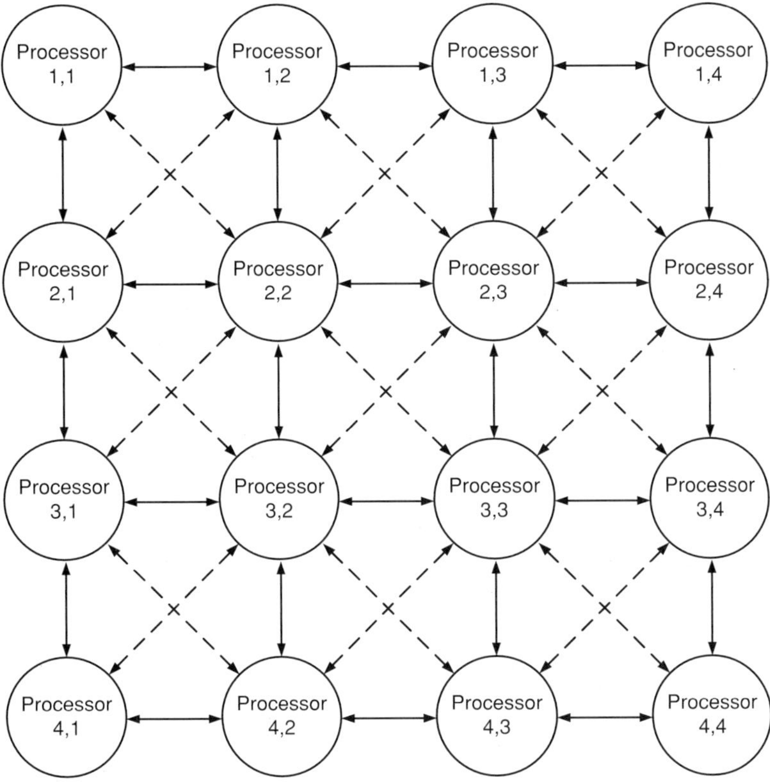

FIGURE 16.12. Mesh with X-connection.

- Hypercube has a simple routing scheme (Akl, 1997).
- Hypercube can be used to simulate (Leighton, 1992) many other topologies such as ring, tree, *etc.*

Disadvantages

- It is more expensive than line, ring and binary tree.

16.5.6 Complete Connection

This connection has the smallest diameter (*i.e.*, 1). It has the highest bisection width and total number of links compared with other network topologies (Leighton, 1992). However, the required number of links per processor becomes extremely

FIGURE 16.13. Zero-dimensional hypercube.

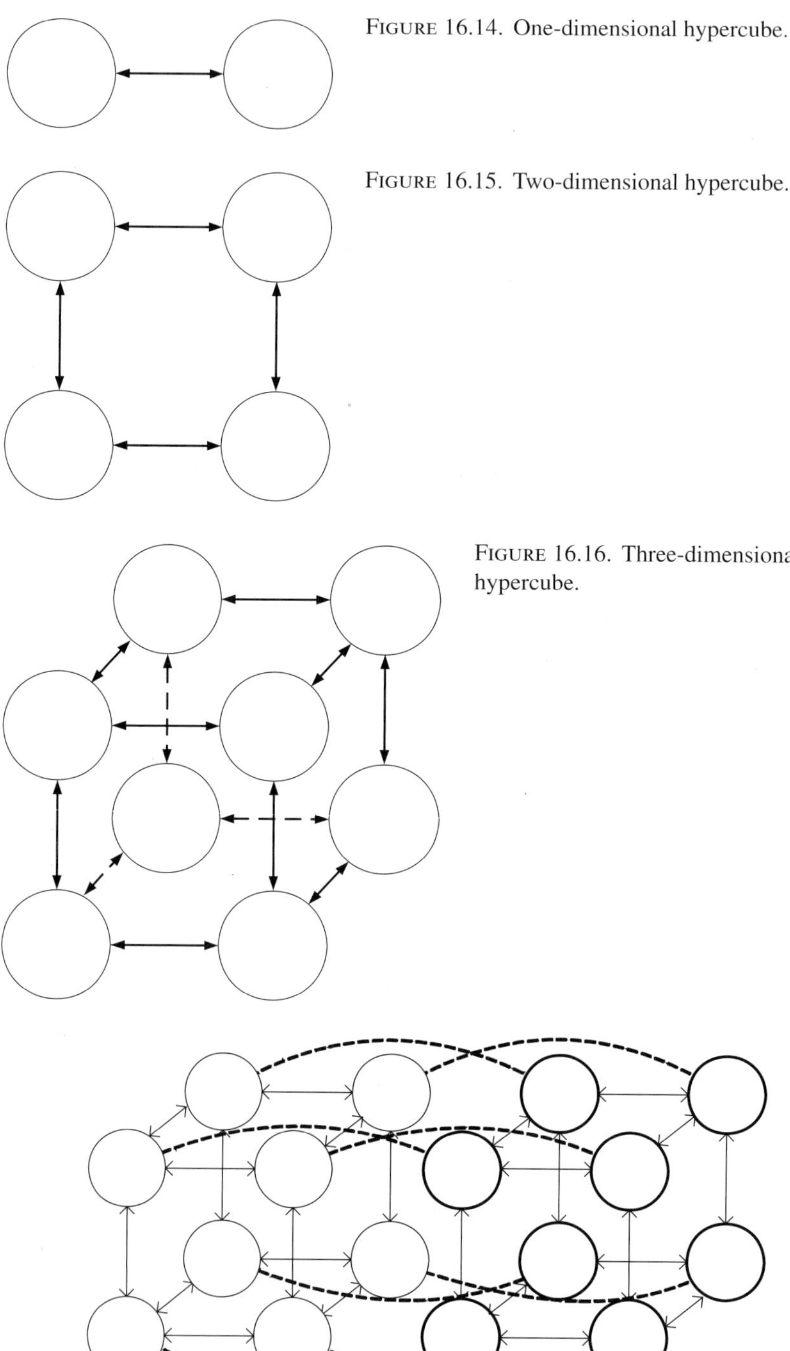

FIGURE 16.14. One-dimensional hypercube.

FIGURE 16.15. Two-dimensional hypercube.

FIGURE 16.16. Three-dimensional hypercube.

FIGURE 16.17. Four-dimensional hypercube.

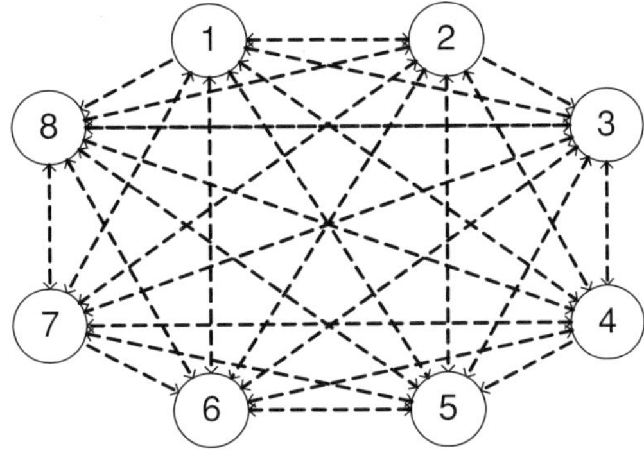

FIGURE 16.18. Complete connection (eight processors).

large as the number of processors increases (Fig. 16.18), thus it cannot be used for large systems.

Advantages

- The diameter is the smallest (*i.e.*, 1).
- It has the highest bisection width and number of links.

Disadvantages

- The requirement for the number of links per processor is $p - 1$ so this architecture is difficult to implement for large systems.

16.5.7 Summary of Characteristics of Network Connections

Linear array is the simplest network. It is easy to implement and inexpensive. Only two links are required for each processor. Although the architecture is simple, it can still support a rich class of interesting and important parallel algorithms (Leighton, 1992). However, it has a large diameter in a large system.

By connecting the two ends of the linear array, a ring can be formed. The diameter is reduced to half. However, its diameter is still not good for large systems.

By increasing the number of links per processor to three (*i.e.*, one more link than the linear array), a binary tree can be built. Its diameter is better than that of a ring. However, the processor at the higher levels might be much busier than other processors at the lower levels. It is difficult to maintain 'load balancing'.

Two-dimensional mesh is a very common architecture for massively parallel computers. The number of links per processor is four (*i.e.*, one more link than the binary tree). The bisection width is better than that of binary tree. However, it has high diameter for systems with large numbers of processors.

The number of links per processor for hypercube is $\log_2 p$. As indicated in Table 16.1, its diameter and bisection width are better than those of mesh.

The complete connection architecture is the best in terms of diameter, bisection width and total number of links. However, it is extremely difficult to build a large system with such architecture.

TABLE 16.1. Characteristics of processor organizations

Organization	No. of links per processor	Diameter	Bisection width	Total number of links in system
Linear array	2	$p-1$	1	$p-1$
Ring	2	$p/2$	2	P
Binary tree	3	$2\log_2((p+1)/2)$	1	$p-1$
two-dimensional mesh	4	$2(\sqrt{p}-1)$	$\sqrt{p}$	$2(p-\sqrt{p})$
Hypercube	$\log_2 p$	$\log_2 p$	$p/2$	$(p\log_2 p)/2$
Complete connection	$P-1$	1	$p^2/4$	$p(p-1)/2$

The characteristics (Hwang, 1993) of the above processor organizations can be summarized in Table 16.1.

16.6 Shared Memory Connection

Shared memory can be accessed by more than one processor. We will discuss two major connection methods:

- Bus and
- Crossbar switch.

16.6.1 Bus

Every processor and memory module in the system is connected to a bus (Fig. 16.19). For example, a sequent computer uses this kind of connection. Bus contention will be serious for systems with a large number of processors and activities in the system. Thus, this connection cannot be used (Fountain, 1994) for a massively parallel system.

16.6.2 Crossbar Switch

A crossbar switch improves performance when there is more than one memory module; thus it has better performance than the bus organization under these conditions (Fig. 16.20). Crossbar architectures provide fast communication (Zomaya, 1995) but are relatively expensive. Switching time is an additional overhead for the system.

16.7 Summary

A parallel system consists of a parallel algorithm and the parallel architectures on which it is implemented. Its performance depends on a design that balances hardware and software. Computer classification methods and architectures of different

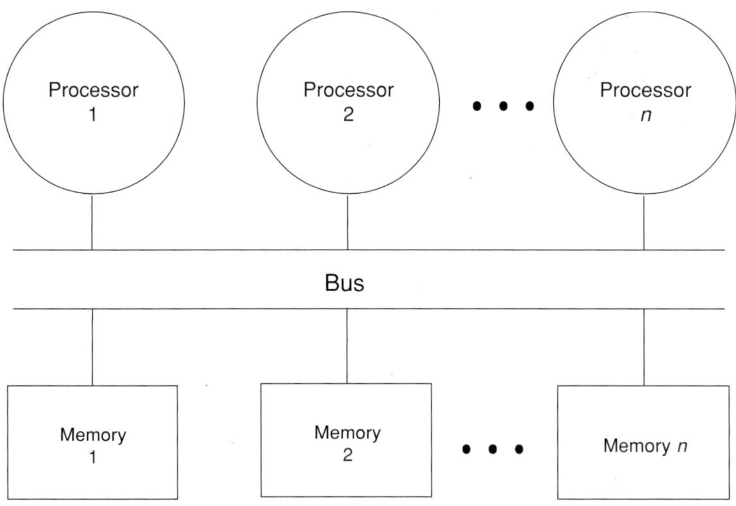

FIGURE 16.19. Bus

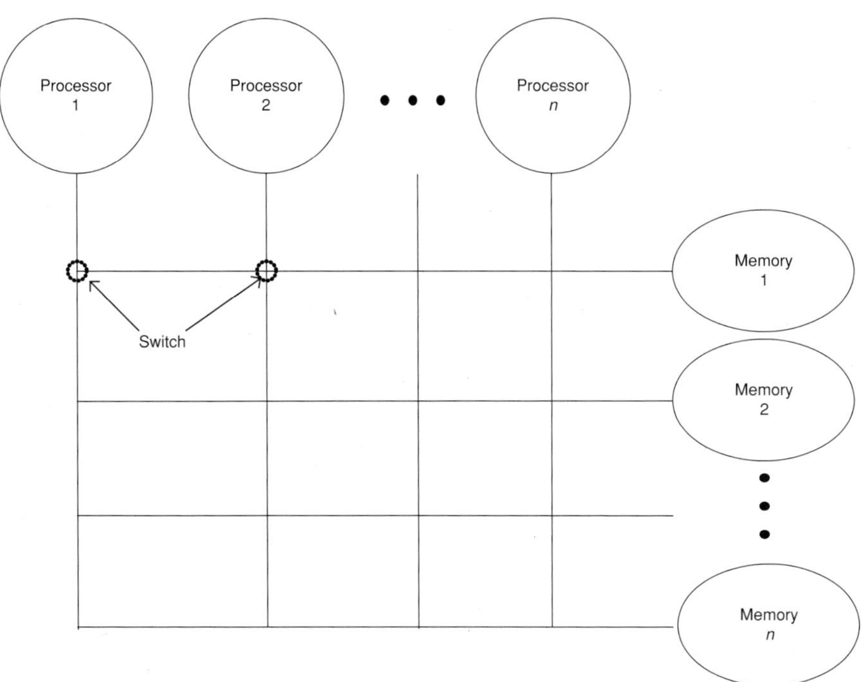

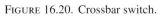

FIGURE 16.20. Crossbar switch.

computers have been discussed. The processor networks were compared according to their diameter, bisection width and number of links. Granularity, choice of processors and shared memory connection methods have also been presented as they affect the design of parallel algorithms. There is no single network that is generally considered best (Siegel, 1992). The cost-effectiveness of a network depends on a large number of factors discussed in this chapter.

17
Distributed and Parallel Algorithms

17.1 Introduction

Many parallel algorithms are derived from serial algorithms. Thus, it is worthwhile to examine serial algorithms before we design our new parallel algorithms. This approach has the following advantages:

- There are a lot of serial algorithms.
- The behaviours of these algorithms have been extensively studied and documented.
- Some of them can be converted to parallel algorithms with minimum efforts.

However, good serial algorithms might not be good candidates for parallel/distributed conversion. Some efficient serial algorithms might become inefficient if we are not careful in the conversion process. In this chapter, we will discuss what can go wrong in this process. Sorting algorithms are chosen as examples in our discussion for the following reasons:

- Everyone knows what sorting is. The idea is simple and sometimes we need to perform it manually (*e.g.*, playing games of cards). Thus, we can concentrate on the discussion of algorithm development.
- Although the concepts of sorting are simple, the evaluation of this class of algorithms is not.
- The sorting process (Aba and Ozguner, 1994; Shaffer, 1997) is executed many times a day in the data-processing function of almost every organization as even trivial operations with databases often involve sorting (Rowe, 1998; Moffat and Peterson, 1992). For example, printing a report or processing a simple query will probably involve sorted output.
- Many organizations now have very large files, and terabyte databases are becoming more and more common (Sun, 1999). Any improvement in sorting will tend to improve the speed of other processes such as searching, selecting, index creation, *etc.*
- Many other algorithms have a sorting process so that later operations can be performed efficiently. Examples (Quinn, 1994) include data movement operations

for problem solving in graph theory, computational geometry and image processing in optimal or near optimal time.

The principles of serial sorting algorithms are presented, and their methods in reducing exchanges, comparisons, memory requirements are discussed in this chapter. Parallel sorting algorithms are presented, and it is shown how they differ from serial algorithms.

17.2 Overview of Serial Sorting

In this section, major serial sorting algorithms are presented so that the characteristics of serial and parallel sorting algorithms can be compared in latter sections. Measuring factors in serial sorting will also be discussed so that they can be compared with the factors of their parallel counterpart.

17.2.1 Insertion Sort

Insertion sorting is based on the 'bridge player' method (Knuth, 2005). Many players sort their hands by examining one card at a time. Each time they get one more card, and they insert it into a group of cards which has already been sorted. This process is repeated until all cards are sorted. An example is presented next.

Original sequence

- First round
  - Compare first number with second number.
  - Exchange the position of first and second number as 11 is smaller than 16.

- Second round
  - Compare second number with third number.
  - No need to exchange positions as 16 is smaller than 45.

- Third round
  - Compare third number with fourth number.
  - No need to exchange positions as 16 is smaller than 45.

- Fourth round

- ∘ Compare the fourth number with the fifth number.
- ∘ Exchange positions of these two numbers as 34 is smaller than 88.

- ∘ Compare the third number with the fourth number.
- ∘ Exchange positions of these two numbers as 34 is smaller than 88.

- ∘ Compare the second number with third number. As 16 is smaller than 45, there is no need to swap. The sorting is complete.

Measurement of sorting algorithms—From the above algorithm, there are two major overheads:

- Number of comparisons.
- Number of swaps.

  This method (McCracken and Salmon, 1989) has different performance under different cases. The numbers of comparisons required to sort a file with n keys in these cases are as follows:
  - ∘ Best case
    - ▪ Number of comparison required is n − 1.
    - ▪ Condition is that the original file is already sorted (in ascending order).
  - ∘ Average case
    - ▪ Number of comparisons and swaps required is $n^2/4$ comparisons.
    - ▪ Condition is that the original file is not in any particular order.
  - ∘ Worst case
    - ▪ Number of comparisons and swaps required is $n^2/2$ comparisons
    - ▪ Condition is that the original file is in descending order.

The disadvantage of this method is that:

- the number of comparisons and swaps grows quickly when n is a large number. It is not suitable for big files.

The advantages are that

- it is easy to write the program (less than 10 statements) for this algorithm.
- additional memory is not required for this process.

17.2.2 Shellsort

The insertion sort is inefficient because it compares only neighbours. If a key is not in the right place, it is moved by a process of comparing and swapping adjacent keys. If this key is far away from its correct position, this process can be very time consuming as there are a large number of swaps and comparisons.

Shell (1959) proposed the Shellsort, which is a modification of insertion sort. Shellsort solves the aforementioned problem by comparing keys at a distance. For example, the key in the first position is compared to the key in fourth position. The fourth key is compared with the seventh key. If the key in a lower position is bigger than the key in a higher position, they exchange their positions. Keys can be moved to the correct position at a faster speed than the insertion sort.

An example is given next.

- First round—step 1. We use insertion sort to sort the first, fourth and seventh keys (*i.e.*, 16, 88.25).

- First round—step 2. The second, fifth and eighth keys are sorted.

- First round—step 3. The third, sixth and ninth keys are sorted.

- Second round—step 1. After the sorting of sub-files, the algorithm uses sub-files with a distance of two. The sub-list with the first, third, fifth, seventh and ninth keys is sorted with insertion sort.

- Second round—step 2. The sub-list with the first, third, fifth, seventh and ninth keys is sorted with insertion sort.

- Third round. The whole list is sorted with insertion sort.

There are several improved versions (Knuth, 2005; Weiss, 1991) of Shellsort. The analysis of this algorithm is extremely difficult, but a empirical study (Weiss, 1991) suggested that the complexity of this algorithm is in the range of $O(n^{1.16})$ to $O(n^{1.25})$.

Advantages

- Its efficiency is better than other algorithms when the file is nearly sorted.
- Its performance is rather stable compared with other algorithms. Thus, it is a good algorithm for critical applications which cannot tolerate even occasional poor performance.
- Additional memory is not required for the sorting process.

Disadvantage

- It is one of the fastest sorting algorithms.

17.2.3 *Quicksort*

Quicksort is a 'partition' sorting method; the original file is partitioned into two sub-files. These sub-files can then be sorted independently with the same technique. This 'divide and conquer' technique reduces the size of the file recursively and thus reduces the number of comparisons and number of swaps effectively.

In the quicksort algorithm, a key value (the pivot) will be selected and used to partition the file into two sub-files. The choice of pivot is important because it affects the efficiencies of the process. The ideal situation is that a pivot can divide the file into two equal (or almost equal) sub-files. There are many methods to select the pivots. We present an example as follows:

Original sequence is given as

- First round
  - The first item '16' is used as pivot.

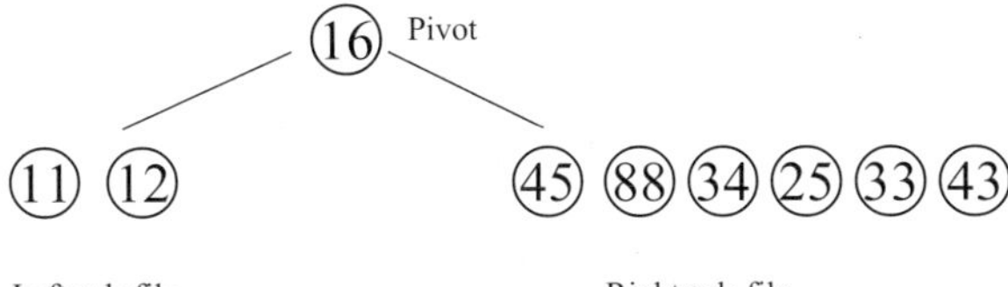

- Second round
  - The second item '45' is used as pivot.
  - Sorting of the right sub-file can be achieved by a single swap.

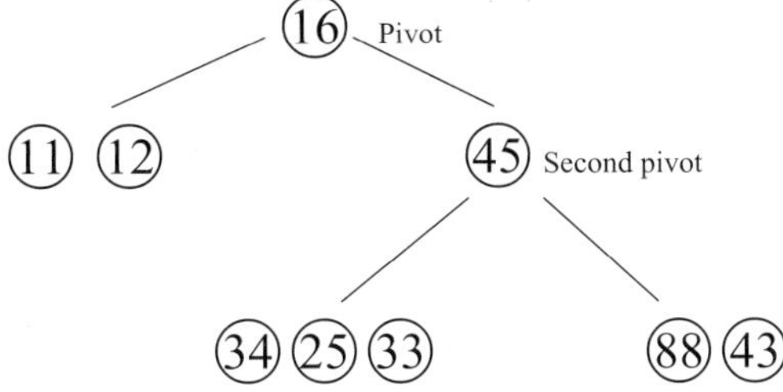

- Third round

- The item '34' is used as pivot.

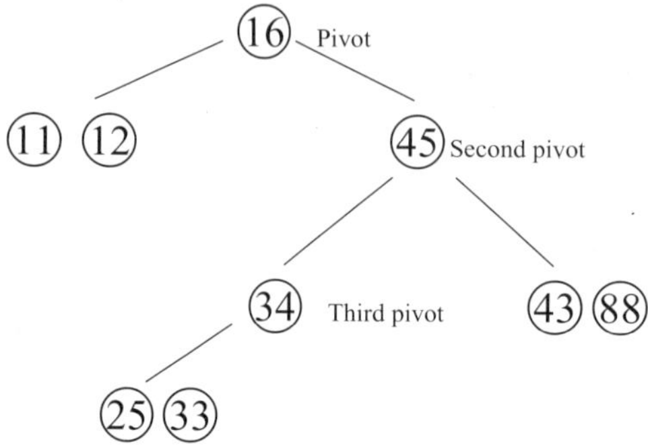

- The above list is sorted after three rounds.

We will have the best case if the sizes of two sub-files are equal in every round. On the other hand, the algorithm will hit the worst case if there is only one sub-file as in the third round of the aforementioned case.

There are many works (Loo, 1990; Motzkin, 1983; Poon and Jin, 1986; Scowne, 1956; Van Emden, 1970; Zhang, 1990) on the improvement of Quicksort. These projects aimed to improve the average case performance. On the other hand, some projects (Cook, 1980; Sedgewick, 1975; Wainwright, 1985) aimed to reduce the probability of hitting the worst cases by devising better methods to select a good pivot.

Quicksort is, on average, the fastest (Weiss, 1991) known sorting algorithm for large files. Its behaviour has been intensively studied and documented (Eddy, 1995; Sedgewick, 1977, 1997). Quicksort's average running time requires $2n \log_2 n$ comparisons and has time complexity of $O(n \log_2 n)$. However, time complexity increases to $O(n^2)$ for the worst case.

Advantages

- It is considered to be one of the fastest sorting algorithms (in terms of average case performance).
- Additional memory is not required for the sorting process.

Disadvantages

- Occasionally, the performance of Quicksort is very poor.
- The coding of the program is tricky, especially if you want to minimize the chance of hitting the worst cases.

17.2.4 Linear Probing Sort

This algorithm is specially designed for sorting n numbers, which are uniformly distributed (Dobosiewicz, 1978). It requires an additional memory of the order of

125% of the original file size. A special function is used to distribute the numbers into the auxiliary storage, and an overflow area is also used.

The average case complexity is $O(n)$. However, the performance deteriorates (Dobosiewicz, 1991) when the original file is not uniformly distributed. The worst case complexity of this algorithm is $O(n^2)$. The large amount of additional memory is a major weakness for this algorithm.

Advantage
- The algorithm is faster than most algorithms when the file is uniformly distributed.

Disadvantages
- Large amount of additional memory is required.
- It is not suitable for files that are not uniformly distributed.

The coding of program is tricky, especially if you want to minimize the opportunity of hitting the worst cases.

17.2.5 Distributive Partition Sort

Distributive partition sort (Dobosiewicz, 1978) is a sorting method which sorts n items with an average time of $O(n)$ for uniform distribution of keys. The worst-case performance is $O(n \log_2 n)$, and it needs an additional memory storage of $O(n)$ for the process. An example of this sorting process is shown in Fig. 17.1.

A special distribution algorithm (Allision, 1982; Meijer and Akl, 1982) is used to distribute items into bins. After the distribution phase, all items in bin i will be greater than items in bin j (where $i > j$). There are several improved versions of this algorithm. Double distributive partitioning sort (Janus and Lamagna, 1985) is one of the improved versions which avoids the poor performance on certain distributions. Thus, it maintains a more stable performance for different types of key distribution.

A major weakness of this algorithm is the requirement for a large amount of additional memory storage (*i.e.*, $2n$ memory is required, while other algorithms such as Quicksort or Shellsort need n memory for a file with n keys).

- Advantage: The algorithm is stable.

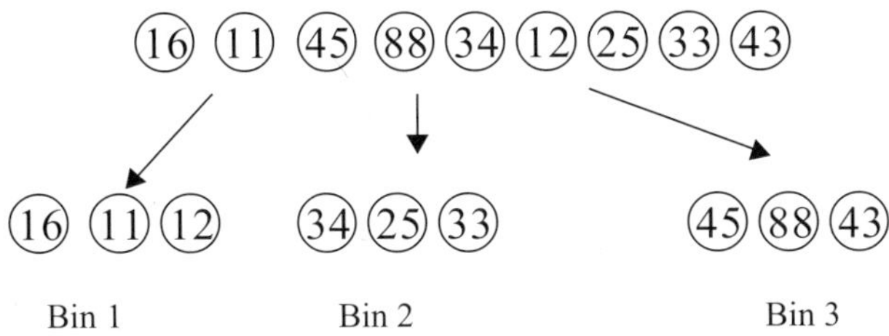

FIGURE 17.1. Operations of distributive partition sort.

TABLE 17.1. Summary of sorting algorithms performance

Algorithms	Average case time complexity	Worst case time complexity	Additional memory required
Quicksort	$O(n \log_2 n)$	$O(n^2)$	None
Insertion sort	$O(n^2)$	$O(n^2)$	None
Shellsort	$\sim O(n^{1.2})$	$\sim O(n^{1.2})$	None
Linear probing	$O(n)$	$O(n^2)$	$O(n)$
Distributive partition sort	$O(n)$	$O(n \log_2 n)$	$O(n)$

- Disadvantage: Large amount of additional memory is required.

17.3 Characteristics of Sorting Algorithms

The characteristics of the discussed algorithms are summarized in Table 17.1.

It is easy to write and debug an insertion sort program. However, its performance is very poor for large files. Shellsort modifies the insertion sort and improves the performance substantially. Although its performance is the best, it is very stable. Shellsort is a good algorithm for applications that need predictable performance at all time.

On the other hand, the average performance of Quicksort is faster than Shellsort. It is considered to be one of the fastest algorithms in term of average case performance. However, occasionally Quicksort's performance will be very poor (*i.e.*, when the input file is nearly sorted). The Quicksort algorithm is a good algorithm for applications that need the best average performance. At the same time, these applications must be able to tolerate poor performance in some rare cases.

Linear probing and distributive partition sort have good average performance. However, the large amount of additional memory required is a major problem of these algorithms. They are not suitable for computer system with small amounts of memory and big files.

17.4 Parallel Sorting Algorithms for MIMD with Shared Memory

It is more difficult to measure parallel algorithms. The number of processors, memory architectures, communication methods, *etc.*, can all affect the performance of an algorithm. Other issues, such as bus contention, queue delay and synchronization, make it more complicated so it is more difficult to measure and compare different algorithms. Thus the design of parallel sorting has attracted a lot of research in the past decade. Although much effort has already been spent on this area, efficient sorting algorithms are still required to utilize fully the power of parallel computers.

We will now present two parallel sorting algorithms to demonstrate what can go wrong.

17.4.1 Parallel Quicksort

A parallel Quicksort algorithm works as follows:

In the beginning, one processor is used to divide the file into two sub-files. The processor will keep one sub-file and pass the other sub-file to an idle processor.
In the second round, two processors are busy. At the end of round 2, there will be four sub-files. Two more idle processors will be assigned for the sub-tasks. These processes will repeat until all processors get their own sub-files. Each processor will then sort their sub-files recursively using serial Quicksort.

Quicksort (Hoare, 1961) is a well-known and very efficient sorting algorithm for serial computers. However, a parallel Quicksort algorithm has low parallelism at the beginning of its execution and high parallelism at the end (Quinn, 1988). A lot of processors will be idle (Lorin, 1975) at the early phases of the sorting process, thus it cannot provide a good 'speedup'.

Parallel Quicksort (Brown, 1993; Loo, 1993; Loo and Yip, 1991; Quinn, 1988, 1994) has the following characteristics:

- A lot of processors are idle at the beginning of the process.
- All processors are busy at the end of the process.
- Suffers from 'load balancing' problems as many processors are idle in the initial steps of the process.
- Poor speedup.

17.4.2 Parallel Shellsort

As discussed in the example of Section 17.2.2, there are sub-files in different rounds:

- First round—three sub-files.
- Second round—two sub-files.
- Third round—one file only.

A simple conversion of Shellsort is to use three processors to sort the sub-files in the first round. In the second round, we use two processors. Only one process is used in the last round.

This design (Quinn, 1994) has very high parallelism at the beginning of its execution so it is better than Quicksort. However, it has very low parallelism at the end and thus it does not eliminate the 'load imbalance' problem. In term of parallelism level, it is similar to Quicksort. Furthermore, parallel Shellsort is inferior to parallel Quicksort because Shellsort has higher time complexity than Quicksort. According to Quinn's (1994) empirical study, the speedup of the parallel Shellsort algorithm is poor.

17.4.3 Possible Improvement

Both parallel Quicksort and parallel Shellsort suffer from the problem of uneven workload between processors. As Quicksort has better average performance than Shellsort, many researchers have designed ways to overcome these problems. We will discuss the basic idea of an improved version of parallel Quicksort in this section.

We have p processors to sort n keys. The idea is to partition the input file into hopefully p equal-sized sub-files according to the known distribution of the keys. Sub-files will then be handled by each processor and sorted independently. The algorithm has three phases:

Phase one—this phase comprises two sub-steps.

Step 1: There are p pivots which are used to separate the file into p sub-files. Only one processor is used to calculate all pivots (refer to Section 17.4.3.1 for the calculation of the pivot).

Step 2: p processors concurrently count the numbers of keys which fall into the p ranges. The results are merged to obtain the actual number of keys in each range.

Phase two—concurrently, each processor i extracts all keys which fall into the range (Pivot_i, Pivot_{i+1}) from the input file, and forms a sub-file. This results in a new file which consists of p sub-files. After this phase, every key element X in sub-file i will satisfy the following conditions:

X $\geq$ for Pivot_{i-1} and X < Pivot_i for sub-file i, when $p - 1 > i \geq 0$

Or

X < for Pivot_i for sub-file i, when $i = 1$

Phase three—concurrently, each processor sorts a sub-file in the newly generated file by either a statistical sorting method (Loo, 1989) or other powerful sorting methodologies.

Each processor divides its own sub-file into two smaller sub-files. It stores one sub-file in a global queue and keeps the other sub-file. This iteration is repeated until it has no more sub-files to keep, and then it will pick up a sub-file from the global queue and start this process again. This method maintains even workload between processors when the distribution of the keys is slightly different from our assumption.

17.4.3.1 Calculation of Pivots

P_i can be calculated with the following formula if the keys follow uniform distribution:

$$P_i = \text{Min} + (\text{Max} - \text{Min}) * i / n$$

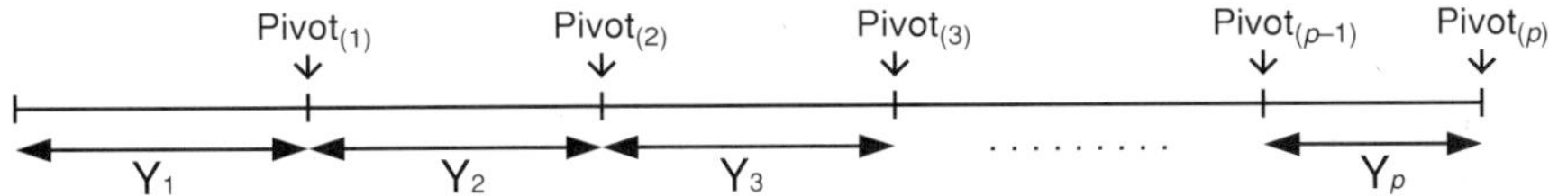

FIGURE 17.2. Schematic diagram of the calculation of pivots.

where Max is the Maximum value of keys, Min is the Minimum value of keys and n is the number of processors in the system. A schematic diagram is presented in Fig. 17.2. Y_i is the sub-file after phase 1.

This formula can still be used for non-uniform distribution. However, pre-processing is required to map the non-uniform distribution to uniform distribution. Before the sorting starts, a cumulative distribution table should be built using the method specified in many standard statistics textbooks. The pivot used in this algorithm can be found by mapping to the cumulative distribution table. A schematic diagram for the mapping is presented in Fig. 17.3. In this figure, we split the file equally over five processors. We maintain the 'load balance' by allocating approximately equal numbers of keys to each processor.

17.4.3.2 Performance

Additional storage of n keys is required only at phase 2 and thus the storage requirement is $2n$. However, the storage of the old array will be released after this phase.

This algorithm has the following properties:

- Better than parallel Quicksort algorithm on average.
- Easily applied to difference kinds of distribution pattern of the input data file.

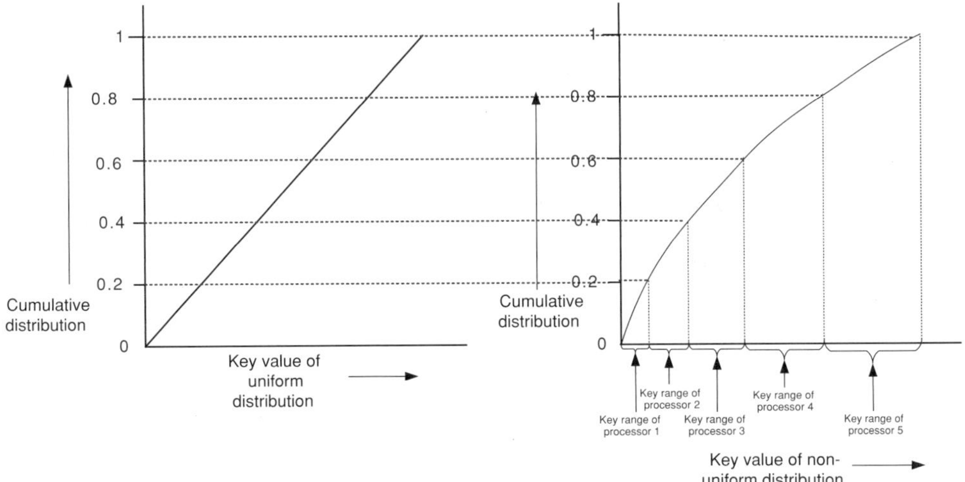

FIGURE 17.3. Mapping of non-uniform distribution.

- Eliminates the low amount of parallelism at the beginning of parallel Quicksort algorithm.
- Has a good speedup.

17.5 Parallel Sorting Algorithms for MIMD with Distributed Memory

Since the final sorted file is distributed over different local memory/computers, a new definition of sorting is required. The sorting model is briefly described in the next section.

17.5.1 Definition of Distributed Sorting

- A large file is physically distributed in the local memory of p processors.
- n records are approximately evenly distributed in p processors (*i.e.*, n/p records for each processor).
- No processor has enough resources to collect all keys and sort the file locally (or do it efficiently).

We denote the elements in the file as $X(i,j)$, where i is the processor number and j—is an integer from 1 to n/p. The objective of sorting is to rearrange $X(i,j)$ elements so that the elements will be in the following order:

$$X(i, 1) < X(i, 2) < \cdots < X(i, n/p)$$

and

$$X(k, n/p) < X(k + 1, 1)$$

where k is an integer from 1 to p.

Communication time is usually much longer than computation time in the execution of algorithms for distributed memory environments. The communication time is thus a major criterion for measuring the performance of a distributed algorithm. Therefore, reducing the number of communication messages and volume of transmissions has become the focus of research (Dechter and Kleinrock, 1986; Huang and Kleinrock, 1990; Loo and Ng, 1991; Loo et al., 1995; Wegner 1982).

17.6 Conclusions

The design of any parallel algorithms will be strongly influenced by the architecture of the computers on which they are to be run. Different priorities will be used in different computer systems.

In MIMD with shared memory, particular attention will be paid to ensure that the processors will be fully utilized. Locking and synchronization overheads should be reduced in the design.

In MIMD with distributed memory, the time for processing the data items is usually much less than the communication time. Thus, the communication time is the most important factor for these kinds of systems.

As we can see from the aforementioned discussion, parallel sorting algorithms are more complicated than serial algorithms. In addition to the factors considered in serial algorithms, additional factors must be addressed in the design process. Those factors are summarized as follows:

- Number of processors required.
- Speedup, scaleability and efficiency.
- Idle time of processors and load balancing between processors.
- Memory contention or conflict.
- Task creation and allocation to processors.
- Locking, synchronization and task scheduling method.

18 Infrastructure and Future Development

18.1 Infrastructure

Building reliable automobiles alone will not solve the transportation problems. We also need highways and gas stations, or no one will be interested in using a car. We need to build computing infrastructure to realize the full benefits of P2P applications.

18.1.1 Coordinator

One problem for our models is the difficulty in finding the power servers. We can solve this problem by adding a coordinator to the system as in Fig. 18.1. The coordinator is a computer which will store the IP addresses of all power servers and the servlets of the applications.

The client stores the servlets on the coordinator. Any computer owner who wants to donate their computer power to the network needs to register with the coordinator and provide the following information:

- IP address of the power server.
- Type of processor on the power server.
- When and how long it is available.
- The size of memory on the server.

The coordinator is not involved in the actual computation. It plays the role of a broker. It will find power servers which will be able to do the actual computation for the requesting user. The tasks of coordinator are as follows:

- Allow new users to register.
- Maintain the database of registered power servers' information.
- Match user's requirements with power servers and pass the IP addresses of power servers to the user.
- Transfer servlets to the power servers.

The user contacts the coordinator to get the IP addresses of available power servers and uses the IP address to initiate the servlet on the power servers (Fig. 18.1).

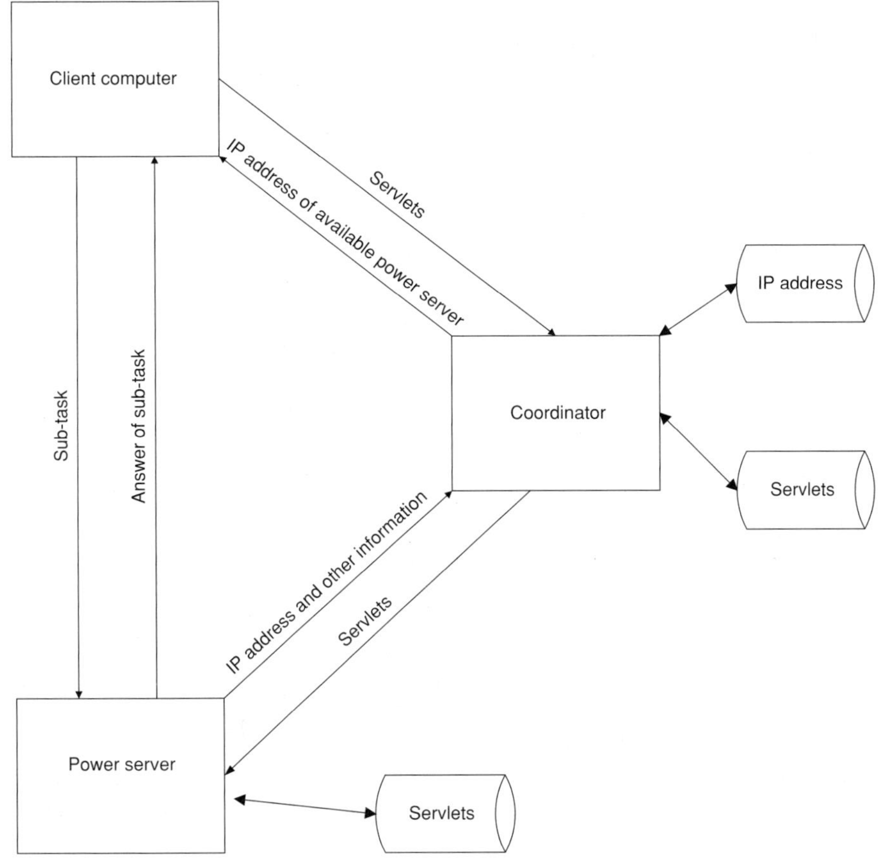

FIGURE 18.1. Coordinator and IP addresses.

For very large P2P systems, multiple levels of coordinators (Fig. 18.2) for each country, city and organization might be necessary. The organization coordinator will record the IP addresses of computers in its organization. The city coordinator will record the addresses of all organization coordinators and power servers in the city. A global system will include many country, city and organization coordinators. The concept is similar to the domain name server (DNS), which successfully enables the Internet.

18.2 Incentives

It is obvious that an organization would like to use the spare power of all available computers. If we want to build a P2P system which consists of different organizations and individuals, we need to provide incentives to the participants.

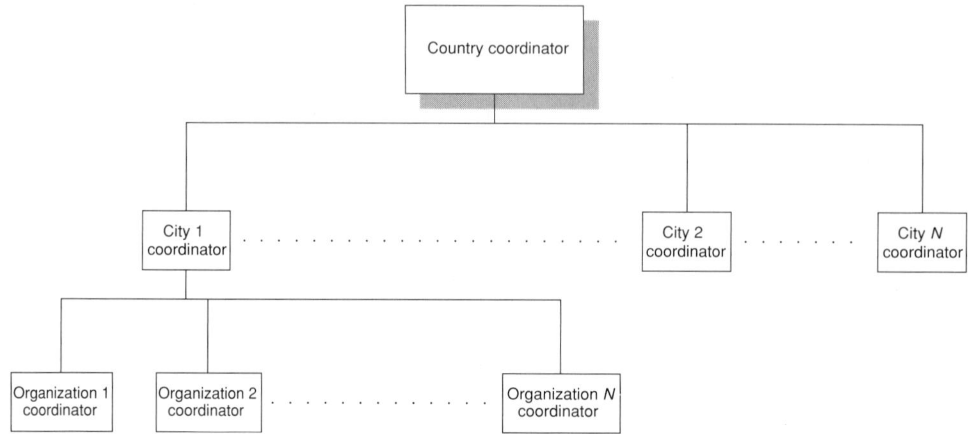

FIGURE 18.2. Multi-level coordinators.

One way to do this is to set up an association in which members (organizations and individuals) can share each other's computing power. In becoming members of the association, users commit themselves to connecting to the Internet for agreed amounts of time, allowing other members access to computing resources.

It might also be possible to create a market for surplus computing power. Brokers would sell the unused processing power of individuals or organizations. Telephone companies or Internet service providers might provide free services to customers if they promise to connect their computer to the Internet. The telephone companies or Internet service provider would then collect and re-sell the unused power from their customers.

18.3 Maintenance

We need to update the server machines one by one in our model. If we have a large number of servers, this maintenance job is very time consuming. This drawback can be overcome by automation. Some web servers have upload functions; the maintenance job can be alleviated by using these functions. This can be achieved by uploading the new version of the servlets and can be automated by use of a special program on the client computer. If the uploading function is not available in the web server, a special servlet can be deployed in each web server to extend its ability to handle such requests from the client.

The maintenance job can be further reduced if all participants are within one organization and their computers are connected in a LAN. Only one copy of the web server and servlet is installed on the network drive as in Fig. 18.3. Every computer invokes the web server and servlet using the single version on the network drive and thus the maintenance job is streamlined.

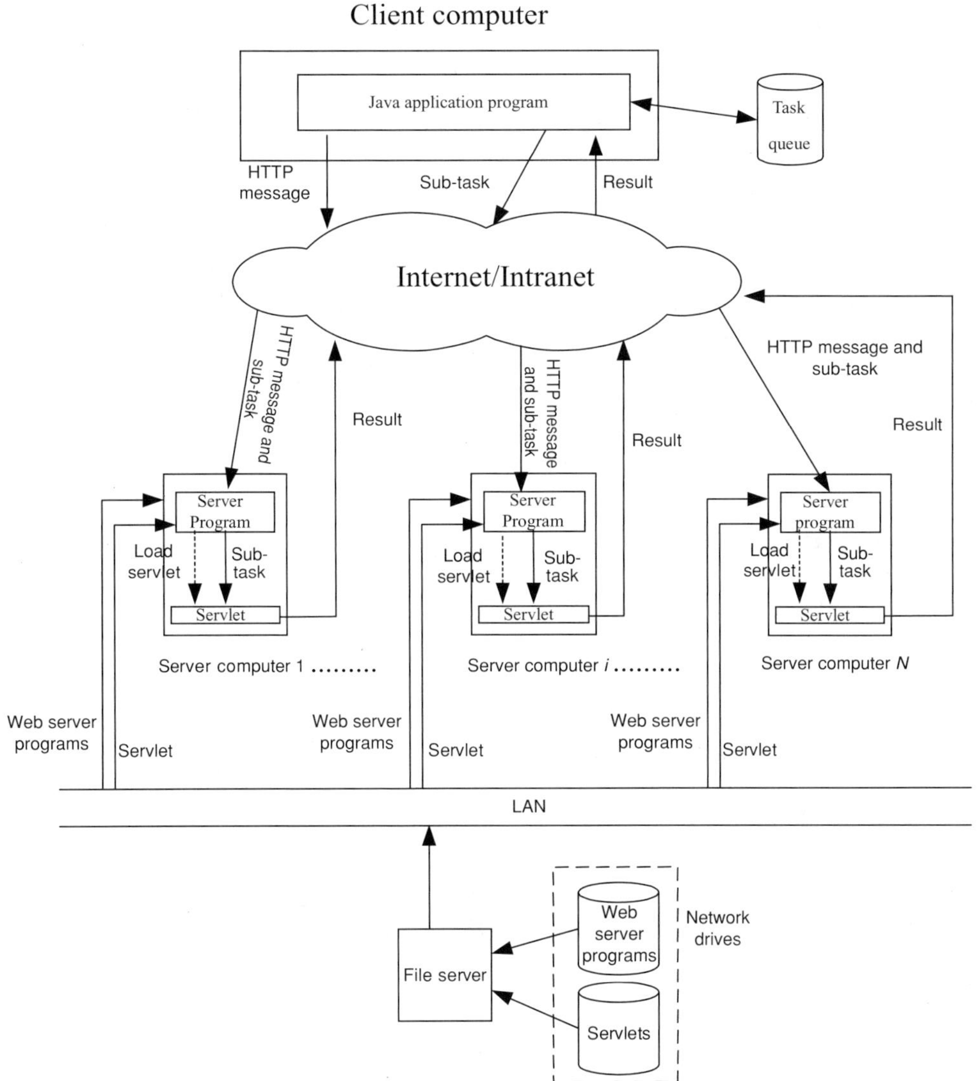

FIGURE 18.3. Server and servlets from network drive.

Many operating systems support the sharing of folders from any computer. This feature can be used if a dedicated network drive is not available in the system. As described in Fig. 18.4, a client computer can allow other computers to access the web server and servlets. In other words, all programs will reside in a single computer. It will be easier to develop and maintain the system.

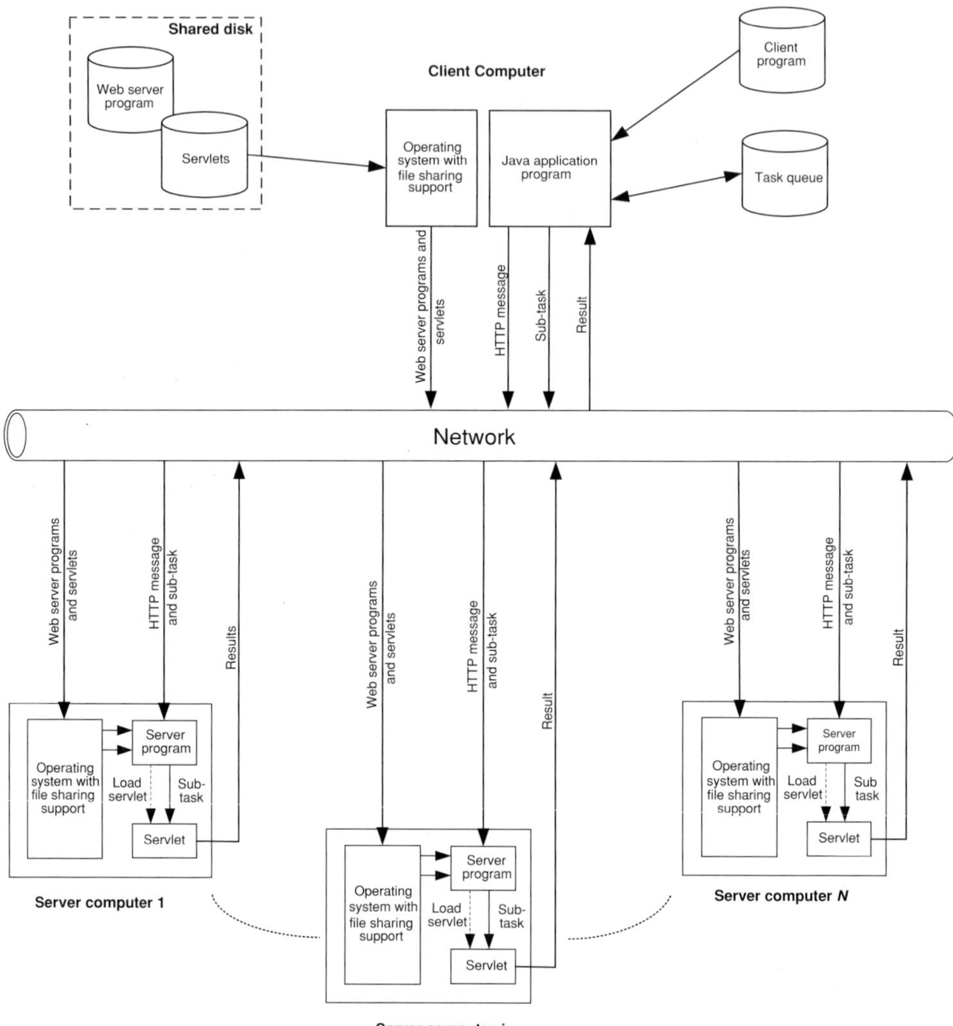

FIGURE 18.4. Web server and servlets from shared disk.

18.4 Future P2P Development

With the advent of new technologies, it is possible to conceive of more complicated P2P applications for organizations. For example, insurance companies need to calculate the premiums for their new products and services. They also need to adjust the premiums for their existing products. Ad hoc calculations are required due to new diseases such as SARS, bird flu, *etc.* However, they need to collect statistical data before they can do the calculations. These data-collecting processes are time consuming and expensive. It would be beneficial if large insurance companies could form P2P systems and share information for such statistical calculations. Any insurance company could request information from the computers of others as and when required. This could reduce the cost and time needed to complete these processes.

These new applications will have different characteristics from those discussed in Chapters 2 and 3. The numbers of computers in the systems are relatively small compared with, for example, the Napster system. The owners of these computers are organizations instead of individuals. More complex database operations are involved, requiring very efficient distributed algorithms. Unlike the Napster or anti-cancer programs, security (and/or privacy) is extremely important as each database belongs to a different organization. They may be happy to share statistical information with other companies, but they also need to protect their own confidential information. They are, after all, competitors. These differences create problems and provide new challenges to researchers in this area.

18.5 Problems of Data-Sharing P2P System

Although P2P has become a buzzword nowadays, there are still problems in building P2P systems (Loo, 2003). One of the most serious problems is in the area of database operations. Many database operations on a single computer can be completed within a very short time. However, on a distributed database system, performing these operations might require many communication messages and so take a much longer time. *Selection* is one such time-consuming operation and an example is available in Loo and Choi, 2002.

One solution is to transfer all data sets to one computer so the operations can be executed in an efficient way. However, this solution is not feasible in many P2P systems for the following reasons:

- Security—Transferring all records to one computer may raise security concerns as each data set belongs to a different owner. Owners of data sets might not be comfortable transmitting all values of even a single field to other computers. For example, 10 large companies want to carry out a salary survey in a city for reference in their annual salary adjustment exercises. With the advent of JDBC (Reese, 2000), Java technologies (Englander, 2002; Herlihy, 1999) and new protocols (Herlihy and Warres, 1999; Merritt et al., 2002), it has become easy to connect heterogeneous computers of these 10 companies to form an ad hoc P2P system. A company can find out the 25th percentile, medium and 75th percentile of salary range in that city. Although these 10 companies are happy to supply data to each other for such statistical calculations, they would not want to transmit the salary values of every employee via the network, even if the name of the employee was not included in the process.
- Capacity—Data sets can be extremely large. Typically, no single computer in a P2P system has the capacity to hold all data sets. Even where one computer

has the capacity to hold all records, this would be inefficient. Holding all the data on a single computer would use the major part of its memory and slow it down.
- Performance of the network—Transferring a large amount of data can also overload a network. It will slow down other users who are using the network.

In order to make such kind of P2P applications successful in the future, many distributed database algorithms need to be reviewed and improved. A case is presented in Appendix 1 so readers can gain better understanding of the problems and operations of data-sharing (not file sharing) P2P systems.

18.6 Efficient Parallel Algorithms

Now you should be able to modify the programs in this book for your applications. As discussed in Section 3.4, it is important to design an efficient algorithm before you develop your programs. As parallel computing is not completely new, you can find a lot of parallel algorithm in research papers and books. It is possible that you can get a good algorithm and modify it for your application. In other words, you do not need to start from scratch and it will take a shorter time to complete your project.

However, many parallel algorithms are designed with particular computer architectures in mind. You need some knowledge of different computer architectures in order to understand these algorithms.

18.7 Re-Visiting Speed Up

As discussed in Section 3.5, speed up is an important metric for parallel computers because these kinds of computers are extremely expensive. A 10-processor parallel computer will usually be more expensive than 10 serial computers with the same processor. It will also take much longer to develop parallel programs than serial programs. If the speed up is not good, that means either we are not using the right facilities for our job or we are using the facilities in the wrong way. Thus, it is not a cost-effective solution for our application.

Speed up is less important for P2P systems in the sense that computer power is free (or almost free) as we are using the unused CPU cycles of peer computers. It will not bother us if the speed up is poor. P2P systems provide a new method for us to solve very large problems which we cannot handle due to lack of computer power in the past. Speed up of a large-scale P2P will usually not be very good due to the following reasons:

- The communication cost (in term of time required) is extremely high, especially for computers in different countries.
- Owners might shut down the peer computer or use it for other purposes during the process.

Having said that, speed up is still a useful tool for us to measure and compare different algorithms in P2P system development. For example, a computation-intensive job can be completed in three months with a poor algorithm, while a good algorithm will reduce it to one month. Although the computer power is free, the completion time is still an important factor for many mission critical applications.

I recommend you to conduct experiments with a small number of computers which are connected by a LAN before the actual deployment of a large-scale P2P project. You can measure the speed up of different algorithms in such controlled environment. Although the actual speed up will be quite different in an Internet environment, these experiments will give you some rough idea of the efficiencies of different algorithms. Thus, you can pick up the best for your implementation.

18.8 Applications

You need to select the application carefully as the models in this book are not panaceas for every problem. Some applications are good candidates for parallel processing, while others are poor candidates. Let us consider two extreme real-life examples:

- A person travels from one place to another; ten identical cars cannot make the process faster than one car. More computers will never be able to speed up the process in some applications.
- From time to time, we heard of cases of wild fire in the forests which last for many days. It is always better to have more fire fighters to put out such fires, especially in the early phase. Fire can spread quickly, and delay means we will only have more fire to fight. More fire fighters can contain the fire earlier. We can expect a very good speed up as we have less fire to fight.

Most applications are somewhere between the above two extremes. Detailed study of problems is required for any serious applications. However, speed up is not the only thing we care about and other factors might be more important for some applications.

Indeed, examples in Section 18.4 and 18.5 will never achieve any good speed up at all. We still want to deploy such P2P systems as they will provide substantial benefits in other areas.

18.9 Further Improvements

Thank you for reading my book! I am a believer in Open Source Software. Please feel free to modify the programs in this book for any purposes. Certainly there will be room for improvement in my models, and I will be happy to hear any suggestions from readers. Updated versions of the programs (contributed by either you or me) will be available in the book's website. I will be glad to receive any feedback (good or bad) from readers (my e-mail address: alfred@ln.edu.hk).

Appendix A: Data-Sharing P2P Algorithm

A.1 New Multiple Distributed Selection Algorithm

The distributed multiple selection algorithm in this appendix was derived from a single selection algorithm in Loo and Choi (2002) by the authors. The distribution pattern of the keys of the file is known before the operation begins, thus statistical knowledge can be applied to find the keys in the file faster than with other algorithms. The objective of this algorithm is to reduce the number of communication messages.

The objective of a distributed single-selection algorithm is to select one key (*e.g.*, the 30th smallest key) from a very large file distributed in different computers. However, it is more likely that we would need to select multiple keys simultaneously in real applications. Thus, an efficient multiple-selection algorithm is required. A special case of the multiple-selection problem is to find $p - 1$ keys, *i.e.*, keys with the ranks of $n/p, 2n/p, \ldots, (p-1)n/p$, in a system with $n$records and p computers. For example, we need to find out the 30th and 60th smallest key of a distributed file.

The distributed system model used in this section is presented as follows:

- All computers are connected by broadcast/multicast facilities. For example, computers connected by a LAN with TCP/IP can use this algorithm for their selection operation.
- A large file is physically distributed among p computers, and n records are approximately uniformly distributed among p computers (*i.e.*, n/p records for each computer).
- No computer has enough resources to collect all records and select the keys with the selected ranks from the file locally.
- We denote the keys in the file as X(i, k) where k is an integer (1–n/p) and i is the computer number. The keys will be in the following order:

$$X(i, 1) < X(i, 2) < \cdots < X(i, k) < \cdots < X(i, n/p) \tag{A.1}$$

There is no particular sequence for any two keys, *e.g.*, X(i, k) and X($i + 1$, k), in different computers.

- The keys follow a known distribution. The algorithm is suitable for any distribution using the mapping method discussed in the work of Janus and Lamagna (1985), but the uniform distribution will be used in the example in this chapter.

The objective of this algorithm is to find $p-1$ target keys. The rank of each key is jn/p (where $1 \leq j \leq p-1$).

For example, find the 30th and 60th smallest key of a distributed file for a system with three computers and 90 keys (*i.e.*, $n = 90$ and $p = 3$).

Note that this algorithm will be able to find more than $p-1$ target keys simultaneously. $p-1$ keys will be used for explanation purposes in this chapter as we frequently need to find $p-1$ keys in real applications.

A.2 Steps of Distributed Statistical Selection Algorithm

Note that an example is available in Section A.4. It will be easier for reader if they could refer to the example simultaneously when they read this section.

The statistical selection algorithm is described as follows:

Phase 1

Step 1. One computer will be selected as the coordinator. Each participant will transmit the maximum and minimum key values in their local file to the coordinator. The coordinator will calculate the initial $p-1$ delimiters' values. We denote MAX as the maximum key value in the global file and MIN as the minimum key in the global file.

$$DELIMITER_j = MIN + \frac{(MAX - MIN)\,j}{p} \tag{A.2}$$

where j is an integer starting from 1 to $p-1$.

Step 2: The coordinator transmits $p-1$ delimiters' value to all participants.

Step 3: Each computer selects $p-1$ pivots. Pivot $_{i,j}$ is the biggest value which is less than or equal to the *delimiter* $_j$ and i is the computer number and $1 \leq i \leq p$.

Note that steps 1 and 2 are optional steps. If the maximum and minimum are known due to some prior operations, then all computers can calculate the first pivot and communication of these two steps is not required. A schematic diagram for phase one is presented in Fig. A.1.

Phase 2—Each computer assumes two roles simultaneously (*i.e.*, pivot calculating and ranks calculating). Sequentially, each computer broadcast pivots with ranks after the calculations once in each round. The following operations are repeated until the answers are found. A schematic diagram for this phase is presented in Fig. A.2.

Ranks calculating role—We denote rank as $R[i,j]$—number of the keys which are smaller than pivot $_{i,j}$ in computer i. Each computer will receive $p-1$ pivots from one broadcasting computer, and they will compare all keys in

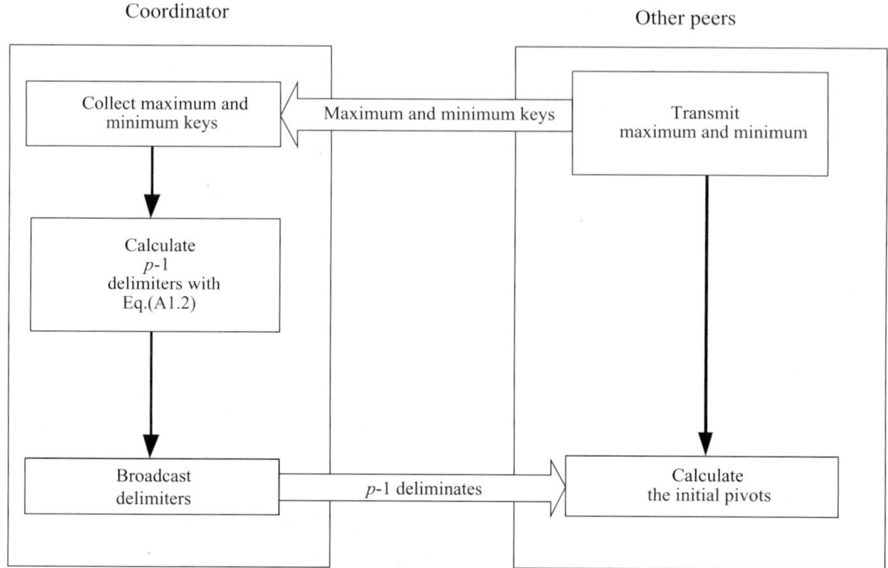

FIGURE A.1. Schematic diagram of the operations in phase 1.

their local files with this pivot. Sequentially, each computer will broadcast these ranks $R[i,j]$ to other computers.

Pivots calculating role—Each computer will receive $(p-1)^2$ ranks from other computers. It will compare its own pivots and calculate the rank of its pivot in the global file using Eq. (A.3). If the sum of these ranks is equal to the target rank, then the answer is found and the operation is completed. Otherwise, each computer will calculate a new pivot according to the method in the next section. The new pivots will be broadcasted to the coordinator together within the ranks.

A.3 Calculation of the New Pivot

We denote G as global rank, calculated as follows:

$$G_j = \sum_{i=1}^{p} R[i, j] \tag{A.3}$$

After each probe, each local file will be split into two sub-files. All keys in the first sub-file will be smaller than or equal to pivot $_{i,j}$, while all keys in the second sub-file will be greater than the pivot. The first sub-file will be used for the next operation if the global rank G_j is less than target rank, otherwise the second sub-file will be used.

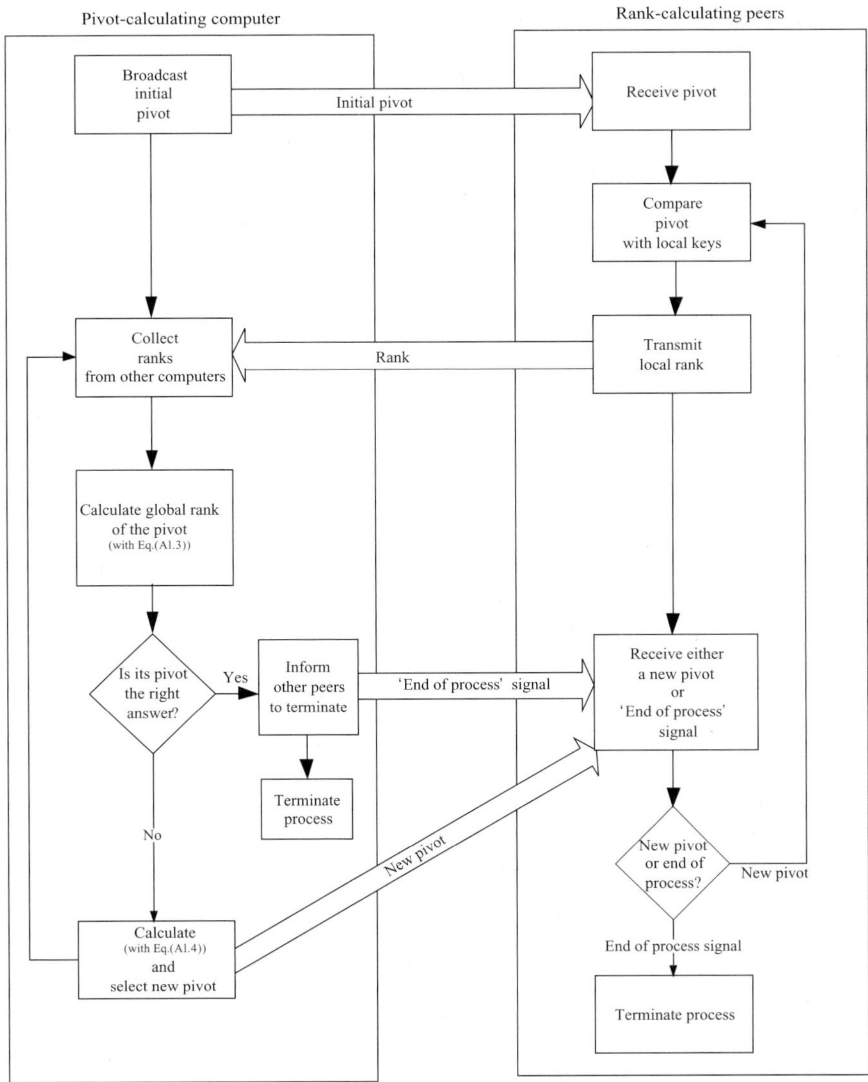

FIGURE A.2. Schematic diagram of the operations in phase 2.

The new pivot $_{i,j}$ will be calculated as follows :

$$NP = OP + (LK - SK) * offset_j / NK \tag{A.4}$$

where *NP* denotes new value of pivot$_{i,j}$, *OP* denotes old value of *pivot*$_{i,j}$, *LK* denotes largest key of the sub-file, *SK* denotes smallest key of the sub-file, *NK* denotes number of keys in the sub-file and

$$offset_j = \frac{\frac{jn}{p} - \sum_{i=1}^{p} R[i, j]}{p} \tag{A.5}$$

The smallest key in the remaining sub-file, which is greater than or equal to *NP*, will be selected as the new pivot.

A.4 Example

The objective in the following example is to find two target keys. The first target key is the 30th smallest key, while the second target key is the 60th smallest key in the global file. It shows all messages broadcasted by all computers from step 2 to step 5 of the algorithm. There are three computers and 30 numbers for each computer in this example. After each computer sorted its own keys, the keys were arranged as in Tables A.1 to A.3.

A.4.1 Phase 1—Calculation of Delimiters and Initial Pivots

In this example, we have the following values:

$Min = 3 \quad Max = 449 \quad p = 3.$

Using Eq. (A.2), we have:

$DELIMITER_1 = 151.6$ *and* $DELIMITER_2 = 300.3.$

TABLE A.1. Keys in computer 1 after phase 1

(1–10)th keys	16	22	38	47	48	66	86	94	101	105
(11–20)th keys	170	191	193	207	226	251	273	305	324	332
(21–30)th keys	337	348	375	381	404	412	425	444	446	449

TABLE A.2. Keys in computer 2 after phase 1

(1–10)th keys	34	35	45	55	77	79	151	185	187	196
(11–20)th keys	200	206	240	244	249	280	294	295	366	367
(21–30)th keys	373	383	393	394	395	423	425	430	443	444

TABLE A.3. Keys in computer 3 after phase 1

(1–10)th keys	3	26	44	45	65	76	101	106	145	167
(11–20)th keys	183	187	193	215	226	246	249	254	255	263
(21–30)th keys	266	319	325	330	342	359	359	399	405	410

In computer 1, 105 is the biggest value which is less than 151.6. Key 273 is the biggest value which is less than 300.3. Thus, 105 and 273 are selected as the pivots for round 1 operation.

Computer 2 selects 151 and 295 as initial pivots, while computer 3 selects 145 and 266.

A.4.2 *Phase 2—Messages in Round 1*

In the first round, computer 1 broadcasted two pivots—105 and 273. As no other computers broadcasted any pivot, computer 1 did not broadcast any $R[i,j]$ so the special character '-' was broadcasted.

Computer 2 compared 105 and 273 (pivots from computer 1) with its keys. Six keys were less than 105, and 15 keys were less than 273. Computer 2 broadcasted these two ranks (6 and 15) together with its pivots 151 and 295.

Computer 3 compared the first pivot (105) from computer 1 with its keys, and seven keys were less than or equal to 105. It also compared the first pivot (151) from computer 2 with its keys, and nine keys were less than 151.

In a similar way, computer 3 compared the second pivot (273) from computer 1 with its keys, and 21 keys were less than or equal to 273. It also compared the second pivot (295) from computer 2 with its keys, and 21 keys were less than 295.

The pivots of computer 3 were 145 and 266. Computer 3 transmitted these pivots together with two pairs of ranks (*i.e.*, 7, 9 and 21, 21). The messages in round 1 are summarized in Table A.4, while a schematic diagram showing the interaction of computers in round 1 is presented in Fig. A.3.

A.4.3 *Phase 2—Messages in Round 2*

In round 2, computer 1 performed the following steps:

Step 1

- The local rank of the first pivot 105 (transmitted by computer 1 itself in round 1) was 10 in computer 1. Computer 1 also received the ranks 6 and 8

TABLE A.4. Communication message in the process.

Round	Message broadcasted by	$k = 1$				$k = 2$			
		Pivot	Response to pivot			Pivot	Response to pivot		
1									
	Computer 1	105	&[a]	—[b]	—	273	&	—	—
	Computer 2	151	6	&	—	295	15	&	—
	Computer 3	145	8	9	&	266	21	21	&

[a]The symbol '&'indicates that this field is not used by the computer as there is no need to broadcast the local rank of its own pivot.

[b]The symbol '—' indicates that the computer is not using this field to broadcast the rank.

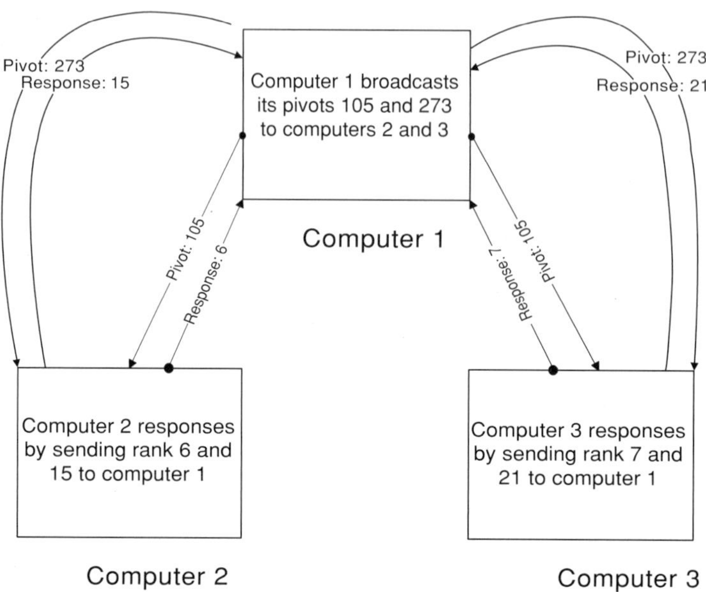

FIGURE A.3. Schematic diagram showing the interactions between computers in round 1.

from computer 2 and 3, respectively (as from Fig. A.3). The global rank of 105 was $10 + 6 + 8 = 24$. Computer 1 knew that key 105 was not the 30th smallest key.

- Using Eq. (A.5), the offset from the target was:

$$(30 - 24)/3 = 2.$$

- Using Eq. (A.4), the new search value was

$$105 + [(449 - 105) * 2]/(30 - 10) = 139.4.$$

- Key 170 was chosen for the next pivot as it was the smallest key which was greater than or equal to 139.4.

Step 2

- Computer 1 examined the number of keys which were less than or equal to pivot 151 (the pivot value transmitted by computer **2**). Ten keys were less than 151.
- Computer 1 examined the number of keys which were less than or equal to the pivot value 145 (the pivot value transmitted by computer 3). Ten keys were less than 145.

Step 3

- The local rank of the second pivot 273 (transmitted by computer 1 itself in round 1) was 17 in computer 1. Computer 1 also received the ranks 15 and 21 from computer 2 and 3, respectively (as from Fig. A.3). The global rank of 105 was $17 + 15 + 21 = 53$. Computer 1 knew that key 273 was not the 60th smallest key.

- Using Eq. (A.5), the offset from the target was

$$(60 - 53)/3 = 2.34$$

- Using Eq. (A.4), the new search value was

$$273 + [(449 - 273) * 2.34]/(30 - 17) = 304.68.$$

- Key 305 was chosen for the next pivot as it was the smallest key which was greater than or equal to 304.68.

Step 4

- Computer 1 compared 151 and 295 (pivots from computer 2 in round 1) with its keys. Ten keys were less than 151, and 17 keys were less than 295.
- It also compared 145 and 266 (pivots from computer 3 in round 1). Ten keys were less than 145, and 16 keys were less than 266.

Step 5

- Computer 1 broadcasted 2 pairs of ranks together with its new pivots 170 and 305.

In round 2, computer 2 performed the following steps:

Step 1

- The local rank of pivot 151 (first pivot of computer 2) was 7 in computer 2. Computer 2 also received the ranks 9 and 10 from computer 1 and 3, respectively. The global rank of 151 was $7 + 9 + 10 = 26$, thus computer 2 confirmed that 151 was not the 30th smallest key.
- Using Eqs. (A.4) and (A.5), key 185 was chosen as the new pivot.

Step 2

- Computer 2 examined the number of keys which were less than or equal to pivot 170 (the pivot value transmitted by computer 1 in round 2). Seven keys were less than 170.
- Computer 2 examined the number of keys which were less than or equal to the pivot value 145 (the pivot value transmitted by computer 3 in round 1). Six keys were less than 145.

Step 3

- Computer 2 compared 305 (second pivots from computer 1 in round 2) with its keys. Eighteen keys were less than 305. It also compared 266 (second pivots from computer 3 in round 1); 15 keys were less than 266.

Step 4

- The local rank of pivot 295 (second pivot of computer 2) was 18 in computer 2. Computer 2 also received the ranks 21 and 17 from computer 1 and 3,

respectively. The global rank of 295 was 18 + 21 + 17 = 56; thus computer 2 confirmed that 295 was not the 60th smallest key.
- Using Eqs. (A.4) and (A.5), key 366 was chosen as the new pivot.

Step 5

- Computer 2 broadcasted these two pairs of ranks together with its new pivots 185 and 366.

In round 2, computer 3 performed the following steps:

Step 1

- The local rank of pivot 145 was 9 in computer 3. Computer 3 also received the ranks 10 and 6 from computer 1 and 2, respectively. The global rank of 145 was 9 + 10 + 6 = 25; thus computer 3 confirmed that 145 was not the 30th smallest key.
- Using Eqs. (A.2) and (A.1), key 167 was chosen as the new pivot.

Step 2

- Computer 3 examined the number of keys which were less than or equal to pivot 170 (the pivot value transmitted by computer 1). Ten keys were less than 170.
- Computer 3 examined the number of keys which were less than or equal to the pivot value 185 (the pivot value transmitted by computer 2). Eleven keys were less than 170.

Step 3

- The local rank of pivot 266 was 21 in computer 3. Computer 3 also received the ranks 16 and 15 from computer 1 and 2, respectively. The global rank of 266 was 21 + 16 + 15 = 51; thus computer 3 confirmed that 266 was not the 60th smallest key.
- Using Eqs. (A.4) and (A.5), key 319 was chosen as the new pivot.

Step 4

- Computer 3 compared 305 (second pivots from computer 1 in round 2) with its keys. Twenty-one keys were less than 305. It also compared 366 (second pivot from computer 2 in round 2); 27 keys were less than 366.

Step 5

- Computer 3 broadcasted these two pairs of ranks together with its new pivots 167 and 319.

The messages in round 2 were summarized in Table A.5.

A.4.4 Phase 2—Messages in Round 3

In the third round, computer 1 calculated the global rank of its two pivots in round 2, and they were not the 30th and 60th smallest keys. Computer 1 compared 185

TABLE A.5. Communication message in the process.

Round	Message broadcasted by	k = 1				k = 2			
		Pivot	Response to pivot			Pivot	Response to pivot		
2									
	Computer 1	170	&[a]	10	10	305	&	17	16
	Computer 2	185	7	&	6	366	18	&	15
	Computer 3	167	10	11	&	319	21	27	&

[a]The symbol '&' indicates that this field is not used by the computer as there is no need to broadcast the local rank of its own pivot.

and 366 (pivots from computer 2 in round 2) with its keys. Eleven keys were less than 185, and 22 keys were less than 366. It also compared 167 and 319 (pivots from computer 3 in round 2). Ten keys were less than 167, and 18 keys were less than 319. Computer 1 broadcasted these two pairs of ranks together with its new pivots 191 and 324.

Computer 2 calculated the global rank of its two pivots broadcast in round 2. The 30th smallest key was 185 so it is one of the answers. It broadcasted four 'E' characters so that other computers stopped searching for the 30th key. On the other hand, 366 was not the 60th smallest key. However, computer 2 confirmed that the answer was not in its sub-file, so it broadcasted an 'E' character in its second pivot field. In other words, computer 2 knew that the 60th key is not in computer 2. Computer 2 also compared 324 (pivots from computer 1 in round 3) with its keys. Eighteen keys were less than 324. It also compared 319 (pivot from computer 3 in round 2). Eighteen keys were less than 319. Computer 2 broadcasted these pairs of ranks.

Computer 3 calculated the global rank of its pivot broadcast in round 2. The 60th smallest key was not 319 so a new pivot 330 was chosen. Computer 3 compared 324 (pivot from computer 1 in round 3) with its keys. Twenty-two keys were less than 324. Computer 3 broadcasted the rank 22 together with its new pivot 330. As computer 2 did not broadcast any rank in this round, there was no need to compare the pivot of computer 2. Computer 3 broadcasted 'E' character in this rank field. The messages in round 3 are summarized in Table A.6.

TABLE A.6. Communication messages in round 3.

Round	Message broadcasted by	k = 1				k = 2			
		Pivot	Response to pivot			Pivot	Response to pivot		
3									
	Computer 1	191	&[a]	11	10	324	&	22	18
	Computer 2	E[b]	E	E	E	E	18	E	18
	Computer 3	E	E	E	E	330	22	E	&

[a]The symbol '&' indicates that this field is not used by the computer as there is no need to broadcast the local rank of its own pivot.

[b] 'E' indicates that the computer is not using this field as it reaches the end of operation.

A.4.5 Phase 2—Messages in Round 4

In the fourth round, computer 1 calculated the global rank of its pivot (transmitted in round 3) and it was not 60th smallest key. Computer 1 compared 330 (pivot from computer 3 in round 3) with its keys. Nineteen keys were less than 330. Computer 1 broadcasted this rank 19 together with its new pivot 332.

Computer 2 did not broadcast any pivot in the last round so it did not need to calculate the global rank of its pivot. Computer 2 compared 332 (pivot from computer 1 in round 4) with its keys. Eighteen keys were less than 332. Computer 2 compared 330 (pivot from computer 3 in round 3) with its keys. Eighteen keys were less than 330. Computer 2 broadcasted this pair of ranks (18 and 18).

Computer 3 calculated the global rank of its pivot in round 3, and it was not the 60th smallest key. Computer 3 compared 332 (pivot from computer 1 in round 4) with its keys. Twenty-four keys were less than 332. Computer 3 broadcasted this rank 24 together with its new pivot 325 (Table A.7).

TABLE A.7. Communication message in the process.

Round	Message broadcasted by	$k = 1$				$k = 2$			
		Pivot	Response to pivot			Pivot	Response to pivot		
4									
	Computer 1	E[a]	E	E	E	332	&[b]	E	19
	Computer 2	E	E	E	E	E	18	E	18
	Computer 3	E	E	E	E	325	24	E	&

[b]'E' indicates that the computer is not using this field as it reaches the end of operation.
[b]The symbol '&' indicates that this field is not used by the computer as there is no need to broadcast the local rank of its own pivot.

A.4.6 Phase 2—Messages in Round 5

In the fifth round, computer 1 calculated the global rank of its pivots in round 4, and it was not the 60th smallest key. Computer 1 compared 325 (pivot from computer 3 in round 4) with its keys. Nineteen keys were less than 325. Computer 1 confirmed the 60th key was not in its sub-file by broadcasting an 'E' character in its second pivot position together with the rank 19.

Computer 2 did not broadcast any pivot in the last round so it did not need to calculate the global rank of its pivot. Computer 2 compared 325 (pivot from computer 3 in round 4) with its keys. Eighteen keys were less than 325. Computer 2 broadcast this rank (18) together with seven 'E' characters.

Computer 3 calculated the global rank of its pivot (325) in round 3. The 60th smallest key was 325 so this was the answer. Computer 3 broadcasted 'E' character on all fields so that all computers stopped.

The communication messages in round 5 are summarized in Table A.8.

TABLE A.8. Communication message in round 5.

Round	Message broadcasted by	k = 1				k = 2			
		Pivot	Response to pivot			Pivot	Response to pivot		
5									
	Computer 1	E	E	E	E	E	E	E	19
	Computer 2	E	E	E	E	E	E	E	18
	Computer 3	E	E	E	E	E	E	E	E

A.4.7 Phase 2—Messages in the Whole Process

It took five rounds to complete the process. All messages are summarized in Table A.9.

TABLE A.9. Communication messages in the process.

Round	Message broadcasted by	j = 1				j = 2			
		Pivot	Response to pivot			Pivot	Response to pivot		
1	Computer 1	105	&[a]	—[b]	—	273	&	—	—
	Computer 2	151	6	&	—	295	15	&	—
	Computer 3	145	7	9	&	266	21	21	&
2	Computer 1	170	&	10	10	305	&	17	16
	Computer 2	185	7	&	6	366	18	&	15
	Computer 3	167	10	11	&	319	21	27	&
3	Computer 1	191	&	11	10	324	&	22	18
	Computer 2	E[c]	E	E	E	E	18	E	18
	Computer 3	E	E	E	E	330	22	E	&
4	Computer 1	E	E	E	E	332	&	E	19
	Computer 2	E	E	E	E	E	18	E	18
	Computer 3	E	E	E	E	325	24	E	&
5	Computer 1	E	E	E	E	E	E	E	19
	Computer 2	E	E	E	E	E	E	E	18
	Computer 3	E	E	E	E	E	E	E	E

[a]The symbol '&' indicates that this field is not used by the computer as there is no need to broadcast the local rank of its own pivot.
[b]The symbol '—' indicates that the computer is not using this field to broadcast the rank.
[c] 'E' indicates that the computer is not using this field as it reaches the end of operation.

Appendix B: Useful Websites

Napster

www.napster.com

BitTorrent

http://www.bittorrent.com

Directory of Gnutella

http://www.gnutelliums.com/

P2P resources

http://www.openp2p.com/

http://crypto.stanford.edu/∼mironov/p2p/

Gnuttela Client

BearShare (Windows)
http://www.bearshare.com/
Gtk-Gnutella (Linux/Unix)
http://gtk-gnutella.sourceforge.net/
Gnucleus (Windows)
http://www.gnucleus.com/
LimeWire (Windows, Linux/Unix, Macintosh)
http://www.limewire.com/
Mactella (Macintosh)
http://www.tucows.com/preview/206631
Mutella (Linux/Unix)
http://mutella.sourceforge.net/

Phex (Windows, Macintosh)
http://phex.kouk.de/mambo/

Qtella (Linux/Unix)
http://www.qtella.net/

Swapper (Windows)
http://www.revolutionarystuff.com/swapper/
XoloX (Windows)
http://www.xolox.nl/

Grid Technology

Grid Computing Environments Working Group
http://www.computingportals.org/

Bibliography

Aba, B. and Ozguner, F. 1993. Balance parallel sort on hypercube multiprocessors. *IEEE Transactions on Parallel and Distributed Systems* Vol. 4 (3).

Akl, S. 1989. *The Design and Analysis of Parallel Algorithms.* Englewood Cliffs, NJ: Prentice Hall.

Akl, S. 1997. *Models and Methods, Parallel Computation.* Englewood Cliffs, NJ: Prentice Hall.

Allision, D. and Noga, M. 1982. Usort: An efficient hybrid of distributive partitioning sorting. *BIT* 22:137–138.

Amdahl, G. 1967. Validity of Single Processor Approach to Achieving Large Scale Computing Capability, Proc. AFIPS., Reston, VA., pp. 483–485.

Barkai, D. 2002. *Peer-to-Peer Computing: Technologies for Sharing and Collaborating on the Net*. Intel Press.

Basham, B., Sierra, K., and Bates, B. 2004. *Head First Java Servlet & JSP.* O'Reilly.

Beaulieu, M. 2002. *Wireless Internet Applications and Architecture: Building Professional Wireless Application Worldwide*. Reading, MA: Addison-Wesley.

Braunl, T. 1993. *Parallel Programming*. Englewood Cliffs, NJ: Prentice Hall.

Brittain, J. and Darwin, I. 2003. *Tomcat: The Definitive Guide*. O'Reilly.

Brown, T. 1993. A parallel quicksort algorithm. *Journal of Parallel and Distributed Computing* 19:83–89.

Campione, M. and Walrath, K. 2001. *The Java Tutorial—Object Oriented Programming for the Internet.* Reading, MA: Addison-Wesley.

Carlsson, S. 1993. Sublinear merging and natural mergesort. *Algorithms* 9:629–648.

Cohen, B. 2003. Incentives build robustness in BitTorrent. The Workshop on Economics of Peer-to-Peer Systems.

Colin, M. 1993. Queue-mergesort. *Information Processing Letters* 48.

Cook, J. 2001. *WAP Servlets: Professional Developer's Guide*. New York: John Wiley.

Cook, R. 1980. Best sorting algorithm for nearly sorted lists. *Communications of the ACM* 23.

Culler, E., Singh, J., and Gupta, A. 1999. *Parallel Computer Architecture, A Hardware/Software Approach.* San Mateo, CA: Morgan Kaufmann.

Curtois, T. 1997. *Java Networking and Communications.* Englewood Cliffs, NJ: Prentice Hall.

Dechter, R. and Kleinrock, L. 1986. Broad communications and distributed algorithms. *IEEE Transactions on Computers*. c-35(3).

Deitel, P. 2005. *Java: How to Program*. Englewood Cliffs, NJ: Prentice Hall.

Dobosiewicz, W. 1978. Sorting by distributive partitioning. *Information Processing Letter* 7:1–6.

Dobosiewicz, W. 1991. Linear probing sort. *The Computer Journal* 34(4):370–373.

Doob, J.L. 1967. *Stochastic Processes*. New York: John Wiley.

Eddy, W. 1995. How many comparison does quicksort uses? *Journal of Algorithms* 19.

Englander, R. 2002. *Java and Soap*. O'reilly.

Erkio and Hannu. 1984. The worst case permutation for medium-of-three quicksort. *The Computer Journal* 27(3):276–277.

Evans, M. and Hastings, N. 1993. *Statistical Distributions*. New York: John Wiley.

Flynn, M. 1966a. Very high speed computing systems. *Proceeding of IEEE.*

Flynn, M. 1996b. Parallel computers were the future and may yet be. *Computer, IEEE.*

Foo, S., Hoover, C., and Lee, W. 2001. *Dynamic WAP Application Development*. Manning.

Foster, I. 1994. *Designing and Building Parallel Programs*. Reading, MA: Addison-Wesley.

Fountain, T. 1994. *Parallel Computing*. Cambridge University Press.

Gropp, W., Huss-Lederman, S., Lumsdaine, A., Lusk, E., Nitzberg, B., Saphir, W., and Snir, W. 1997. *MPI-The Complete Reference, Vol. 2, The MPI Extensions*. Cambridge, MA: MIT Press.

Hamilton, G., Cattell, R., and Fisher, M. 1997. *JDBC Databases Access with Java: A Tutorial and Annotated Reference*. Reading, MA: Addison-Wesley.

Harold, E. 2001. *Java I/O*. O'Reilly.

Harold, E. 2004. *Java Network Programming*. O'Reilly.

Herlihy, M. 1999. *The Aleph Toolkit: Support for Scalable Distributed Shared Objects*. Network-based parallel computing–communication, architecture and applications. Lecture Notes in Computer Science 1602, Springer.

Herlihy, M. and Warres, M. 1999. A Tale of Two Directories: Implementing Distributed Shared Objects in Java, Concurrency. *Practice and Experience* 12(7): 555–572.

Hinton, J. and Pinder, A. 1993. *Transputer Hardware and System Design*. Englewood Cliffs, NJ: Prentice Hall.

Hoare, C.A.R. 1961. Quicksort. *Computer Journal* 5(1):10–15.

Hockney, R. and Jesshope, C. 1998. *Parallel Computers 2: Architecture, Programming and Algorithms*. London: Adam Hilger.

Hord, R. 1999. *Understanding Parallel Supercomputing*. IEEE Press.

Huang, J.H. and Kleinrock, L. 1990. Distributed selectsort sorting algorithms on broadcast communication networks. *Parallel Computing*.

Hughes, M., Shoffner, M., and Hamner, D. 1999. *Java Network Programming*. Greenwich: Manning.

Hunter, J. 1998. *Java Servlet Programming*. O'Reilly.

Hunter, J. 2001. *Java Servlet Programming*. O'Reilly.

Hwang, K. and Briggs, A. 1984. *Computer Architecture and Parallel Processing*. McGraw Hill.

Hwang, K. and Xu, X. 1998. *Computer Architecture and Parallel Processing*. McGraw Hill.

Hwang, K. 1993. *Advanced Comptuer Architecture*. McGraw Hill.

Ian, O. 1993. *Programming Classics: Implementing the World's Best Algorithms*. Englewood Cliffs, NJ: Prentice Hall.

Janus P. and Lamagna E. 1985. An adaptive method for unknown distributions in distributive partitioned sorting. *IEEE Transactions on Computer* c-34(4):367–371.

Jebson, B. 1997. *Java Database Programming*. New York: John Wiley.

Johnson, N.L. and Kotz, S. 1969. *Distributions in Statistics.* New York: John Wiley.

Kamath, C. 2001. The Role of Parallel and Distributed Processing in Data Mining, Newsletter of the Technical Committee on Distributed Processing. IEEE Computer Society, Spring.

Khermouch, G. 1994. Large computers—parallelism to the fore. *IEEE Spectrum* January, 1994.

Knuth, D.E. 2005. *The Art of Computer Programming.* Reading, MA: Addison-Wesley.

Kumar, V. 1994. *Introduction to Parallel Computing.* Reading, MA: Addison-Welsey.

Lakshamivarahan, S. and Dhall, D. 1990. *Analysis and Design of Parallel Algorithms.* McGraw Hill.

Lamm, G., Falauto, G., Estrada, J., and Gadiyaram, J. 2001. Bluetooth wireless networks security features. *Proceedings of the 2001 IEEEE Workshop on Information Assurance and Security.*

Lea, D. 1997. *Concurrent Programming in Java.* Addison Wesley.

Leighton T. 1992. Tight bounds on the complexity of parallel sorting. *IEEE.*

Leuf, B. 2002. *Peer to Peer.* Reading, MA: Addison-Wesley.

Li, X., Lu, P., Schaeffer, J., Shillington, J., Wong, P., and Shi, P. 1993. On the versatility of parallel sorting by regular sampling. *Journal of Parallel Computing* 14.

Lin, S., Wang, H., and Zhang, C. 1997. Statistical tolerance analysis based on beta distributions. *Journal of Manufacturing Systems* 16(2):150–158.

Liu, X. 1992. An efficient parallel sorting algorithm. *Information Processing Letter* 43.

Long, L. and Long, N. 1998. *Computers.* Englewood Cliffs, NJ: Prentice Hall.

Loo, A. July 1989. Application of "key distribution" in very large database. *Proceedings of International ASME Conference*, Brighton, UK, 165–169.

Loo, A. 1990. Pivot selection in sorting algorithms.;*roceeding of ASME Conference*, China.

Loo, A. and Ng, J. 1991. Distributed statistical sorting algorithm. *Proceeding of SICON*, Singapore, 222–225.

Loo, A. and Yip, R. 1991. Parallel statistical sorting algorithms. *Proceeding of International Conference on concurrent Engineering and Electronic Design*, UK, 165–168.

Loo, A., Chung, C., Fu, R. and Lo, J. 1995. Efficiency measurement of distributed statistical sorting algorithms. *Proceeding of Applications of High Performance Computing in Engineering*, Italy.

Loo, A. and Bloor, C. 1999. Parallel computing with java and Intranet/Internet. *Microcomputer Applications* 18(3).

Loo, A. and Choi, C. 2002. Peer to peer selection algorithm for Internet. *Internet Research* 12(1).

Loo, A. 2003. The future of peer-to-peer computing. *Communications of ACM* 46(9):57–61.

Loo, A. 1993. Performance evaluation of efficient parallel sorting algorithms for supercomputers. *Proceedings of Applications of Supercomputers in Engineering 93 Conference*, UK.

Loo, A. 2005. Distributed multiple selection algorithm for peer-to-peer systems. *Journal of Systems and Software* 78(3).

Loo, A., Bloor, C., and Choi, C. 2000. Parallel computing using web servers and servlets. *Journal of Internet Research: Electronic Networking Applications and Policy* 10(2).

Looseley, C. and Douglas F. 1998. *High Performance Client/Server: A Guide to Building and Managing Robust Distributed Systems.* New York: John Wiley.

Lorin, H. 1975. *Sorting and Sort System.* Reading, MA: Addison-Wesley, pp. 347–365.

Maufer, T. 1998. *Deploying IP Multicast in the Enterprise.* Englewood Cliffs, NJ: Prentice Hall.

McCracken, D. and Salmon, W. 1989. *A Second Course in Computer Science with Pascal.* New York: John Wiley.

Meijer H. and Akl S.G. 1980. The design and analysis of a new hybrid sorting algorithm. *Information Processing Letter* 10:213–218.

Miller, C. 1998. *Multicast Networking and Applications*. Reading, MA: Addison-Wesley.

Miller, M. 2001. *Discovering P2P*. Sybex.

Moffat, A. and Peterson, O. May 1992. An overview of adaptive sorting. *Australian Computer Journal*.

Moldovan, D. 1993. *Parallel Processing.* San Mateo, CA: Morgan Kaufmann.

Moodie, M. 2005. *Pro Jakarta Tomcat 5*. Apress.

Moore, D. and Hebeler, J. 2002. *Peer-to-Peer: Building Secure, Scalable, and Manageable Networks*. Osborne.

Moretti, G. 2001. *Is Anyone Talking*. EDN.

Morse, S. 1994. *Practical Parallel Computing.* Cambridge, MA: AP Professional.

Moss, K. 1999. *Java Servlet.* McGraw Hill.

Motzkin, D. 1983. Meansort. *Communications of the ACM* 26(4).

Noga M.T. 1987. Sorting in parallel by double distributive partitioning. *BIT* 27:340–348.

Olariu, S. 1995. A fast sorting algorithm in the broadcast communication model. *The Nineth International Parallel Proceedings Symposium.*

Oliver, I. 1993. *Programming Classics: Implementing the World's Best Algorithms.* Englewood Cliffs, NJ: Prentice Hall.

Oram, A. 2001. *Peer-to-Peer*. O'Reilly.

Orfali, R. and Harkey, D. 1998. *Client/Server Programming with Java and CORBA.* New York: John Wiley.

Osterhuag, A. 1989. *Guide to Parallel Programming.* Englewood Cliffs, NJ: Prentice Hall.

Panda, D. and Wi, L. 1997. Special issue on workstation clusters and network-based computing. *Journal of Parallel and Distributed Computing 40*:1–3.

Park, S., Ganz, A., and Ganz, Z. 1998. *Security Protocol for IEEE 802.11 Wireless Local Area Network, Mobil Network and Application*. pp. 237–246.

Perry, B. 2004. *Java Servlet and JSP Cookbook*. O'Reilly.

Pitzer, B. 2002. *Using Groove 2.0.* Que.

Poon, S. and Jin, Z. 1986. Multiqueue quicksort. *Journal on Research and Development in Computer* 23.

Quinn, M.J. 1994a. *Parallel Computing : Theory and Practice.* McGraw Hill.

Quinn, M.J. 1988. *Parallel Sorting Algorithms for Tightly Coupled Multiprocessors, Parallel Computing.*

Quinn, M.J. 1994b. *Designing Efficient Algorithms for Parallel Computer.* McGraw Hill.

Reese, G. 2000. *Database Programming with JDBC and Java*. O'Reilly.

Rowe, W. 1998. *Introduction to Data Structures and Algorithms with C++*. Englewood Cliffs, NJ: Prentice Hall.

Scowen, R.S. 1956. Quicksort: Algorithms 271, *Communications of the ACM*, 8.

Sedgewick, R.S. 1975. Quicksort. *Ph.D. Thesis.* Stanford University.

Sedgewick, R. 1977. The analysis of quicksort program. *Acta Information* 7:87–97.

Sedgewick, R. 1997. *An Introduction to the Analysis of Algorithms*. Reading, MA: Addison-Wesley.

Shaffer, C. 1997. *Data Structures and Algorithm Analysis.* Englewood Cliffs, NJ: Prentice Hall.

Share, J. 1973. Second thoughts on parallel processing. *Computer Electronic Engineering* 1:95–109.

Shell, D. 1959. A high speed sorting procedure. *Communications of the ACM* 2:30–32.

Siegel, H. 1992. *Interconnection Networks for Large-Scale Parallel Processing.* McGraw Hill.

Smith, G. 1994. *Statistical Reasoning.* McGraw Hill.

Standish, T. 1998. *Data Structures in Java.* Reading, MA: Addison-Wesley.

Steelman, A. and Murach, J. 2003. *Java Servlets and JSP*. Mike Murach & Associate, Inc.

Steinmetz, R. and Wehrle, K. 2005. *Peer-To-Peer Systems and Applications.* Springer.

Stone H.S. 1978. Sorting on star. *IEEE Transactions on Software* 2.

Stone, H. 1980. *Introduction to Computer Architecture.* Chicago, IL: Science Research Associates.

Sun Microsystems. 1999. High-Speed Database Backup on SunTM Systems [online]. Available from: www.sun.com.

Treleaven, P., Brownbridge, D., and Hopkins, R. March 1982. Data driven and demand driven computer architecture. *Communications of the ACM* 14(1):95–143.

Trew, A. 1991. *Past, Present, Parallel.* Springer Verlag.

Tull, C. 2002. *WAP 2.0 Development*. Que.

Van Emden, M. 1970. Increasing the efficiency of quicksort, algorithm 402. *Communications of the ACM* 13.

Wainwright Roger L. 1985. A class of sorting algorithms based on quicksort. *Communications of the ACM* 28:396–277.

Walsh, A. 1996. *Foundations of Java Programming for the World Wide Web.* IDG books Worldwide, Inc.

Watson,W.A., Philipson, T., and Oates, P.J. 1981. *Numerical Analysis.* London: Edward Arnold.

Wegner, L.M. 1982. Sorting a distributed file in a network. *Proceedings of Conference Information Science System,* New Jersey.

Weiss, M.A. 1991. Empirical study of the expected running time of shellsort. *The Computer Journal* 34(1):88–90.

Wilson, G. 1995. *Practical Parallel Processing*. MA: Massachusetts Institute of Technology.

Yousif N. and Evans D. 1984. Parallel distributive partitioned sorting methods. *International Journal of Computer Mathematics* 15:231–255.

Zhang, Z. 1990. The research of increasing the efficiency of quicksort. *Proceeding of ASME Conference*, China, 1–9.

Zomaya, A. 1995. *Parallel Computing: Paradigms and Applications.* International Thomson Company Press.

Index

Printed in the United States of America